PIAF

PIAF

A Passionate Life

David Bret

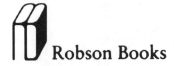 Robson Books

First published in Great Britain in 1998 by Robson Books Ltd,
Bolsover House, 5–6 Clipstone Street, London W1P 8LE

British Library Cataloguing in Publication Data
A catalogue record for this title is available from the British Library

ISBN 1 86105 218 9

Printed in Great Britain by WBC Book
Manufacturers Ltd., Bridgend, Mid-Glamorgan.

This book is dedicated to
BARBARA
(1930–1997)
and
DOROTHY SQUIRES
(1915–1998)

Les plus grandes chanteuses de
notre age, et Les Enfants de Novembre.
N'oublie pas . . .
La vie sans amis c'est comme
un jardin sans fleurs.

FOREWORD

I like to think that I helped introduce the British to Edith Piaf's work. I was doing a revue in London, and the producer wanted a show-stopper, so I suggested 'La vie en rose'. He was quite horrified when I said that I wanted to sing it properly, in the original French, instead of using the Kennedy translation, 'Take me to your heart again'. London audiences weren't all that sophisticated in those days, and he said the public wouldn't know what I was singing about. I argued that hardly anyone understood what was being sung in opera, but that it didn't stop them from enjoying it! So I did the song, and it was a big hit.

I never met Piaf, more's the pity. I flew on the same plane as her when she came to London for a private show at the Mayfair Hotel, I saw her many times in Paris, and I saw her again in America when they'd made her feel very uncomfortable by turning her into a Hollywood-style glamourpuss . . . though I can understand her mentality for allowing them to do that when you think of what she came from. I even appeared on the same bill as her, at the Olympia when she was with the Greek boy, Théo Sarapo, towards the end of her life. She was very sick, then, and disorientated. He had to follow her on to the stage and turn her around to face the audience.

By this time I was used to the shock – and it was a shock – of seeing the spot move over to the wings and picking up this little thing in a black serge dress and flat, tied-up shoes, the sort schoolgirls used to wear. She looked like something off the streets, no make-up only bright red lipstick, her hair an absolute mess. I never saw such a sight! But when she opened her mouth – my God, the beautiful sound that came out, and the way you saw only her hands and her face when she was singing! It was the most astonishing thing I ever witnessed in my life. And believe me, I've seen them all!

Elizabeth Welch

ACKNOWLEDGEMENTS

Writing this book would not have been possible had it not been for the inspiration, criticisms and love of that select group of individuals whom I still regard as my true family and *autre coeur*: Barbara, Irene Bevan, Marlene Dietrich que vous dormez en paix; Montserrat Caballé, René and Lucette Chevalier, Jacqueline Danno, Hélène Delavault, Tony Griffin, Roger Normand, Betty Paillard, Annick Roux, Monica Solash, Terry Sanderson, John and Anne Taylor, Francois and Madeleine Vals. God bless you all!

Very special thanks to Charles Aznavour, Francois Bellair, Marcel Blistène, Christian Bourgois, Damia, Pierre Desgraupes, Jean Dréjac, Marc Bonel, Louis Dupont, Charles Dumont, Catherine Jan, Sylvie Galthier, Claude Lableau, Fernand Lumbruso, Charley Marouani, Bernard Marchois, Simone Margantin, Betty Mars, Hughes Vassal, Manouche, Claude Sounac, Félix Marten. Dorothy Squires.

Un grand chapeau-bas for Elizabeth Welch for her kind words, laughter and support.

Especial thanks to my agent, David Bolt, and to the magnificent team at Robson . . . and to my wife, Jeanne, still the keeper of my soul!

INTRODUCTION

I'm not afraid of death. I don't think I've ever harmed anyone, so I don't fear chastisement. If you act with sincerity you haven't much to fear when you present yourself to the Great Judge!

This was Edith Piaf, speaking on the eve of her premiere at the Paris Olympia, in December 1960. Hers had been a truly magnificent career. For twenty-five years this diminutive, black-clad woman had battled against seemingly unsurmountable odds of hardship, heartbreak, illness and near-despair. Her life, its every triumph and tragedy shared by an adoring public, had closely resembled one of her songs: its beginning had been hesitant, its zenith lively and colourful, and now its close was a catalogue of sadness and catastrophe. And yet she could stand there and defiantly declare, 'I regret nothing!'

I've never been deceived! The men I loved brought me a great experience. I regret nothing I've done or known. If I could, I would begin again. I thank heaven for giving me this life to live to the full!

Piaf's life never lacked her quintessential qualities of courage and love: courage to face the inevitable, and a love of those less fortunate than herself. During the war, she worked for the Resistance and risked her life helping prisoners to escape from a concentration camp. She chartered a ship to bring some of these to England and narrowly missed being executed by the Gestapo. This is why the French flag was draped over her coffin, and why all over the world her admirers held a two-minute silence . . . even in Russia and China, where she had never sung. And after the war, with tireless energy and often limitless patience, she launched a whole new generation of French and international entertainers: Yves Montand, Paul Meurisse, Les

Compagnons de la Chanson, Eddie Constantine, Charles Azna-vour, Félix Marten, Robert Lamoureux, Georges Moustaki . . . and Théo Sarapo, the young man she married and who inherited her millions of francs worth of debts.

Piaf was unique in that she was capable of transcending conventional language barriers. She only gave a handful of private engagements in Britain, yet she is still immensely popular here. However, because most of her lyricists worked in a Parisian *argot*, not unlike our own Cockney, many of her songs cannot be translated literally. Paraphrases are included therefore in the English adaptations of her works throughout this book.

For many of us, Piaf is not dead. Her magic and knowledge of the often unfathomable human condition will live on for ever.

Chapter One

MON COEUR EST AU
COIN D'UNE RUE

'I believed that when a boy sought out a girl, she
should never turn him down. I genuinely thought it
to be part of a woman's role in life.'

Edith Piaf loved to tell the tale of how she had been born on a
policeman's cape in front of the steps of 72 Rue de Belleville –
the building which contained her parents' tawdry room –
during the early hours of 19 December 1915, adding that the
gendarme had been summoned by a neighbour after the horse-
driven ambulance had failed to turn up. Her birth-certificate,
however, tells another story – stating that she was born at the
Hôpital Tenon, at 4 Rue de la Chine in Paris, and at the bottom
of the document, proving the fact, is the signature of the
midwife, Jeanne Crauzier. Even so, Edith's account is sufficiently amusing to fit in with the subsequent legends which
abounded throughout her tragically short life, some real, most
of them figments of an overworked imagination.

Her father, Louis Alphonse Gassion, worked as a street
acrobat and contortionist and came from a family of circus
entertainers. Two sisters, Mathilde and Zéphoria, enjoyed a
modest success in France and Belgium under the name Tante
Zaza, and another sister, Louise, formed one third of Kragg's
Trio, at that time popular on both sides of the Channel. Born in
1881 in Falaise, Normandy, Gassion was a far from handsome
man who measured just 4 feet 11 inches, though what he lacked

1

in looks and stature he more than made up for in the virility stakes – fathering at least nineteen children, mostly to teenage girls. Of his many offspring, the future Edith Piaf was the only one not have been brought into the world a bastard.

Her mother, half-Italian, half-Berber, and born Annette Maillard in Leghorn, Italy, was professionally known as Line Marsa – though when not singing rowdy *revencharde chansons* in the local *beuglants* and *bal-musettes* she earned a more meagre living, selling nougat and working a roundabout at the fairground at Pantin, on the outskirts of Paris.

Gassion and Line Marsa had actually married on 14 September 1914, soon after Marsa's sixteenth birthday, and though they never got around to divorcing, neither did they spend much time together after Edith's birth. It has even been suggested that Gassion was a coward and conscientious objector, who only married in the first place because army regulations unofficially stated that any man about to be married was sent home on compassionate leave, and not always recalled to fight. If this was so, the plan backfired, though Gassion was allowed to return to Paris for the baby's birth and subsequent christening. The child was baptized Edith, after the heroic English nurse, Edith Cavell, recently executed by the Germans, and for a second name her mother chose Giovanna, so that she might always be reminded of her Italian ancestry. Edith hated both the name *and* the woman who had given her life, and never made a secret of the fact when asked. 'She might just as well have gone all the way and added Said Ben Mohammed,' she once said bitterly, referring to her equally loathsome maternal grandmother, though everyone in the district called her Mina, the name she had used whilst directing a flea-circus sideshow.

In January 1916, Louis Gassion returned to the Front, leaving the baby with his wife. Line Marsa likewise dumped Edith upon her mother, in order to fulfil a music-hall contract with an entrepreneur who had promised to make her a star. In 1974 I shared a jug of wine with an elderly couple in a Montmartre bar who had actually seen Line Marsa on the stage. Her performance, they recalled, had been tense but not unprofessional, her voice fully vibrant but harsher than those of her more celebrated contemporaries, Damia and Fréhel. Marsa also cut several records – 'Les filles de joie' and 'Une dernière cigarette' are reminiscent of Yvonne George's later songs, with the voice trailing off at the end of each line or even breaking completely, as if she is desperately trying not to choke. She also sang 'De l'autre côté de la rue', one of Piaf's earlier hits, several weeks before her daughter, having persuaded a friend to steal the sheet music from the publisher. The only reason Line Marsa did not achieve lasting success, one must conclude, having listened to these scratchy recordings, was simply because luck was never on her side.

Home for the infant Edith was an indescribably filthy hovel in Rue Rebeval, not far from where she had been born, and such was Mina's stupidity that she put red wine in the child's feeding bottle to make her sleep, so that she could go off on benders with her cronies. Needless to say, Edith soon fell ill, and when Louis Gassion returned home in September 1917 he found her covered in eczema sores and crawling with fleas. Without further ado he had her sent to Bernay, a small town in Normandy, to be cared for by his own mother, Louise. Though the environment here was a great deal warmer, healthier and more opulent than the one she had been snatched from, there was one detail which could hardly be overlooked . . . the house at 7 Rue Saint-Michel, where Madame Gassion worked as head cook, was the region's most notorious bordello!

What happened at Bernay remains an integral part of the Piaf legend. The prostitutes, eight in all, adopted Edith as their mascot – they made her dolls, took her on outings, and dressed her in pretty clothes. She was also taught how to play the piano, for the bordello owned one of those wonderful mechanical instruments which, later on, would regularly turn up in her songs. 'Le vieux piano', written by Henri Contet in 1960, came about only after she had told him about her childhood in Bernay.

> Qu'il était beau, le piano, bon piano,
> Vieux piano, à l'époque des copains . . .
> Vers trois heures du matin
> Quand elle buvait son demi d'oubli . . .
>
> [How lovely it was, the piano, good piano,
> Old piano, when there were pals around . . .

Around three in the morning
When she was drinking herself into oblivion . . .]

And of course the song ends, in true Piaf-fashion, with the now old woman drinking alone at the bar, seeing imaginary fingers on the keyboard, whilst kids in jeans talk about an outdated bar, its has-been piano, and the soldier who once walked in . . .

The prostitutes at Bernay were surprised to discover Edith had an astonishing ear for music – even at the age of three she was able to tackle several basic chords, and whenever anyone put a record on the wind-up gramophone she only had to hear the song a few times to pick up the melody. Then, quite suddenly, she fell ill, developing cataracts on her eyes, and the bordello doctor diagnosed conjunctivitis. Though we will never know for sure if she lost her sight completely, witnesses have described how for some time she would wander around with her eyes glued shut, constantly bumping into things, and Edith referred to her 'years of darkness' many times in interviews. Also, considering her lifelong faith and devotion towards the saint who she claimed had restored her sight – almost certainly a 'miracle' effected by medicine as opposed to divine intervention – there is absolutely no reason why she should have wanted to fabricate *this* story. Indeed, such was the intensity of her superstitious nature that she would never have *dared* tamper with fate!

Initially, the prostitutes paid for Edith to see a specialist: he applied silver nitrate directly to her eyes, a horrendously painful procedure which did not effect a cure. She was then seen by the local doctor who visited the bordello each week, a man who was more used to treating colds and venereal diseases and who joked that the establishment might be better off spending its money on a white stick. Therefore, as a last resort the girls closed shop for the day and took her on a pilgrimage to Saint Thérèse's shrine at Lisieux – something of a 'risk' considering that Thérèse Martin, the watchmaker's daughter from Alençon who had died in a Carmelite convent aged just twenty-four, eighteen years before Edith's birth, was not actually canonized until 1925.

Edith later claimed that her sight had returned on 21 August 1921, and few people ever doubted her – for the rest of her life

Thérèse, with her shower of roses, would remain the key figure in her personal and religious development, a curious mixture that embraced Catholicism, superstition and instinct. She *always* wore the saint's talisman around her neck, and on one occasion actually believed herself to be close to death after it had been misplaced. Saint Thérèse's picture also shows up in many of Edith's later off-scene photographs – most of them sadly taken when she was in some hospital bed or other – wedged between the Bible and the essential bottle of pills. She also confessed to 'speaking' to her before going on stage – once she had performed the obligatory ritual of kissing the floorboards and making the sign of the cross.

There was a major problem, however, now that Edith could see, for she had suddenly become aware of her surroundings, even if she did not understand why the 'ladies' greeted a steady succession of soldiers, sailors and businessmen in the salon, only to see them off again an hour or so later. Louis Gassion was therefore served with an ultimatum by the priest at the local École Paul Bert, where Edith had been registered a few months before – unless Gassion took his daughter away from the bordello, she would be forced to leave the school. Gassion ignored the priest's threats, and over the next few years father and daughter – in their ramshackle caravan – toured the provinces, entertaining in streets and market-squares with a fair amount of success.

In spite of what has been said or written, Edith never sang with her father: it was her job to unroll his tattered piece of matting on the pavement and act as his stooge. Gassion would bawl to passers-by, 'Mesdames et messieurs, you are about to see the finest *contortioniste-antipodiste* in France! My little girl, Edith, will make the collection and afterwards, providing you pay well enough, she will execute her perilous somersault!' But although Edith always made the collection, she never performed the somersault – her father always came up with the excuse that she was frail, or under the weather. By and large, the couple lived reasonably well. They slept in hotels, and whenever they stayed in any particular town for a number of weeks Gassion sent his daughter to school – not because he was interested in Edith getting a good education, but so that she could take advantage of the concessionary handout of shoes and clothes.

He was not, however, a patient man. Although Edith remembered him as a loving, caring father, she was often the butt of his temper whenever things were not going according to plan, and occasionally felt the back of his hand. Louis Gassion was also a very heavy drinker: for the poorer classes in France between the two world wars there was little else to do if one was not employed, and needless to say the alcohol was rough and cheap, as absinthe had not yet been outlawed by the government. As her father was very much a womanizer, Edith learned about sex perhaps earlier than she should have done, particularly as there was only ever one bed in their hotel room . . .

The mighty singing career began quite by chance one December day in 1926 when Louis Gassion fell ill and had to be confined to his bed. There was no money for food, and the concierge had already threatened the pair with eviction if they did not cough up their rent. Edith simply shrugged her shoulders, put on a dirty overcoat which was several sizes too big for her, and descended to the local square where she sang the only song she knew all the way through, 'La Marseillaise'. In fact, she earned as much singing this *one* song as her father had made over three days! Then on, whenever Louis Gassion was 'busy' with one of his mistresses, Edith would go out into the streets and sing. She very quickly put together a repertoire of *chansons-réalistes* popularized by the great stars of the day: Damia, Fréhel and Yvonne George were her favourites. Damia (Marie-Louise Damien, 1890–1978) was known as *La Tragédienne de la Chanson*, and as such was the most popular singer in France after Piaf. She was the first of the *réalistes* to sing entirely in black, with the spotlight directed on her face, and she had a big hit with 'Just a gigolo' in Europe and the United States. Another famous song was 'Gloomy Sunday', which was also sung by Billie Holiday. Fréhel (Marguerite Boul'ch, 1891–1951) sang in the café concerts and later became a friend. Yvonne George (Yvonne de Knopf, 1896–1930) had amassed a cult gay following in France, though she was hopelessly addicted to cocaine and the bottle, and she had an overt fondness for bisexual American sailors. It was after spending the night with several of these that she was found dead of a suspected drugs overdose in a Swiss hotel room in May 1930, though some contemporary reports stated that she had actually died of the consumption which had ravaged her frail body over the years. Edith is alleged to have witnessed her funeral at the Père Lachaise cemetery, and learned Yvonne's most famous song by heart – to 'cash in' on the pathos that same evening. It is a great pity that she never recorded 'Pars' later in her career.

> Mon désespoir reste mon secret,
> Nous ne sommes que deux étrangers,
> Pars, sans un mot d'amour,
> Pars, laisse-moi souffrir . . .
>
> [My hopelessness stays my secret,
> We are but two strangers,
> Go, without a word of love,
> Go, leave me to suffer . . .]

At the age of fifteen, and allegedly no longer a virgin, Edith left her father to make her own way in life. It was at this time that she met the young woman whom she would later call 'my demon spirit', and who would many years later broadcast to the world, 'I am Piaf's sister'. Her name was Simone Berteaut, but as Edith always shortened the names of her loved ones – unless they had done something to displease her – she always called her Mômone. Over the next thirty or so years their relationship would be in turn stormy and embarrassingly compassionate. They were together at every major stage of Edith's life and career, fought and made up in public with equal vociferousness, and once faced each other in a fierce courtroom drama which would have done justice to any song, only to emerge arm in arm and head for the nearest bar!

When she published her famous book, in 1969, Mômone herself was on the receiving end of countless injunctions and threats from those who accused her of being a charlatan, until she was forced to confess to a packed courtroom that she had made up the 'family connection'. Yet if she was not Piaf's half-sister, in the singer's eyes she was as good as. In 1930, Louis Gassion – approaching fifty and apparently terrified of dying alone – had placed an advert in a newspaper lonely hearts column, and this had resulted in a brief but fruitful liaison with

Georgette L'Hôte, a young woman just six years older than
Edith, but with a temperament far removed from that of Line
Marsa. Ten months later their daughter Denise had been born,
and like Simone Berteaut she would cash in on her sibling's
fame by publishing *two* biographies. Whilst Mômone's tome
was a smash hit all over the world, Denise Gassion's white-
washed accounts of Piaf's 'no-drugs, no-alcohol' life were barely
noticed outside of France.

With Mômone, Edith began singing in the streets on a regular
basis. They earned a lot of money, and spent it without so much
as thinking where their next meal would be coming from. They
slept in cold, rat-infested cellars and disused buildings, and
were not always choosy about their company. They were gloriously content, however, because for the first time in their lives
they were able to please themselves. Mômone's mother was
little better than Edith's had been, and so long as the girl paid
her a weekly allowance out of the 'salary' she earned working
for Edith, she did not create too much of a fuss over the fact
that both girls were breaking the law because they were minors.

Edith's first serious love affair began on an auspicious date:
21 March 1932. Louis Dupont, whom I met in 1975, told me
that he had been enjoying a first day of spring stroll through
the streets of Romainville, on the outskirts of Paris, when he
had stumbled on this scruffy little kid, singing her heart out:

> The song was Damia's 'J'ai le cafard', a rather depressing
> piece for one so young, and she really did look as though
> she had just stepped out of a dustbin, and for weeks after-
> wards I kept asking myself what she'd had to make me
> fall head-over-heels in love with her. I guess it must have
> been her personality, or her cheek. And as for her temper
> – let me tell you, when Edith got out of bed the wrong
> side on a morning, *everyone* darted for cover!

According to Dupont, Edith baptized him P'tit Louis not
because he was small – on the contrary, he was over six-feet tall
– but so that he would never be confused with her father.
He was handsome, naturally – throughout her life, with one
exception (Marcel Cerdan), Edith managed to ensnare only
those men she regarded as having 'Valentino qualities', though

none of them was quite as poor as Louis Dupont, who worked part-time as a delivery boy. His first move, once he had decided that he and Edith were about to become an item, was to take her to meet Madame Georgette, his formidable, alcoholic mother. Needless to say, Edith took an instant dislike to this woman who, she said, reminded her of her own mother, and instead of living with Madame Georgette in Romainville the couple rented a room in the inaptly-named Hôtel de l'Avenir, on Rue Orfila, in Edith's native Belleville, at that time one of the most run-down districts of Paris. And neither was it an ideal love-nest . . . for Edith insisted that Mômone move in with them, even though the room only possessed one bed.

Almost at once, P'tit Louis began putting his foot down. He was decidedly against Edith's singing in the streets, claiming than this amounted to little more than common vagrancy. She was so infatuated with the young man – at nineteen, he was two years her senior – that for a while she relented and accepted a job in Taupin et Masquet's clog factory. The money was good, but even so she missed the freedom of the streets, and when she became ill she was convinced that it was due to the lack of fresh air. In fact, she was pregnant, and as soon as the factory manager was told this – by Mômone – she was dismissed for breaking one of the house rules!

Edith's next job was in another factory, varnishing army boots – this time she was fired for swearing at the boss. Mômone then found them both a job in a wreath factory, and she actually went into labour whilst on duty. Her daughter was born on 11 January 1933 – Ste Marcelle's Day – at Hôpital Tenon, and was baptized Marcelle Dupont a week later at the church in Belleville. The factory employees then had a whipround to pay for the child's first layette, and for the rest of her short life Marcelle never wore anything that was not brand-new. Neither Edith nor her two companions were in any way domesticated, and Edith never would be. If anything needed washing, it was thrown out and replaced.

Now that she had become a mother, P'tit Louis *forbade* Edith to ever sing in the streets again, and on top of this his mother began interfering in their relationship. Further complications occurred with Mômone, though Edith refused to give her friend her marching orders when told to do so. Edith then took her revenge on her lover by joining forces with a young couple named Zéphrine and Jean, who had already enjoyed some success in café-concerts and some of the local *salles des beuglants* – quite literally the bawling halls, which were famed for the atrocious behaviour of their clientele. When Edith became their 'central vocalist' they took up entertaining in the army barracks, and through this Edith developed her lifelong passion for men in uniform. Her favourites were the *légionnaires* and the *coloniales*, both of whom featured in famous songs, and the re-named trio Zizi, Zozette and Zouzou were so popular in some quarters that they often caused near-riots and mass-hysteria in the mess-halls. This was a two-year-long episode of one-night stands and broken promises, and all the time Louis Dupont was going frantic with worry over his 'wife' and daughter – for wherever Edith and Mômone went, Marcelle went with them.

It has to be remembered that in spite of her 'family' status, Edith was still legally a minor. On top of this, Jean was wanted by the police because he had refused to pay a fine for stealing, and Zéphrine was on a good-behaviour bond after being bound over for under-age importuning. Their association ended abruptly when Louis Gassion filed a search petition with the commissariat in Place des Fêtes.

> One evening we slept rough in an alleyway which stank of dustbins. Zéphrine was frightfully ugly, and she had mumps. Suddenly the beam of a pocket-torch fell on our faces and a surly voice ordered us to get up. We had been surprised by a police sergeant and two officers on bicycles, but as luck would have it the sergeant looked into Zéphrine's seductive eyes. It was a tough sacrifice to make, but our only chance of evading prison. Zéphrine went off into the night with the sergeant, and Jean and I were let off the hook . . .

Edith's adventure, typically perhaps, did not end there. The incident caused a heated argument between Jean and Zéphrine – this resulted in the girl walking out on him and returning to the family home, in effect a caravan in the gipsy camp at Pantin, on the northern edge of the city. Edith was given the ubiquitous task of reuniting the couple, but the moment she entered the camp she was set upon by Zéphrine's family. When Jean saw the state she was in, he decided to declare war, and the whole of that afternoon was spent touring the cafés and bars of Belleville and Montmartre gathering an army of drop-out friends, most of whom had at some time in their young lives been in trouble with the law. During the ensuing scrap at Pantin, several people were badly injured and someone called the police. Edith and Jean were arrested, with some forty others, and herded in single file along the peripheral zone which bordered Paris in those days. Aware that they would almost certainly be sent to a correction house if found guilty, they decided to make a break for it across the wide expanse of scrubland which was the forerunner of today's concrete metropolis. The police shot at them, and missed. Edith scratched her legs on the brambles, and twisted her ankle. They eventually ended up at P'tit Louis' house, but instead of finding her lover Edith was confronted with his angry mother. Madame Georgette had never forgiven Edith for taking her son away from her. Although blind drunk, she grasped a poker and would have hit the hapless girl with it had she not lost her balance and crashed to the floor, banging her head on the coal scuttle. At that moment – and Madame Georgette's injuries were apparently fatal – her son barged into the room and yelled that he never wanted to see Edith again as long as she lived. Edith fled, and for the rest of the night lay low in a friend's café, hiding from the police. When she returned to the Hôtel de l'Avenir the next morning, Mômone broke the most terrible news to her – Louis Dupont had taken away their little daughter.

Unable to face singing in the streets any more, and still in fear of being picked up by the police, Edith secured herself a job in Le Tourbillon, a *bal-musette* in the heart of Pigalle's red-light district. Here she washed glasses and mopped the floor, and occasionally sang a couple of songs if any of the resident acts failed to turn up. She also changed her name to Denise Jay, and had fallen in love with a *légionnaire*, hoping that the news of the affair would bring Louis Dupont to his senses, and that she would be asked back into the fold. Little is known of this man, other than the fact that he was 'incredibly handsome', but a few years later their brief affair would form the basis of one of her most famous songs. And Edith was right in one respect

– the association would bring P'tit Louis back to her, but in the most tragic circumstances.

In the summer of 1933 Edith left Le Tourbillon, changed her name to Huguette Hélia, and took up as *chanteuse-en-résidence* at one of the most notorious gay bars in Paris, the Juan-les-Pins in Pigalle. This was run by a huge butch lesbian named Lulu, a woman not without powerful contacts in the Parisian under-world. Yet despite its clientele of criminals, thugs and drug-addicts who mixed freely with the toffs and gangsters, the Juan-les-Pins was much favoured by respectable artistes such as Maurice Chevalier, Mistinguett, Suzy Solidor and Charles Trenet, who many years later recalled 'a little thing in a blue satin sailor's suit' singing 'Nous irons à Valparaiso', a vulgar sea-shanty popularized a few years earlier by Yvonne George.

> Nous irons à Valparaiso, all-away!
> Pour la saler, pour faire la paix,
> Pour foutrer les filles
> Et quelques mat'lots!
>
> [We're going to Valparaiso, all-away!
> To fleece it, to make peace,
> To fuck the girls
> And a few sailors!]

It was at the Juan-les-Pins, one evening after the show, that P'tit Louis informed Edith that their daughter had been taken to Hôpital Tenon, where doctors had diagnosed spinal-meningitis. By the time Edith reached the hospital, Marcelle had been given a lumbar-puncture and the doctor told her that the next nine days would be critical – in fact she died on the tenth day, just as the parents were growing confident that she had got over the worst. Edith was devastated, but in spite of her grief she would have nothing more to do with Louis. Returning to the Hôtel de l'Avenir she consoled herself in the arms of her légionnaire . . . and even Mômone had the sense to stay away.

Edith's friends did not desert her in her hour of need. The staff and clientele of the Juan-les-Pins clubbed together to pay for the child's funeral. Even so, she was ten francs short and, terrified of insulting everyone's generosity by asking for more, she went out on the beat. She picked up a man not far from the nightclub, and this stranger took her to his hotel room. Ten francs was not a great deal of money, though in her shabby state Edith probably could not have demanded much more. However, when she told her 'client' *why* she needed the money, he gave her the ten francs and asked her to leave. Many years later, Edith regretted this dreadful occasion.

In my career I have earned millions of francs, and I have squandered it all away because being a spendthrift was so much fun! It was my revenge on myself for having slept on the pavement as a child. I have conquered my own destiny, which caused me to be born at the bottom of the social scale – in the gutter where hope hardly exists at all. But even the greatest of my triumphs would never compensate for the most atrocious memory of them all – the night when I was so poor that I wanted to sell myself for ten francs.

A few weeks after Marcelle's death, a new man entered Edith's life. His name was Albert, and he was a handsome, irascible but menacing pimp – so menacing, in fact, that within hours of meeting her he told her that she would be expected to go on the beat. She should have ended the whole thing there and then, but her daughter's demise had left her confused and wondering what to do next. Though she refused to work as a prostitute, she did agree to hand over a modest proportion of her earnings to Albert in return for his protection. This is not as unusual as it seems – even established entertainers like Damia and the British star Harry Fragson doled out protection money to pimps. Even so, when Edith returned to the Juan-les-Pins in September 1935 Albert was not satisfied that she was earning enough, and he forced her to work as a 'prospector'. This involved visiting some of the better class nightclubs and bars and making a mental note of where all the wealthy women hung out. This information was passed on to Albert, who then lay in wait for them and robbed them of their jewels and cash. Another girl who worked for Albert was not as submissive as Edith: her name was Nadia, and when she disobeyed Albert's instructions, he informed her that she would have her face 'rearranged'. A few days later Nadia was fished out of the Canal Saint-Martin, and in desperation Edith tried to break free of her mentor. This resulted in a nasty confrontation in a bar opposite the Juan-les-Pins where Albert pulled a gun on her and fired. The bullet missed, grazing her neck . . .

This unfortunate episode should have taught Edith a valuable lesson, but it did not. Albert was the first of many leeches – some claiming to be lovers or friends – who would ultimately bleed Edith dry. What is so utterly remarkable is that she hardly ever seemed to mind, so long as she was getting something in return. In later life that 'something' almost invariably came in the form of a song, and she always had to fight to hang on to a man. In 1935, however, there were no songs other than the ones she had picked up whilst hanging around outside *café-concerts*, and the men were often more trouble than they were worth.

Following the incident with the gun, Albert was arrested by the police – no doubt more to do with the muggings he had perpetrated than for what he had done to Edith, for in her then small world, such was the *loi du cercle* that problems were usually dealt with internally, by fellow thugs, without involving the police. And yet she boldly states in her memoirs that she immediately took up with *two* men, both infinitely worse than Albert – Léon, one of the regulars from the Juan-les-Pins, and a young sailor named Pierre, whom she had met whilst working with Zéphrine and Jean.

Louis Dupont could not remember Léon, but he knew Pierre well, as he explained:

Everyone called him Le Balafré [Slasher] because he always walked around with a cutthroat razor in his pocket. He was very good-looking, almost like a girl, and he would sleep with absolutely anyone – any age, either sex, so long as they could afford the going-rate, which was high. Edith, of course, always charmed him into giving it her for free . . . well, in exchange for the commission he charged on her earnings. Le Balafré's hang-out was Gerny's, an expensive cabaret near l'Étoile. He was knocking off the owner, Louis Leplée . . .

Gerny's, one of the most fashionable nightclubs in Paris, stood on Rue Pierre-Charron, just off the Champs-Elysées, and Louis Leplée – a nephew of the great comic, Polin, who had died in 1927 – was its sixty-year-old director. He was also a man with a shady reputation, as Louis Dupont confirmed:

> For years he'd made his living as a drag-artiste, working the halls until taking over the reins at Chez Liberty, in the twenties home to some of the most notorious perverts in Paris. He was never interested in any man older than twenty-five, and of course he had the money to pay whatever they asked, and not always honestly earned. Leplée ran a crime-ring which peddled drugs and under-aged prostitutes, and Gerny's was merely a cover. And neither was the meeting between himself and Piaf an accident – it was engineered by Le Balafré, so that he could screw Edith for more money. Contrary to popular belief, she was no longer an unknown street-singer. Though she had never done more than four or five songs in any one performance, she was popular with the Pigalle crowd and had developed quite a following in that part of town. She didn't have to sing in the streets, not any more, but she did so because to her the smell of the traffic was like a drug. She couldn't stand to be cooped up. Even when she was the biggest star in France she would occasionally put on old clothes and go out there for the sheer hell of it!

According to Edith, and the legend she innocuously instigated, she and Mômone were working the junction of Rue Troyon and Avenue MacMahon, near the Champs-Elysées, when Louis Leplée just 'happened' to be passing. Indeed, had it not been for the arrangement with Le Balafré, they would never have ventured near the area known as l'Étoile: despite its opulence, the pickings here were virtually non-existent because the locals did not wish to identify with the poverty that was rife on the other side of town, whereas in Belleville, everyone helped everyone else.

The song was 'Les deux ménétriers', a Damia number which had proved popular at the Juan-les-Pins, and at first Edith ignored her elderly admirer, as Le Balafré had instructed her to. He was wearing smart clothes, but what really annoyed her once he began chatting to her was the fact that he was wearing gloves and carrying a cane. Leplée asked her why she was ruining her voice by singing in a dusty street, and she replied, sarcastically, that she did not have a contract to sing elsewhere! Then, scribbling his name and address on a scrap of paper and folding this inside a banknote, he asked her to attend an audition at his club the next day, so they would go through her repertoire. Edith and Mômone then took the Métro back to Belleville, where Le Balafré was waiting. Their little plan had worked, Leplée had been none the wiser, and though Edith was not sure that she would secure an engagement at Gerny's, her lover certainly was.

Edith's repertoire was more extensive than Leplée could possibly have imagined: besides the dramatic works of Damia, Yvonne George and Fréhel, to name but a few, there were several operatic arias! Neither was she impressed with Gerny's. She could not abide snobs, and loathed the fact that it cost the same for a bottle of champagne in such an establishment as could feed a poor family for a week. What she did look forward to was the chance to prove herself in front of a cabaret crowd who had most likely never known what it had been like to go without food or shoes. Louis Leplée introduced her to his pianist, Jean Urémer, and the young musician was amazed that this girl's untrained voice was so pure that even the flaws within it became qualities. Leplée asked her her name, and she replied that she had several: the latest was Tania, she said, though she had always preferred Huguette Hélia because she thought it sounded artistic. The entrepreneur may not have sounded very flattering when he told her that, in his opinion, she looked more like a bedraggled sparrow who had spent the night in the gutter than any exotic artiste. When Jean Urémer suggested that maybe she should call herself La Môme Moineau, Edith told him that there was already an entertainer by that name – a topless singer-dancer who had risen to prominence during the early twenties and who had since married and left the stage. Leplée thought about this. The slang word for 'sparrow' is *piaf*, and he told her, 'From now on you'll be known as "La Môme Piaf"!'

She had been baptized for life!

Leplée engaged Edith to open at Gerny's on Friday 26

September 1935, allowing her just three days to learn four new songs: 'Les mômes de la cloche', 'La valse brune', 'Nini peau d'chien', and Lucienne Boyer's recent success, 'Si petite'. She was also given extensive last-minute publicity, and was apparently so concerned over the cost of this that she admitted to Leplée that he had been duped into hiring her. According to Louis Dupont, Leplée at once summoned Le Balafré to his office, but instead of bawling him out gave him a *reward* for having such intuition! He knew secretly, of course, that if the venture failed he would become the laughing-stock of the Parisian social set, particularly as he had invited a host of celebrities to the première.

It was at this stage that Edith panicked, for she had nothing to wear for her opening night. The songs also caused her a number of problems: she did not think 'Nini peau d'chien' realistic enough for what she had in mind, and she was not keen on emulating anyone else, least of all Lucienne Boyer. The first problem was easily remedied when a friend loaned her some money to buy wool and needles to knit a dress. The songs she was stuck with, for her new mentor would not compromise. Edith went out and purchased several large hanks of black wool, gave half of it to Mômone, and her new stage garb began to take shape. Two important precedents were thus set: the black dress which would rapidly become her trademark, and a mania for knitting – though she would begin knitting sweaters for almost every one of the men in her life, she allegedly never finished a single garment! Neither did she finish this one – Friday came, and literally minutes before her performance Leplée discovered her in the lavatory, frantically knitting the second sleeve of her dress. She then began unravelling the other sleeve, declaring that she would sing with her arms bare, in the Damia tradition. Leplée would not hear of such a thing. Her arms, he declared, were like matchsticks and in any case there was only one Damia, just as there would only be one Piaf. Again, the situation was given a comic touch when Yvonne Vallée, the then wife of Maurice Chevalier, walked into the lavatory whilst Edith and Leplée were arguing what to do about the missing sleeve. By tradition, *chanteuses-réalistes* usually wore white or red scarves. Yvonne Vallée gave Edith her own violet silk scarf: henceforth Edith's favourite colour would be violet.

There then followed another panic-attack, for if Chevalier's wife was in the auditorium, then surely the great man himself must have been there too? He was, sitting at the same table as his ex-lover, the awesome Mistinguett!

Leplée introduced her personally. 'I was strolling past Rue Troyon the other day when I heard this young girl singing. Her voice overwhelmed me, and I am presenting her to you now as I first saw her – unkempt, and without make-up. La Môme Piaf!' Her reception was decidedly frosty when she walked on to the bare stage, but by now most of her first-night nerves had gone. The resident accordionist at Gerny's was a young man by the name of Robert Juél, and he had re-arranged Edith's four songs to suit the harsh timbre of her voice. Her opening number, 'Les mômes de la cloche', had actually been written for Mistinguett by Vincent Scotto some twenty years before; the great star had sung it in a revue at the Folies-Bergère, when she had played a motherless waif. And now, the champagne-and-glitter set were about to be entertained by a *real-life* guttersnipe, and many of them felt ill at ease as Juél and Jean Urémer struck up the first bars of Piaf's first song. Not sure what to do with her hands, Edith kept them planted firmly on her hips – another future trademark – and sang from the guts.

> C'est nous les mômes, les mômes de la cloche,
> Clochards qui s'en vont sans un rond en poche!
> C'est nous les paumées, les purées d'paumées,
> Qui sommes aimées un soir, n'importe où . . .
>
> [We're the kids, the guttersnipes,
> Tramps who roam around broke!
> We're the outcasts, the clapped-out outcasts,
> Who are loved for one night, no matter where . . .]

Halfway through the first verse of the song, those customers who had ordered meals began eating. During the second verse when those sitting closest to the stage observed that Chevalier and Mistinguett had set down their knives and forks, everyone else followed suit. By the third verse she had them in the palm of her tiny hand. Then, as the song was finishing Edith forgot herself and raised her arms: Yvonne Vallée's beautiful silk scarf slithered from her shoulders, revealing her missing sleeve. Not one person laughed. Mistinguett is said to have begun dabbing her eyes – though insincerely, for in the future she would never disguise her contempt for Piaf, at her politest referring to her as 'cette petite en noir' – and Chevalier shouted encouraging words. King Faud shook hands with her after the performance, and Jean Mermoz, the world-famous aviator, invited her to sit at his table . . . where she was treated to her very first glass of champagne, and the entire basket of violets from the flower-girl.

Paris had a new star! La Môme Piaf had taken it by storm!

Chapter Two

RAYMOND ASSO: THE FIRST SVENGALI

Within a matter of days, word passed along the social grapevine that it was the 'in-thing' to go and hear La Môme Piaf at Gerny's. Yet despite the obvious adulation from the public, a great many of Piaf's contemporaries disliked her – not because they thought her to be lacking in talent, or on account of her vulgarity, but quite simply because they were jealous of her rapid success and afraid that she might steal some of the limelight from them. Damia, who later became a friend, was one of them.

> In her early days, Piaf was a thief! She didn't have any songwriters of her own, so she stole ours. One of my big numbers in those days was 'Les deux ménétriers', the one she was supposed to be singing when Leplée discovered her. Piaf went around telling everyone that it was *hers*, and as you can well imagine, that really stuck in my throat. She also stole material from Marie Dubas and Marianne Oswald, and began copying *my* style, until my agent went to see Asso and told him that this would have to stop. Then one evening I came off stage at the Concert-Pacra and she was waiting in my dressing-room with a huge bunch of flowers. After that she began respecting me, and we became rather good friends. She loaned me several of her songs and even wrote three especially for me!

Several important people also found it necessary to engage Edith for private parties and functions – as she herself remarked,

'They wanted to see this crude little nine-day wonder and have a little fun with her before she returned to the gutter.' One publicized incident was a dinner-party hosted by the cabinet minister, Jean de Rovera – and yes, she *did* drink out of the finger-bowl, though as soon as she learned why she had been invited, she gave as good as she got and was admired for doing so, most especially by the poet, Jacques Bourgeat, who became one of her closest friends – indeed, theirs was to remain the most secretive relationship of her life. Even today, virtually nothing is known about it, other than that it seems to have been entirely platonic – Bourgeat was in his late-forties, and regarded as her third 'Papa', after Louis Gassion and Leplée.

After her performance at Gerny's, Edith and Bourgeat would head for the Sans-Souci, a bar in Pigalle which stayed open until dawn. Here, drinking very little, they would spend hours discussing the arts and would occasionally be joined by 'boozy' pals such as Mômone and Robert Juél, though more often than not if Edith saw a tramp shuffling by he would be invited in for supper, with Edith always insisting that she pick up the tab. 'Even when she had next to nothing, her generosity was boundless,' Bourgeat later recalled. 'She would swallow absolutely anyone's sob-story, and then as later in her career spent her money as quickly as she earned it – sometimes *before* it was earned. She told me that her greatest ambition had always been to feed the hungry.'

Through Jacques Bourgeat – whom she always referred to as her 'domesticated ray of sunshine' – and several years before meeting Cocteau, Edith became a semi-intellectual. Over the next quarter of a century the pair exchanged more than two hundred highly-personal letters, confidential documents which the poet subsequently bequeathed to the Bibliothèque Nationale, and which will not be made available to the public until the year 2004. Bourgeat also wrote her one of her most lyrical early songs, ''Chand d'habits', which she recorded in October 1936.

> Dis-moi, 'chand d'habits . . .
> Parmi le lot de mes vieilles défroques
> Que ce matin je te vendis à regret . . .
> N'as-tu trouvé tout en loques,

Triste, lamentable, déchiré,
Un douloureux coeur abandonné?

[Tell me, second-hand clothes seller . . .
Amongst my old cast-offs
That I regretfully sold you this morning . . .
Have you not found all in rags,
Sad, lamentable, torn,
An aching, abandoned heart?]

Another aquaintance who sometimes dropped in on the scene at the Sans-Souci was Raymond Asso, an ex-légionnaire who was the secretary of Marie Dubas (1894–1972), one of the most popular entertainers in France at the time and an artiste probably most comparable with our own Gracie Fields in that she had an uncanny ability to switch from intense drama ('La prière de la Charlotte') to buffoonery ('Pédro') within the space of a song. In interviews, Edith very rarely spoke about Damia and Fréhel, her closest living rivals, but she always had a tremendous affection and respect for the woman she called 'La Grande Marie', and met her in October 1935, courtesy of Asso, who since his discharge from military service had also enjoyed considerable success as a songwriter.

This monumental meeting between Piaf and Dubas, in the latter's dressing-room at the Empire, inadvertently added a vital chapter to the history of the *chanson*. Marie, it seems, had heard Edith at Gerny's and she had been so impressed that she now invited her to sing into the machine which she always carried around with her to monitor her audiences' reactions to certain songs – quite likely a machine which produced acetates. The recording of 'La java en mineur', with Asso accompanying her at the piano and yelling instructions at the stagehand working the machine, was later transferred to a tape and played for the first time on France-Inter radio in June 1981, though so far as is known Edith never sang it on the stage. Many years later, she wrote:

Marie Dubas was my inspiration, my joy and sadness. *She* alone created the chanson as we know it today, with its three verses and refrains. *She* knew how to make the public

laugh, whereas I only know how to make them cry. Marie
is the greatest star there has ever been. I owe her *everything*.

Although within a few months of their meeting there would be
a rift between the two women on account of their *Légion* songs,
this would prove but temporary – as would the furore caused
by Edith's 'acquisition' of her first hit: Robert Malléron's
'L'étranger', which had been commissioned by the chanteuse
Annette Lajon, and set to music by her pianist, Marguerite
Monnot.

This was the age when relatively unknown entertainers had
a tough time securing new songs. These were expensive to
commission and launch, and were invariably offered to established stars long before the others got wind of them. Several of
these exercised an unwritten law of the music-hall by
demanding that new songs should remain their 'property' until
six months after they had recorded them – Damia took this one
step further by singing her most popular songs for *years* before
committing them to shellac. Even so, after several weeks of
singing the four songs given to her by Leplée, Edith was desperately in need of a change, and began doing the rounds of the
publishers' offices. One of these was run by Maurice Decruck,
and it was there that she heard Annette Lajon – a mezzo-
soprano who had recently sung *Carmen* with the Opéra
Comique, and who for some inexplicable reason had switched
to the *chanson* – rehearsing two numbers: 'Les lumières dans
l'eau' and 'L'étranger'. Never lacking in nerve, Edith took
Decruck to one side and asked if she might have the latter song,
the story of a prostitute who picks up a sailor who is later found
drowned in the harbour. Naturally, he declined, so Edith politely
requested Lajon to go through the song again, declaring that it
was the most beautiful she had ever heard. The chanteuse was
flattered, and sang it twice – wholly unaware that Edith was
memorizing it. When Edith told Leplée that afternoon that she
intended adding it to her repertoire he hit the roof, and forbade
her to do so, terrified that he would be sued by Decruck. Edith
ignored him. She hummed the tune to her accordionist, Robert
Juél, and it took him less than an hour to rewrite the arrangement – and when Edith sang it at Gerny's that same evening,
she brought the house down.

'D'où viens-tu? Quel est ton nom?'
'Le navire est ma maison,
La mer mon village,
Mon nom, nul ne le saura . . .
Vends-moi donc un peu d'amour,
J'ai soif de caresses!'
Il avait un regard très doux,
Il venait de je ne sais où.

['Where do you come from? What's your name?'
'The ship's my home, the sea my village,
No one will ever know my name . . .
So, sell me a little love,
I'm thirsty for caresses!'
He had a very sweet look,
He came from I don't know where.]

Needless to say, Annette Lajon was furious when she learned that La Môme Piaf had stolen her song, and a few evenings later turned up at Gerny's for the inevitable showdown. Firstly, however, she decided to give Edith the benefit of the doubt by *listening* to her version of the song – and instead of giving her rival a piece of her mind she embraced her, and the two remained friends for the next three decades. Edith recorded the song, coupled with 'Les mômes de la cloche', on 18 October 1935 – the eve of her twentieth birthday – and though it was played endlessly on the radio and has since sold *millions* of copies on compilation albums, in honour of Annette Lajon she never sang it on the stage again. Lajon's own interpretation gained her the prestigious Grand Prix du Disque, which is in itself baffling, for in France today they only remember Edith's recording, and the cover-version by Damia – and sixty years on, the emotion remains as intense at it was back in 1936.

Edith's first gala concert – effectively, her first appearance on an actual music-hall stage – took place at the Cirque Médrano on 17 February 1936 when she performed two new songs: 'La fille et le chien' and 'Reste', which she had just recorded for Polydor. The event, to raise money to aid the widow of the recently deceased clown-female impersonator, Antonet, brought about a number of very nasty backstage cat-fights because the organizers had insisted that everyone appear in alphabetical order. Therefore, in a full bill which included Mistinguett, Chevalier, Marie Dubas, Damia and Fréhel, Edith came on immediately after the controversial Hungro-American dancer, Harry Pilcer. During her first song, the microphone failed – quite likely sabotaged by an angry colleague – but no one seemed to notice as Edith's powerful voice soared above the eleven-piece orchestra.

Sitting in the audience was the Bulgarian-born director of Radio-Cité, Jacques Canetti, who twenty years hence would launch the careers of Jacques Brel and Georges Brassens. Canetti signed her up for a series of fifteen-minute broadcasts, and these began on 15 March 1936. Immediately afterwards the station's switchboard was swamped with callers pleading to hear more of La Môme Piaf, unusual in those days, and Canetti – who had already agreed to supervise her future recording sessions with Polydor – signed her up for a second series of broadcasts, and a third! One of the songs which caused a sensation was Charles Borel-Clerc's moving 'Fais-moi valser'.

> Sur terre tu sais bien je n'avais que toi,
> Tu veux déjà partir, je comprends pourquoi,
> Va-t'en vers ton bonheur,
> Mais avant de partir,
> Fais-moi valser une dernière fois . . .

> [You know well that on earth I only had you,
> You want to leave already, I understand why,
> Go towards your happiness,
> But before leaving,
> Waltz with me one last time . . .]

Tragedy, however, was just around the corner for Edith. For many years, Louis Leplée had been involved in shady deals with the Parisian underworld and his enemies were legion. Then, on 6 April 1936, he was found shot dead in his luxurious apartment at 83 Avenue de la Grande Armée, not far from the Arc de Triomphe. Edith had been out celebrating with friends, but knowing how 'Papa' Leplée always worried about her whenever she stayed out until the early hours of the morning, she telephoned him to arrange a rehearsal of several new songs for the following afternoon. A detective took the call, ordering her to return without delay. Outside the apartment block she was greeted by a storm of press photographers and reporters, two detectives, and an inquisitive crowd of onlookers. The story emerged that in the early hours four young men had barged into the apartment, and after gagging the maid they had entered Leplée's bedroom to demand money which he had most likely owed them. The enquiry was clumsily handled by a Commissaire Guillaume, who was told by the housekeeper that Leplée had often taken young men home for the night. A possible conclusion was that Leplée had been murdered by one of these 'rent-boys' because he had failed to pay for services rendered. There had also been a great deal of money in the apartment.

What made the enquiry worse, from everyone's point of view, was the fact that it was both continued publicly and filmed – over the next few weeks it was shown on newsreel film in cinemas all over France, and even featured as a 'strip-cartoon' in one of the tabloid newspapers. Edith was not spared by Guillaume who, though never suspecting her of firing the actual shot, did believe that she knew the killer's identity. It is quite probable that this man was a lover shared by Edith and Leplée (Louis Dupont stated that he could only have been Le Balafré, who left the city immediately afterwards), though Edith, who throughout her entire life believed that her men had eyes for her and her alone, would not have known this. And of course, *had* she known the truth, she would have been terrified of letting on in case her 'circle' took it upon themselves to eliminate her too. Now, she was shunned by most of her colleagues from the now defunct Gerny's. Robert Juél, who would enjoy a brief spell as her lover, stuck by her, as did two of the cabaret's 'warm-up' singers, Germaine Gilbert and Laure Jarny. Jacques Canetti extended her radio series by several weeks – primarily because the Leplée scandal had increased audiences – and she was befriended by Annette Lajon's twenty-six-year-old pianist, Marguerite Monnot, who very quickly became her *frangine*, or soul-sister, and who ultimately would be responsible for some of her best-known songs.

Publicly, Edith was defended by Marcel Montarron, a young journalist who worked for *Le Détective*, the top-selling weekly crime publication of the day. She appeared on the cover of the edition dated 16 April 1936, pictured at Leplée's funeral, weeping on the arm of a friend. The editorial read, 'THE FOUR KILLERS! Disowned by his comrades of vice, Louis Leplée had only women, La Môme Piaf, and Laure Jarny to weep at his funeral.'

In his piece, Montarron attacked those scandalmongers who had mocked Edith in their comic-strips, raking up numerous episodes of her 'pathetic, weary life' which might have been best forgotten. This had a positive effect on her popularity, particularly as far as record sales were concerned: then as now, there was nothing quite so good for business as a meaty scandal, and Robert Juél, who had taken on the mantle of temporary manager, was inundated with offers of work. Edith accepted an open-ended season with Chez Odette, a seedy gay club in the heart of Pigalle, though she refused to sign a contract, declaring that the establishment would have to take her on trust, or not at all. Its director was Bruno Coquatrix, a young entrepreneur from Ronchin who, two decades on, would become one of her most trusted friends. Coquatrix took one look at the knitted dress she had been wearing since her Gerny's debut, and told her that she would not be singing in *his* club looking like a tramp – to which she replied, 'Fine. You want me to have a new wardrobe, then you *buy* me one!'

Bruno Coquatrix took Edith to a couturier, and she immediately chose the most expensive gown in the shop – having decided that wearing black at Gerny's had only brought her bad luck, this was a floor-length, scarlet chiffon gown which, Coquatrix later said, made her look like a pregnant garden gnome. It was therefore left to him to decide what she would wear for her premiere, and he selected a simple short black frock, with pockets. Edith herself asked the seamstress to add a white lace collar, for effect. The engagement with Chez Odette, however, proved a disaster. She was introduced by a grossly overweight Master of Ceremonies who wore drag, and was not even applauded after her first song – customers here were not interested in La Môme Piaf, but in feasting their eyes on the girl at the centre of the Leplée scandal. The final straw came when someone whistled – in France, a sign of derision – and, agreeing to stick it out until the end of the week because she was terrified that Coquatrix would expect her to pay for the dress, she asked Robert Juél to find her something else.

For a while, she toured the local cinemas, singing three or four songs between features. This did not work out, and through Jacques Canetti she met Fernand Lumbruso, at that time the manager of the avant-garde *diseuse*, Marianne Oswald, the darling of the intellectuals.

I met Fernand Lumbruso in 1990 – a sprightly octogenarian, he was still 'up to his tricks', as he put it, directing the Mogador and presenting a new season of recitals by Barbara. His reminiscences of La Môme Piaf, however, brought about the odd shudder.

Piaf was by far the most important thing that ever happened to me, now that I look back. But oh, what a pain in the ass! I too engaged her to play the cinemas between features. The first stop was Troyes, where she turned up with two men – a young thug who, she said, had told her he loved her almost as much as his flick-knife, and an accordionist called Juél who would take any man apart as soon as look at him! Troyes wasn't too bad, but the real problems began in Brest, where a newspaper had announced the arrival of the next Yvonne George. As you know, the sailors were absolutely crackers about *her*, so they all piled into the cinema, looking for a brawl with anyone who might not like her, even though most of them had never heard her. She came on, did the three or four songs expected of her, then made the mistake of telling them she would be back after the main feature. This was *Lucretia Borgia*, so as you can imagine they were not in a very responsive mood. Then, when everyone should have been going home, she came on and and announced that she was going to sing a song popularised by Marianne Oswald. She had sung 'Embrasse-moi' many times before, but this time she gave them 'En m'en foutant' [While fucking myself]. Well, you can only imagine what happened! The cinema had to be evacuated!

Neither did Mômone's arrival in Brest, the next morning, help matters. Edith's 'protector' was sent packing, Robert Juél found himself kicked out of her room, and the two women took a leaf out of Yvonne George's book and began doling out free passes to the handsomest of the sailors lined up outside the cinema. This led to a great deal of scrapping, though no one was actually killed as had happened in Paris when George had played the Empire. Even so, when fighting broke out again inside the building whilst she was on the stage – this time singing 'Les hiboux', a self-mocking essay on prostitution – the manager rang Fernand Lumbruso, and the next morning Edith was summoned back to Paris.

In Paris, Edith had a brief affair with the singer-songwriter Roméo Carlès, and this resulted in two songs being commissioned especially for her by Jacques Canetti: 'Simple comme bonjour' and 'La petite boutique'. She was not, however, offered anything in the way of work – not that she was ready to give up hope.

> It was at that moment that I remembered Raymond Asso. I was hard pressed; I had hit rock-bottom. So I rang him, and confessed, 'I'm lost, Raymond, and I'm afraid that I'll do something stupid.' He told me to take a taxi, and I left for his place with nothing – not even a suitcase. I had humoured myself by wallowing in stupidity and ugliness – making a mess of the good things in life. Raymond taught me how to become a human being again, though it took him three years to disintoxicate me of Pigalle and my miserable, corrupted childhood.

Fourteen years Edith's senior, Asso was a tall, gaunt-looking individual with sleeked back hair and a large nose. Edith immediately baptized him 'Cyrano', and he retaliated by calling her his 'Spanish beggar', which was probably apt at the time. When he became her mentor he was living with Madeleine, his common-law wife, in Pigalle's Hôtel Piccadilly, and Edith was still encumbered with Mômone. As with Louis Dupont, however, it was love at first sight, and Asso was ordered to get rid of Madeleine, 'or else'. For the time being, he refused to be manipulated, and compromised by securing her a contract with the Boîte à Vitesse, in Nice – the cabaret-room in the basement of Maxim's. Asso was hoping that by the time Edith returned to Paris, she would have rid herself of her fascination for him. He also offered her a song called 'Mon légionnaire', which she always maintained had been based on an actual event in her life.

> Il était plein de tatouages,
> Son cou portait: 'Pas vu, pas pris',
> Sur son coeur on lisait, 'Personne',
> Sur son bras droit un mot, 'Raisonne',
> J'sais pas son nom, je n'sais rien d'lui,
> Il m'a aimée toute la nuit,
> Mon légionnaire . . .

> [He was covered in tattoos,
> On his neck, 'Neither seen nor taken',
> Across his heart, 'Nobody',
> On his right arm one word, 'Truth',
> I don't know his name,
> I know nothing about him,
> He loved me all night long,
> My légionnaire . . .]

According to Edith's confession, she had attempted to woo the hapless Louis Dupont back into her arms – and inflame his jealousy – by cheating on him with her hunky *légionnaire*, but the affair had ended abruptly when the soldier had been transferred to North Africa, where he had subsequently died. This was later proved to be untrue, for in her memoirs she recounts how, many years later, he turned up at one of her recitals – fat and balding – and the pair are reputed to have 'shared a bottle' in her dressing-room. For the time being, Edith refused to have anything to do with the song, and Asso gave it to Marie Dubas, who at once put it into her already extensive repertoire. Edith laughed at this, vowing that not even La Grande Marie would make the song a success. Then she left for Nice, on the start of an adventure which began even before she had got off the train. Because she did not have much money, she travelled alone and third class, sharing a compartment with a handsome young man who did not say a great deal, but who apparently smiled rather a lot before moving next to her and taking her hand.

Throughout most of the journey Edith slept with her head on his shoulder, but when the train reached Marseilles two detectives were waiting for her companion, and she watched helplessly as he was handcuffed and led away. The story formed the basis for another Asso song, 'Paris-Méditerranée'.

> Le soleil rédoublait ma peine,
> Et faisait miroiter ses chaines.
> C'était peut-être un assassin . . .
>
> [The sunshine doubled my pain,
> And made his shackles shimmer.
> Maybe he was a murderer . . .]

In fact, the Leplée scandal had followed Edith all the way to Nice. Posters advertising her show had been posted on hoardings – next to them were slogans: DID LA MÔME PIAF KILL LEPLÉE? WHY NOT COME AND SEE FOR YOURSELVES? At first, she thought about calling Raymond Asso and breaking her contract. Then she decided to stick it out – primarily because her accompanists, Robert Juél and René Cloërec, refused to leave Nice without being paid, but partly because she hoped that the adverse publicity might work to her advantage. It did. Though the premiere attracted possibly every newspaper reporter in the region, once the general public realized that she could sing she was on to a winner – her contract was extended by six weeks, and she always performed to capacity audiences. She also celebrated her twenty-first birthday at the Boîte à Vitesse – with Mômone, of course. Then, at the end of the December, Edith returned to Paris, and the first of her slanging matches with Raymond Asso. What happened next was typical of Edith's later tyranny – Madeleine left, and Mômone found herself a husband!

Edith and Asso moved into the Hôtel Alsina on Avenue Junot, in Montmartre, and here he set about moulding his protégée into the national institution she would very quickly become. Like almost every one of her relationships, the Asso-Piaf affair was not an easy one. She was short-tempered, vulgar, loud-mouthed but above all exceptionally gifted when it came to choosing the material for her shows. He was impatient, sometimes violent, and stubborn. Edith had to be knocked into shape – often literally – and Asso never spared her feelings. Initially, their bouts of screaming brought complaints from the neighbours, but whenever the gendarmes called round to deal with the situation, they were too infatuated with Edith's singing to take any action. To make up for giving 'Mon légionnaire' to Marie Dubas – the chanteuse had scored a tremendous commercial success with the song – Asso presented her with another 'military' piece, 'Le fanion de la Légion'.

Ah! La-la-la-la belle histoire!
Ils restent trois dans le bastion,
Le torse nu, couverts de gloire.
Sanglants, meutris et en haillons,
Sans eau, ni pain, ni munitions . . .
On leur a volé le fanion,
Le beau fanion de la Légion!

[Ah, what a fine story!
There are three left in the bastion,
Bare-chested, clothed in glory.
Bloodstained, battered and in rags,
With neither water, bread nor munitions . . .
They've stolen the flag,
The beautiful flag of the Légion!]

Edith was delighted with the song – until she learned that Marie Dubas had recorded it on the flipside of 'Mon légionnaire', whereupon she purchased a copy of the offending disc and smashed it over Raymond Asso's head! She then told him that she would never even *consider* performing it until he had 'persuaded' Marie to remove it from her repertoire. When Asso warned her that if such a thing happened, he would prevent *her* from singing all the other songs he had written for her – and when Marguerite Monnot, who had composed the music, defended his decision – Edith backed down. Even so, when she recorded the two *Légion* songs for the first time in January 1937, to spite the pair she substituted the verse-melody of 'Le fanion' with one of her own.

Edith's actions sparked off a furious row with Asso, who

stayed away from the Hôtel Alsina for several weeks, hoping this might teach her a lesson. It did not. Edith took up again with Roméo Carlès, demanding that he replace Asso as her personal songwriter. Carlès refused, arguing that he was a poet and not a machine which could be switched on and off to suit her whims, so she went to see Fernand Lumbruso. 'She frightened the life out of me when she barged into my office,' Fernand told me. 'I thought she was expecting me to send her on another tour, and God knows I hadn't recovered from the last one. So I put her in touch with André Mauprey, another of Marianne Oswald's composers.'

Mauprey, who had adapted Kurt Weil's *The Threepenny Opera* into French, very quickly wrote her a new song, 'Entre Saint-Ouen et Clignancourt', and by the end of the month several of his friends had provided her with three more – 'Corrèque et reguyer', 'Dans un bouge du vieux port', and 'Mon coeur est au coin d'une rue'. High drama prevailed when Asso turned up at the studio, yelling that she would never get away with lending her name to such drivel, to which she responded, 'Big deal, I'll use somebody else's!' On the record labels and sheet music she is billed simply as 'Edith Piaff' and over the next year or so, whenever there was a row with Asso, she would do the same thing again... genuinely believing that, just as she had acquired the songwriting services of the man, so too he owned copyright on the name La Môme Piaf!

Asso, of course, knew just what side his bread was buttered on – Edith's record sales and the sale of her sheet music vouched for that, and once he had sulked for a while he returned to their love-nest, and introduced Edith to the most famous music-publishers in France at that time. The couple, Raoul Breton and his wife, known fondly as La Marquise, had recently launched Charles Trenet, and in future years they would take on the mighty talents of Montand and Barbara. La Marquise took Edith on futile trips to beauty salons and couturiers, in an attempt to mould her into the woman she hoped Edith might have wanted to become. Edith had different ideas. Beauty in a woman, she declared, came from within and had nothing to do with powder, paint and pretty frocks. And she told Madame Breton *exactly* what to do with her solfége and elocution classes, adding, 'The *only* lessons I'm interested in are hearing Marie Dubas sing!'

Edith Piaf never emulated the woman revered as 'La Fantaisiste des Années Folles'. She simply learned from her – and from a certain extent from Damia – how to nurture an audience, how to arrange the songs in each programme so as to 'spread out' the drama and intensity. Thus, over the next two weeks she attended every one of Marie's recitals at the ABC, and ordered Asso to organize an interview with the theatre's director, with a view to offering her a slot in a future production. What she did not expect was Asso's reaction, for he told her that *he* would never settle for anything less than top-billing!

Until Bruno Coquatrix re-opened the Paris Olympia in 1954, the ABC on Boulevard Poissonnière was the most prestigious music-hall in Paris though its director, an ebullient Hungarian émigré named Mitty Goldin, was renowned all over France for his extreme stinginess. Asso went to see him, explaining that as Edith's records were selling well, she should be given the chance to prove herself. Goldin showed him the door. For several weeks he persisted, making such a nuisance of himself that the director threatened him with legal action. Asso took no notice of this, and Goldin eventually yielded – however, Edith was not given top-billing, but the position of *vedette amèricaine*. This was the artiste second in importance to the star of the show, who closed the first half of the programme. Meanwhile, Edith tried out two of the new songs written for her by Asso in a gala for the French Popular Front at the Vélodrome d'Hiver – this was almost a repeat performance of the Cirque Médrano, with the microphone failing *before* her first song. And yet again she managed to evoke tremors of emotion with a number loosely based on her own life.

> Elle fréquentait la rue Pigalle,
> Elle sentait l'vice à bon marché,
> Pourtant y avait dans l'fond d'ses yeux,
> Quelqu'chose de miraculeux . . .
>
> [Her beat was the rue Pigalle,
> She smelled of cheap vice,
> Nevertheless there was something miraculous,
> Deep within her eyes . . .]

Edith opened at the ABC on 26 March 1937 – but not as La Môme Piaf. Mitty Goldin insisted that if she *did* have to sing in his theatre, then it would not be under the pseudonym which linked her with the Leplée scandal. Thus she was billed as Edith Piaf. For rehearsals she had worn a short black dress, with mid-length sleeves and a white lace collar. Goldin insisted that this should stay the same, though he asked her to remove the collar when it interfered with the spotlight on her face. On the eve of the premiere Edith also 'adapted' the dress by adding pockets, for she still had problems wondering what to do with her hands – and she was an absolute triumph. Many people were so enraptured by her that they left the theatre after the interval, thinking her incapable of being followed by anyone, and over the next month every performance was a sell-out! Her biggest success, apart from the *Légion* songs, was 'Browning', the hapless story of the playboy gangster, whose nationality Asso changed from French to American because it was based on Pierre Le Balafré, whose body had recently been discovered in a back-alley. It was supposed to be a dramatic piece, though almost every time Edith sang it she had the audience in stitches.

> Il a roulé sous la banquette
> Avec un p'tit trou dans la tête . . .
> Oh, c'n'a pas claqué bien fort,
> Mais tout d'même il en est mort . . .
> Et puis quelqu'un dans le silence,
> A dit, 'Maint'nant à quoi tu penses?'
> Bye-bye, Browning!

> [He rolled under the bench
> With a little hole in his head . . .
> Oh, it didn't make a very big bang,
> But all the same he died of it . . .
> And then in the silence, someone said,
> 'What are you thinking about now?'
> Bye-bye, Browning!]

Most of the music for Edith's recital had been composed by the phenomenally talented Marguerite Monnot, now her very best friend and invariably referred to as Guite. As a child prodigy she had played Mozart in the Salle des Agricultures, and had later been a pupil of Nadia Boulanger before studying under Alfred Cortot. Her first commission had been for 'Ah, les jolis mots d'amour', which Claude Dauphin and Alice Tissot had hummed in a film, but it was her association with Edith that brought her world-wide fame. Likewise, had it not been for Guite, Edith's own rise to fame might not have been quite so sudden.

At around this time, it was revealed that Edith had appeared in a film, some time in 1936 – even her closest friends had no idea how she had managed this without their knowledge, and Edith herself later confessed that she had been very apprehensive about portraying a 'cucumber', as she dismissed her role in Jean de Limur's *La garçonne*. The story was extremely controversial for its day, and ran into immediate trouble with censors: a woman who is deserted by her husband seeks solace in a lesbian opium den. Its stars were Marie Bell, Arletty, and the chanteuse Suzy Solidor – Edith appeared for just a few minutes, singing Jean Wiener's 'Quand-même'.

Between 29 May and 4 June 1938, Edith topped the bill in 'Le Spectacle de la Chanson Française' at the Bobino – for this Asso wrote her 'Madeleine qu'avait du coeur', a sarcastic piece aimed at the woman he had been compelled to oust from his affections in order to keep Edith exclusive to him. On 28 October, she gave her first ever one-woman show, again at the Bobino, when the programme contained only Asso and Monnot songs. One, 'Je n'en connais pas la fin', the first of her records to sell half-a-million copies in France, would later be recorded in English and become a massive hit around the world.

On 11 November, as part of the Armistice Day celebrations, Edith shared top-billing with Marie Dubas at the ABC, an honour which she described as one of the proudest evenings of her life and a lucky omen. From now on there would be no looking back, though now she had attained such a high-point in her career, Raymond Asso found himself taking a back-seat in personal *and* professional development. Twenty-five years later, she incorporated an apology into her memoirs.

Raymond, I have already begged your forgiveness, and today I am asking you to forgive me once more. You were so good and kind, and I think you understand that, just because I went from one man to the next, it wasn't because I was a whore. It was simply because I was searching for one love great enough to transform my whole life . . .

Therefore, when Asso was called up on 4 August 1939 – setting herself yet another precedent as to how to treat the man in her life, once the flames of passion had started to cool – Edith had already found a replacement.

Chapter Three

LA COQUELUCHE
DES INTELLECTUELS

During the summer of 1939, Edith was singing at Le Night-Club, a cabaret on Rue Arsène-Houssaye. As her performances usually took place around midnight, she would often drop in at the nearby Caravelle Bar 'for a drop of Dutch courage' before going on stage, and it was here that she met Paul Meurisse, a twenty-six-year-old singer-conjuror who was appearing at L'Amiral, an establishment in direct competition with the one that had contracted Edith. Good-looking, with smouldering dark eyes and a winning smile, Meurisse was nevertheless snobbish and sophisticated, and therefore must have been something of a culture-shock to the sharp-tongued, fiery little singer from Belleville. Edith was actually startled, the first time he asked her out to dinner – no one had ever helped her on and off with her coat, or held her chair whilst she was sitting down. 'I was on my best behaviour all evening,' she recalled. 'Though when Paul asked me for an honest opinion about his *singing* voice – he used to do Valentino impressions and croon "Le tango c'est le tango" – I couldn't resist telling him how lousy it was!'

It was, once again, love at first sight. A few evenings later, Meurisse invited her to a cocktail party at his apartment and she stayed with him for another two years. And if her relationship with Asso had been merely tumultuous, this one would be nothing short of catastrophic from start to finish. Indeed, with her well-voiced loathing of snobs, one wonders whatever Edith saw in Meurisse in the first place.

When they met, Meurisse had just ended a relationship, and

was living on fashionable Rue Anatole-la-Forge, near l'Étoile. Edith, however, refused to spend the night in an apartment which had housed a former lover, so until alternative accommodation could be found Meurisse was compelled to move into Edith's room at the Alsina. Then, to enable herself to move up in the world, she rented the next room – for her recently-acquired secretary and for Tchang, her Chinese cook. And if the snooty Meurisse did not feel sufficiently humiliated and downgraded, he was told that Mômone would also be moving in, though for once her needs were genuine – her husband had been one of the early casualties of the war.

It was Mômone, the eternal gold-digger, who finally persuaded Edith that she was on to a winner with Meurisse, and a few weeks later she decided to move into the apartment on Rue Anatole-la-Forge. From this point, their relationship plummeted to the depths of neurosis. Meurisse had a habit of infuriating Edith by spending most of the day lounging around in his dressing-gown, reading the newspaper or listening to the wireless. Their rows brought a flood of complaints from the neighbours. Edith smashed most of the crockery, crept up on him when he was fast asleep to burst blown-up paper bags in his ear, rehearsed in the middle of the night, and worst of all smashed his valuable wireless set to the floor and trampled it underfoot before going out and getting blind drunk. And whilst all this was going on, Meurisse acted indifferently, giving her the impression that he could not have cared less, though in reality he was fuming within.

What Edith really wanted, of course, was for Meurisse to begin knocking her around the way Raymond Asso had done. According to Mômone, and a number of others, Edith never really had any respect for a man until he had slapped her.

On one occasion, Edith grew so weary of Meurisse's over-bearing, gentle manner that she stormed out of their apartment and went on the town with the singer Tino Rossi, though during their subsequent meal Rossi grew so fed up with hearing Meurisse's name that he rang the apartment and told him where to pick her up. This caused the most dreadful fracas. When Meurisse arrived at the restaurant, Edith tried to smash a champagne bottle over his head, though fortunately he managed to 'disarm' her before dragging her out to his taxi, screaming obscenities and yelling that somebody was trying to kidnap her. In the end he had to restrain her by laying her out on the pavement and sitting on her until the chauffeur had opened the door! Finally, she was given her reward – a shiny black eye which she proudly showed off to all her friends!

One of Edith's closest friends was the actress Yvonne de Bray, a larger-than-life character who shared her passion for drinking and having fun. It was during one particularly arduous session that Edith poured out her troubles, which had been building up for some time, and Yvonne in turn repeated the story to Jean Cocteau, who lived with his actor-lover Jean Marais on Rue de Beaujolais. Cocteau was fascinated. He had already seen her at the ABC, and he now invited Edith to join his social set – most of whom were as bizarre as he was, although everyone adored Edith because she had absolutely no airs and graces. Therefore they nominated her as their *coqueluche*, or darling. Cocteau was impressed by what she told him about her relationship with Paul Meurisse. Edith had suggested that he should write her a song about it, along the lines of 'Anna la Bonne', which Marianne Oswald had spoken over his piano accompaniment a few years earlier, but Cocteau had ideas of his own, and wrote her a one-act play which he entitled *Le bel indifférent*.

Edith was reluctant to accept a straight play, particularly when Cocteau announced that it would be sharing the bill with another of his works, *Les monstres sacrés*, starring Yvonne de Bray and Madeleine Robinson. She had never considered herself anything but a singer, and was afraid of what the critics might say, should she be pitched against such competition. However, when she learned that Meurisse would be playing 'the dummy lounging on the bed' she no longer hedged.

Le bel indifférent opened at the Bouffes-Parisiens during the spring of 1940, and was an unprecedented triumph. Meurisse, who a few years later would become renowned as an actor, did not have to utter a single word in the play – this was left to his 'mistress', who of course had had plenty of practice over the last few months!

The scene is a cheap hotel room, and the curtain rises to find the woman pacing up and down: she is waiting for Émile, her lover, to come home. She goes to the gramophone, and puts on one of her own recordings ('C'est lui qu'mon coeur a choisi'), and he enters. Ignoring her, Émile puts on his dressing-gown, lights a cigarette, and lounges on the bed with his newspaper. The woman speaks to him: he is indifferent to her presence and her moods change almost with every line of dialogue – passion, hatred, adoration, near-insanity, spite, pleading. Émile gets up to leave: she knows that he is on his way to see his mistress, whose photograph (one of Damia!) is on the wall. She threatens to kill him, then begs him to stay, and unable to stand any more he slaps her and walks out as she flings herself on to the bed, sobbing hysterically!

Edith actually told one journalist who accused her of going over the top in her characterization that there was little difference between the events in Cocteau's play and the real-life situation at home, which was steadily getting worse. She added, 'At home we don't have an audience – well, apart from the neighbours!'

In 1970, when interviewed for BBC Television's famous film-biography, *I regret nothing*, Paul Meurisse commented that if Piaf *was* a bad actress, she acted well in the Cocteau play inasmuch as General de Gaulle, himself a very poor singer, had made a good job of performing 'La Marseillaise'! Not an affable compliment, perhaps, though the reviews for the play spoke volumes for Edith's abilities as *une tragédienne par excellence*. Few people know that one evening, when Madeleine Robinson was taken ill, she took over *her* role in *Les monstres sacrés*! Meurisse, however, did not stay with the play until the end of its run – he received his call-up papers. Edith then contacted one of her friends, who knew the French Minister of War, and won a ten-day reprieve whilst a replacement could be found for the role of Émile. This was given to a young actor named Jean Marconi. During the run of the play she took a night off to appear in a concert for the Red Cross at the Bobino, and for one of the rare occasions in her career was unfaithful to her little black dress. Because there were hundreds of RAF boys in the audience, she wore an air-force blue suit and received a standing ovation for 'Où sont-ils mes petits copains?' – During the final verse the spotlight on her face fanned out to form a massive tricolour, which covered the entire stage.

Où sont-ils tous mes copains
Qui sont partis un matin faire la guerre?
Où est-il, mon beau p'tit gars?
Qui chantait, 'On reviendra,
Faut-pas s'en faire!'

[Where are all my mates
Who left one morning for the war?
Where's my handsome lad
Who sang, 'We'll be back –
Don't you worry!']

Paris had been sucked into the war. Raymond Asso had been called up, but Paul Meurisse had failed his medical, a situation which Edith put to good use: when *Le bel indifférent* closed in Paris, she and Meurisse travelled to Toulouse, where they began a long and successful tour of the Unoccupied Zone. Cocteau also informed her that he was writing her another play, now that he too was sheltering in the South. This was an adaptation of his own story, *Le fantôme de Marseille*. It told a somewhat woeful tale of an elderly man who falls in love with a young girl, only to discover that 'she' is a boy in disguise, on the run from the police. Edith never gave an official reason for turning the part down, though most of her friends agreed that it smacked too heavily of her association with Jacques Bourgeat.

Edith was unhappy working in the Unoccupied Zone. Unlike many of her fellow artistes, who had fled south or out of the country for reasons of their own, she pined for Paris and returned the day after *Le bel indifférent* closed. In doing so she became one of the unsung heroines of the Resistance. Like everybody else, she had to report regularly to the German *Propagandastaffel* on the Champs-Elysées so that the lyrics of her songs could be vetted. One, Marc Helly's biting 'Il n'est pas distingué' – Edith had recorded this old Fréhel song back in 1936 on the flipside of 'Les deux ménétriers' – had been played on the radio 'in error', and she had received a ticking-off from the Gestapo, but Edith had completely ignored an order to remove 'Où sont-ils mes petits copains?' from her repertoire. She fared well under the Germans, not because she kow-towed like many of her colleagues but because she was unafraid of standing up to them, and in doing so she earned their respect. Some of her Jewish friends were not so fortunate. Marcel Blistène (of whom more later) and Michel Emer fled to the South. Marie Dubas had her house seized by the Gestapo; she would spend the rest of the war in Portugal.

Edith despised the Germans, yet she was pragmatically circumspect in her relations with the *Propagandastaffel* personnel, in order to achieve her goal – to sing for French prisoners-of-war in Germany.

Mindless of the personal danger, and of what her colleagues may have been whispering behind her back – Maurice Chevalier was to find himself severely criticized and almost murdered for doing the same thing – she elected to become *marraine de guerre* (godmother of war) to the inmates of Stalag III. She chose this particular camp because of its large quota of Jews and homosexuals from the Belleville-Montmartre area of Paris. Early in 1940 she had engaged a young woman called Andrée Bigard as her secretary – in those days a job which amounted to little more than opening letters and answering the telephone. Though never short of male company, her friend Jacqueline Danno told me that Edith always needed a woman close at hand to confide in – most of the time this was Mômone, though in later years she would have Ginette Richer and Marlene Dietrich, amongst others.

Edith was sickened by some of the things she witnessed in the internment camp, as was Andrée Bigard, who formed part of her entourage, and between them the two women formulated a plan to help the Resistance. The Germans were knocked sideways by the Piaf voice, and the officers of Stalag III could not do enough to please her. What is utterly astonishing is the fact that she was still performing the Fréhel song, *and* 'Le fanion de la Légion', which the Germans had also banned, along with one or two others which would have got her into serious trouble, had she been singing them in Paris . . . especially the one which, she declared, expressed her appreciation of the Third Reich. When Edith begged the kommandant's permission to sing her own 'special adaptation' of the Hitlerian anthem, with his limited knowledge of the French language he did not know that she had 'spiced' it up a bit . . .

Dans le cul! Dans le cul!
Nous aurons la victoire!
Ils ont perdu toute espérance
De gloire, ils sont foutus!
Et l'monde en allégresse!

[Up your arse! Up your arse!
We shall have victory!
They've lost all hope of glory!
They're fucked!
And the world rejoices!]

Edith's performances in Stalag III were nothing short of explosive, and would have been even more so had the kommandant been told the truth! Some of the officers, of course, did understand but reported nothing back to their superiors – to have done such a thing would have robbed them of Edith's magnificent voice! And there was more! After each show Edith and Andrée Bigard were allowed to mingle with the prisoners: they chatted to them whilst memorizing their names and addresses. Edith then craved permission to have her photograph taken with everyone, insisting that the officers should also be included in the shots, so that everyone back home could see for themselves what a happy environment the prisoners were enjoying. The ruse worked every time. The films were taken back to Paris and developed, and the photographs enlarged, so that the heads and shoulders of some prisoners could be snipped off and mounted on to forged identity papers. Edith then sneaked these back into the camp – she never had any trouble being asked back for a repeat performance – and the prisoners were smuggled out a few at a time. The camp authorities trusted her so implicitly that they never realized that she was arriving with an entourage of seventeen, and actually leaving with twenty-five. She did almost slip up once, in the summer of 1942, when she was interviewed by the Gestapo, who suspected her of chartering the ship which their spies in the south had found moored in the docks at Marseilles, waiting to transport a cargo of prisoners to Dover. Had she not talked her way out of this exceedingly tight corner she would certainly have faced a firing squad. Moreover, she gave her interrogators free passes to her show that night and the Perroquet Club, and invited them to the party afterwards!

Ultimately, Edith helped almost three hundred prisoners-of-war to leave France, or travel to the Unoccupied Zone, and not enough may be said in praise of her exploits. This is why, twenty years later, the tricolour was draped over her coffin.

During the spring of 1940, another man entered Edith's life: a gawky-looking youngster with bottle-bottomed spectacles, Michel Emer, who a few months before his death in 1984 told me about his extraordinary stroke of luck, *chez* Piaf:

Edith was preparing for a new season at the Bobino, and I must have caught her in a bad mood. When her secretary announced that there was a young man at the door with a song she might be interested in, I heard her yell, 'Any excuse. Tell him to come back after the war!' So I shouted back, 'And if I'm killed, madame, you'll have missed out on one of the best songs you never heard!' At this, she came to the door, took one look at me and barked, 'Bugger me, it's Tojo. You'd better come in!' Then she added insult to injury by pointing to my corporal's uniform and saying, 'Well, until now I've never been able to resist a man in uniform, but it looks like even I'm going to have to draw the line somewhere. Tell me about yourself – you've got five minutes!' There was little to tell: I was in my early thirties, from a respectable Jewish family, and I was stationed at Val-de-Grace, off Boulevard Port-Royal . . . and I'd been given explicit instructions to return there by midnight, or risk a court-martial. So, I sat at the piano and began singing 'L'accordéoniste'. All the way through, Edith had her fingers in her ears and I was sure she was displeased with the song. Later she said it had been my voice – I've always been tone-deaf. Then, she asked me to play it again *without* singing, and after I'd finished she threw her hands in the air and cried, 'Formidable. I'm going to sing it at the Bobino premiere!' I was absolutely horrified, for that was only twenty-four hours off, and I was worried about getting back to base. Then she told her secretary to get my commanding officer on the line. God alone knows what she said to him, but I stayed with her until five the next morning, going over the song more than a hundred times. And there was no court-martial!

'L'accordéoniste' remains the archetypal *chanson-réaliste*, with its story of the prostitute who falls for the accordionist at the local dance-hall. And though all does not go according to plan, the couple can still aspire towards the future ...

> La fille de joie est triste,
> Au coin d'la rue là-bas,
> Son accordéoniste il est parti soldat.
> Quand il r'viendra d'la guerre,
> Ils prendront une maison,
> Elle sera la caissière et lui sera l'patron ...
>
> [The prostitute's sad,
> Over there on the street-corner,
> Her accordionist's gone off to be a soldier.
> When he returns from the war,
> They'll take over a 'house',
> She'll watch the till and he'll be boss ...]

The man does not return from the war, and in desperation the girl goes back on the beat, only to find that another accordionist has taken the place of her lover. Finally, unable to stand any more she screams for him to stop.

> Arretez! Arretez la musique!

The song was not a big success when Edith introduced it at the Bobino, primarily because of the last verse where the music runs on for several bars whilst the singer buries her face into the crook of her arm – the audience were not sure when to applaud. Within a few months, however, it had become her biggest hit thus far in her career, and it was the first of her recordings to sell a *million* copies, very unusual in France in those days. Michel Emer's only payment for the song, for the time being, was a free pass into the Unoccupied Zone, where he stayed until after the Liberation.

Still under the influence of Cocteau, and the unexpected

success of *Le bel indifférent* – and hanging on to their relationship by a decidedly slender thread – Edith and Paul Meurisse were approached by the film-director Georges Lacombe and shown the script for *Montmartre-sur-Seine*. Again, there was no hesitation. Edith had been wanting to make a film of her own since appearing briefly in *La garçonne*, and she hoped that this would prove the perfect vehicle. Again, the plot was uncomplicated. She played a flower-seller from Montmartre who falls in love with a local boy who, ironically perhaps, is madly in love with someone else. And in order to cope with her distress she dreams of becoming a famous singer. Part of the story is alleged to have been based on the Louis Dupont episode, which Edith had related to Lacombe much as the Meurisse affair had been repeated to Cocteau. The film was not a great commercial success in 1941, though it has since earned cult status amongst Piaf's fans, and is surprisingly well-made and entertaining.

One scene in the film remains memorable, and is reminiscent of the earlier 'Sous les toits de Paris': this is when Edith's character sings 'Tu es partout' on a bridge overlooking the Seine, 'accompanied' on the accordion by Henri Vidal, before assaulting the crowd that had gathered about her with an ungainly Bellevilloise patter in an attempt to sell copies of the sheet-music. For a while, she became amorously interested in Vidal, one of the most beautiful French actors of his generation, but quickly gave up on him when he failed to respond to her flirting. Her admirer in the film was played by a young actor named Jean-Louis Barrault, who would later star opposite Arletty in Marcel Carné's masterpiece, *Les enfants du paradis*. Later on, Lacombe would direct Gérard Philipe in the triumphant *Le pays sans étoile*, and Jean Gabin and Marlene Dietrich in the almighty flop, *Martin Roumagnac*.

Edith herself collaborated with Marguerite Monnot on the film's four-song soundtrack: besides 'Tu es partout' there was the jazzy 'J'ai dansé avec l'amour', 'L'homme des bars', and 'Un coin tout bleu'. Edith had also wanted to include Roméo Carlès 'Simple comme bonjour', a request which brought a vociferous complaint from the otherwise placid Monnot, who would never forgive Carlès for taking Edith under his wing after the argument with Raymond Asso over the *Légion* songs. Unable to hurt her friend's feelings, Edith agreed to drop the song, not just from the film but from her repertoire ... then caused more uproar when Damia visited the set, ostensibly to hear for herself if the rumour was true that these particular songs were the best that Piaf had ever sung. Edith, well-versed in the art of 'theft', sussed her out and demanded her opinion. Damia, whose extremely dramatic and frequently morbid songs were revered by the Germans – it is alleged because she had been born in Alsace-Lorraine at a time when it had been annexed to Germany – had caused a great deal of anguish, of late, amongst her 'Hun apaches' by substituting all of these with light-hearted ones, *besides* trading her classic floor-length black gown for a white one. She told me:

> Two of the songs were only so-so, but the others, 'Tu es partout' and 'Un coin tout bleu', were years ahead of their time. So, swallowing a huge piece of humble pie, I told her this. And what do you think happened? This tiny slip of a thing with the vocabulary of a docker suddenly burst into tears and said, 'Madame, they're yours!' She even accompanied me to the studio to supervise the session, and from that day I completely changed my opinion of her. She even wrote a song especially for me, 'Mon amour vient de finir, mon amour vient de partir, Je n'ai plus aucun désir ... Mon amour vient de mourir,' and so far as I know she never sang the song herself.

The publicity posters for *Montmartre-sur-Seine* were designed by Charles Kiffer, and though not always flattering, Edith liked them and because of this, Kiffer enjoyed a successful fifty-year career. Most important of all, however, was her introduction in December 1940 to Henri Contet, the man doubling as George Lacombe's press-attaché whilst reporting for *France-Soir* and *Cinémondiale*. Tall, good-looking and blond, Edith fell in love with the thirty-seven-year-old Contet on sight, and shortened his name to Riri – always a good sign, for their relationship brought her some of the finest songs she ever sang, though unlike her other lyricists, Contet is thought to have never gone through his work with Edith's composers. '*She* would decide who would be setting them to music,' he later said. 'And *always* with excellent results. I never had a say in the matter!'

The fact that Contet was as good as married mattered little to Edith, and after finishing the film – once the bronchitic Meurisse had vacated their apartment – her new lover was asked to move in. This he refused to do and, believing that Contet's reticence must have had something to do with the 'bad vibes' left behind by her former lover, Edith moved into another place a few blocks down the road. Contet, however, *still* refused to ditch his girlfriend, so Edith did as she had with Meurisse – she attempted to make him jealous by flirting with Yvon Jean-Claude, a young singer who was just breaking into the Parisian cabaret scene.

Denise Gassion later wrote of how, unable to make up her mind between Contet and the younger man, Edith had asked *her* to choose which of them should be her lover, and that she had plumped for Contet, personally holding herself responsible for the beautiful songs which followed. This, of course, is non-sense: throughout her entire life Edith *never* asked for anyone's advice about her lovers, and from the very start *she* had set her sights on Contet. She *did* sing a song with Yvon Jean-Claude, 'Le vagabond', which she wrote herself and which clearly marks the beginning of the Great Piaf years. As this had no effect on Contet, she went one step further by writing and recording 'C'est un monsieur très distingué', so clearly aimed at pricking his conscience.

> Il est d'la haute société,
> C'est c'qu'on appelle un homme du monde . . .
> Ses enfants seront très bien él 'vés . . .
> Je n'suis pas née dans son grand monde . . .
> C'est un monsieur très distingué!
>
> [He belongs to high society,
> What you call a man of the world . . .
> His children will be very well brought up . . .
> I haven't been born into his refined world . . .
> He's a very distinguished gentleman!]

The song gained Edith her lover's undying affection, but Contet insisted that they would never live together and he wrote *her* a song instead ... 'C'était une histoire d'amour', for which she thanked him by singing it as a duet with Yvon Jean-Claude! Even so, Contet knew that in writing for Piaf, he was on to a winner, for she was one of the few people in the world with an equal fondness for intense melodrama within her work. A few years before, he had written 'Traversée' for Lucienne Boyer, of 'Parlez-moi d'amour' fame – a real soot-and-flame piece so far removed from her usual gentle style that she had been devoured by the critics. During his first few months with Edith, Contet also regarded himself as the official replacement for Raymond Asso, whose songs she would only perform spasmodically over the ensuing years – her way, she said, of avenging him for deserting her. Things would not work out quite this way, as will be seen, yet in a songwriting career spanning forty years, though Contet would not work exclusively for Edith, few would argue that all his best songs were performed by her.

At the beginning of 1942, just weeks after the release of *Montmartre-sur-Seine*, Edith was offered the second female lead in another film, *Le chant de l'éxilé*, which had been devised for Tino Rossi. She spent some time working through the script, changing whole lines of dialogue and even composing the score with Henri Bourtayre, who had just set Henri Contet's 'Le chasseur de l'hôtel' to music for her. However, she very quickly ditched the idea of having anything to do with Rossi when informed by a Resistance contact that the Corsican chanteur's wartime activities were 'suspect', and for the rest of her life she would loathe him.

A few weeks later, with the advent of fuel-rationing adding to the fact that her expenditure was by far outweighing her income, Edith gave up her apartment and asked Contet to find her somewhere more suitable – she was also probably hoping that, like Asso, he would get rid of his 'wife' and ask her to live with him. This did not happen. The composer was on friendly terms with Madame Billy, who ran the infamous brothel on Rue Villejuste (now Rue Paul-Valéry), and Edith subsequently rented the entire third floor. Living *chez* Madame Billy, she declared, would bring her luck because the brothel, like the one at Bernay, had two pianos. She was certainly more content living there than she had been with Paul Meurisse, and she stayed there for almost two years, until the brothel was closed down on account of Madame Billy's black-market racketeering. She moved in at once, bringing Andrée Bigard, Tchang, and of course Mômone with her, and was never short of company, day or night. Regular visitors included the actresses Marie Bell, Yvonne de Bray and Madeleine Robinson, and Cocteau spent a lot of time there with Jean Marais and the actor, Michel Simon.

It mattered little to Edith that 'home' was a favourite haunt of German officers – by being seen to be friendly with them, she was offered an invaluable cover for her Resistance work. She was also visited by her parents. Louis Gassion, retired now and in poor health, came to collect the food parcels she had had made up: for years she had been trying to get him to move away from Belleville, but he was still living in the run-down apartment block on Rue Rébéval. Edith had recently provided him with a manservant, which of course had made him the talk of the district. Absolutely no one in that part of town could afford hired help! As for Line Marsa, she made a nuisance of herself by scrounging money not for food, but for drink and drugs. She had already served a prison sentence for trafficking, but the worst insult of all came when Michel Emer sent Edith the sheet-music for 'De l'autre côté de la rue', which he had written whilst in exile. Edith's mother had rubbed salt into Edith's wounds by performing the song in public.

> Des murs qui se lézardent,
> Un escalier étroit,
> Une vieille mansarde et me voilà chez moi!
> De l'autre côté de la rue y'a une fille,
> Une belle fille . . .
> Vivre un seul jour sa vie,
> J'n'en demand'rais pas plus . . .
>
> [Cracked walls, a narrow staircase,
> An old attic room, that's my place!
> On the other side of the street
> There's a beautiful girl . . .
> I would ask for nothing more
> Than to live one day of her life . . .]

Because Line Marsa had purloined the song, Edith came close to refusing it, but if her mother's plight – albeit self-inflicted – had *almost* succeeded in moving her to pity, this singularly selfish act made her decide never to have anything to do with her again. Manouche, the famous former mannequin who became the mistress of the Corsican gangster, Paul Carbone, had recently befriended Edith. Having rebelled against her convent-school education, met Mistinguett backstage at the Casino de Paris and been unofficially adopted as her god-daughter, Manouche had just been 'widowed' when Carbone's train had been blown up by the Resistance. She told me:

Piaf – and I never once called her by her first name – offered me a shoulder to cry on in those days. Whenever you were with her, there was never a dull moment. We were in Billy's sitting-room, and Piaf was singing Misting-uett's 'Mon homme' when all of a sudden this other voice came floating in through the half-open window – almost a copy of Piaf's voice, singing 'Mon légionnaire'. Piaf screwed up her face and bellowed at Cocteau, 'It's my fucking mother. Quick, pass me the piss-pot!' When I rushed to the window, I saw Line Marsa out in the street. She was dressed in red, rocking back and forth as if in pain. Cocteau ignored Piaf's instruction, and threw her a banknote. Line Marsa hoisted her skirts, pretended to wipe her backside on it, and left. Piaf slammed the window shut, and I think she assumed she'd seen the last of her. No such luck. Every morning for two weeks she was out there, crowing until one of us threw her some money to shut her up.

The only good that came from these unwelcome 'invasions' was that one day Line Marsa brought along a young man named Herbert Gassion. If this woman's story is to be given any credence, when they had separated some twenty years before, Edith's mother had been carrying Louis Gassion's child. The more plausible theory, however, given Line Marsa's character, is that Herbert could have been fathered by almost anyone. Even so, he does *appear* to have been her half-brother, and history had repeated itself when his mother abandoned him to be brought up by the Public Assistance. Just how close Edith was to him is not easy to determine: like Mômone and Denise Gassion he received the occasional letter and sometimes posed for photographs with her, though none of these people warranted sufficient importance to be mentioned in her two autobiographies.

'De l'autre côté de la rue' would also spark off another row – between Edith and Michel Emer. Convinced that she would not record the song now that it had been 'sullied' by her mother, Emer gave permission for it to be recorded by Renée Lebas, a young singer who had acquired a sizeable following amongst the Left Bank café society. Unfortunately, most of her songs had been 'borrowed' from established stars. She had already annoyed Edith in the past with her cover-versions of 'Le grand voyage du pauvre nègre' and 'On danse sur ma chanson' – the latter, an Asso composition, had been released on the same *day* as Edith's version, causing Edith to contact Lebas and warn her in no uncertain terms what might happen, should she pull such a stunt again. Lebas had subsequently vowed never to record another Piaf song in a French studio. Two years later, however, she had got around this by cutting a 78rpm whilst on a tour of Switzerland – 'Le vagabond', coupled with 'L'accordéoniste'. When Edith was told that she had most recently recorded 'De l'autre côté de la rue', she was *so* furious that she went around all of her songwriters and made them swear on the Bible that they would neither write for Lebas nor allow her to sing any of their existing songs, even the ones which had not been performed by Piaf. Because of this, Renée Lebas' career took a sudden nosedive, and today she is remembered only by very serious devotees of the *chanson*. As for 'De l'autre côté de la rue', Edith would not record it until 1945, when it would feature in her very last session for Polydor.

On 17 October 1942 Edith began a three-week stint at the ABC, where her programme featured twelve songs by Henri Contet. These included 'Le chasseur de l'hôtel', 'Le brun et le blond', and a number of others which she recorded between December 1942 and April 1943 – recordings which, along with several cut by Marlene Dietrich and Gracie Fields during visits to Paris, have never been released. One theory is that the master copies were destroyed by the Germans, though I *have* heard the first pressing of 'Le disque usé'. Edith closed her ABC recitals with 'Monsieur Saint-Pierre', a bold piece which tells the story of the sinner who turns up at the gates of heaven, where she begs St Peter to let her in because she never *meant* to be so bad. On account of the subject, Edith first recorded the song with an 'angel' choir, but was so appalled by the result that she ordered the engineer to destroy the acetate. He did not, and after spending more than fifty years in a Polydor vault it was dis-covered in 1996, and released on a compilation – a welcome antidote to the faulty 'regular' recording of 1943, which has a pronounced 'wobble' in the first few bars.

There was also grand drama at the ABC, minutes before the curtain rose on the premiere. When Edith observed that the first three rows of the stalls were filled with German officers, she stormed into Mitty Goldin's office and demanded an expla-nation. Goldin told her that it was 'house policy' for French theatregoers holding tickets for the stalls to swap seats with any Germans who had only been able to acquire seats for the galleries. Upon hearing this, Edith rushed to her dressing-room and put on her coat – after announcing over the tannoy *why* she was leaving. Fortunately, her Bellevilloise *argot* was too strong for the Germans to comprehend, and Goldin came up with a more tactful solution. The officers were told that, as Madame Piaf was very small and likely to be obscured from view by the footlights, they would be far better off sitting in the dress-circle. Edith then rewarded them by singing a few bars from 'Dans le cul'!

On 30 January 1943 Edith opened at the Folies-Belleville, and her supporting act was billed as Le Chanteur Sans Nom, quite a good publicity gimmick until his name was revealed to be Roland Avelys. The pair became close friends, though never lovers as has been suggested. Avelys was also a great practical joker. Edith was once halfway through a recital, in 1960, when she suddenly doubled up as if in great pain. Thinking her about to collapse, her impresario rushed on to the stage to witness the spectacle, within the orchestra-pit and out of sight from the audience, of Avelys' bare backside, into which he had inserted a lighted pipe! Le Chanteur Sans Nom's biggest commercial success, 'Tous mes rêves passés', which he recorded in 1953, was penned by Edith.

Je me revois lorsque j'avais vingt ans,
Que de chagrins j'ai dû faire à ma mère,
Que de tourments et combien de misères,
D'espoirs perdus emportés par le vent.

[I see myself again when I was twenty,
Such worries, torments and distress
That I must have caused my mother,
Lost hopes carried off by the wind.]

The next few months were extremely busy for Edith. On 15 April 1943 she participated in the 'Revue des Chansons', an important event in the music-hall calendar, and on 10 May she opened at La Vie en Rose, a small cabaret in the heart of Pigalle. Five days later she sang at the Casino de Paris – one of the rare occasions that the establishment, famed for its revues, opened its doors to a serious singer – and on 19 May she appeared in a gala at the ABC with Damia and Charles Trenet. And whilst all this was going on, she spent what little spare time she had rehearsing new songs for a forthcoming season at the ABC! These recitals proved more popular than anything she had ever done before. She opened on 11 June and was accompanied by the Claude Normand Ensemble. Her biggest successes were her own 'C'est l'histoire de Jésus', and Michel Emer's 'Le disque usé', which ended with her impersonating a cracked old record. She also introduced Jacques Besse's doleful 'Un monsieur me suit dans la rue', a song which had a strange, ironic twist. During the last verse, a piano plays a few bars from the Funeral March, and just six weeks after the record was released, Edith was informed of her father's death, at the age of sixty-two. She was devastated, but took some consolation in the fact that Louis Gassion had not died alone: his faithful manservant had remained at his bedside until the end. No expense was spared for his funeral, which was described by Denise Gassion in *Piaf, ma soeur*.

Edith took Papa in her arms. Yvon Jean-Claude was there: he had been touring Switzerland and had promised to bring Papa some chocolate. Too late, he made up for this by removing his gold cross and wrapping it around Papa's wrist. I will never forget that gesture. Thank you, Yvon! Then, on Wednesday 8 March, at St-Jean-le-Baptiste in Belleville – the service took place. Edith had had the chancel decked out in black: there was a long black carpet leading to the altar, and even the chairs were draped in black. It was my thirteenth birthday . . .

The prostitutes from the bordello in Bernay filed into the church to pay their last respects, and the surviving members of Louis' family travelled from Falaise, in Normandy. He was buried in the vault which Edith had bought for herself, within the 97th Division of the Père Lachaise cemetery. There then followed an event which would be repeated some six years later for someone else she loved dearly: that same night Edith gave a recital, telling her audience that the applause would be not for her, but for her father.

On 8 April 1945, Edith's mother would die, aged forty-six, of a drug overdose. For several months Line Marsa had been living with her bisexual lover, André Comès, a fellow addict twenty years her junior. When Comès found her dead on the floor he panicked, thinking that if the nature of her death was disclosed, he would be hauled in by the police. He therefore dragged the body into the next-door apartment whilst the occupant was at work. By the time the undertaker arrived it had been wrapped in a piece of sacking and dumped in the gutter.

Edith refused to have anything to do with Line Marsa's funeral, and did not even attend the ceremony. The arrangements were made by Henri Contet, by now hanging on to his relationship with Edith by the skin of his teeth – she was still two-timing him with Yvon Jean-Claude. She then gave instructions for Marcelle Dupont's body to be exhumed from the churchyard at Thiais, just outside Paris: she was laid next to her grandfather in Père Lachaise. Line Marsa was then interred in Marcelle's old grave, and if some years later Edith wrote lovingly of her mother in her memoirs, this was only to placate her readers, who she feared might criticize her for her lack of sensitivity. In fact, she had absolutely nothing to reproach herself for – few mothers could have been more callous towards their offspring than Line Marsa.

Chapter Four

UN REFRAIN COURAIT
DANS LA RUE

In April 1944, Edith celebrated her tenth anniversary as a professional entertainer. Her records were selling well, every one of her performances was playing to a packed house, and she was earning a more than modest income. On the negative side, however, she still did not have an apartment of her own, there had hardly ever been a man in her life who had not been married or attached, and there was no regular impresario to look after her affairs. Intermittently, she had been handled by the OSA, the agency which managed artistes as diverse as the singer Lucienne Delyle and her bandleader husband, Aimé Barelli, the boxer Marcel Cerdan, and Michel Emer. Their headquarters were at the Club de Cinq, in Montmartre, where Emer's renowned Swing-Band played most nights, accompanying impromptu performances from regulars such as Lucienne Boyer, Suzy Solidor, and even Maurice Chevalier.

In those days, Edith's fees were paid directly to her, or to Andrée Bigard, who always tried her utmost to put a little aside for the proverbial rainy day once Edith's expenses had been met. These, of course, were colossal. Not only were there the endless overnight revelries, but Edith had already started to attract the leeches who, in later life, would bleed her dry. None of them were worse than Mômone, who was using her 'sister' as a meal-ticket for the upkeep of her family. Then, in April 1944, Edith met Louis Barrier – not in some expensively-furnished office, but in the street when he almost knocked her down with his bicycle!

By way of an apology, Barrier asked Edith if *she* would do

him the honour of allowing him to become her agent, and she was so bowled over by the young man's audacity that she agreed! 'Loulou', as he was re-christened, would represent Piaf for the rest of her life and stand by her through the very worst of her traumas. Aside from Marlene Dietrich, Jacques Bourgeat and Marguerite Monnot, he was the only person in the world she trusted implicitly.

Within a week of becoming 'Piaf's right-hand man', Barrier had secured her a two-week season at the Moulin-Rouge, then a temple for the *chanson* and very far-removed from the dollar-and-yen-trap of the present day. For the first time, too, Edith was allowed to choose the artiste who closes the first half of the programme, and she set her sights on Roger Dann, a popular operatic-style singer then very much in demand. He, unfortunately, was not available, and as she could think of no one else, Edith told the management to choose. They came up with Yves Montand, a young Italian-born crooner who would set another precedent as the first in a long, distinguished line of artistes she would alternately love, nurture, mould and bully towards national and international fame.

Montand had been born Yvo Livi in Monsumano Alto, in October 1921, but when young had moved with his family to Marseilles, in order to evade the fascism of Mussolini. Leaving school at the age of fourteen, he had taken a number of jobs before becoming a docker. Three years later, he had begun supplementing his meagre income by singing in suburban theatres and cinemas, emulating cowboy songs and the semi-surrealistic works of his idol, Charles Trenet. Edith had first seen Montand in 1944 at the ABC, when he had been *vedette-américaine* to André Dassary, the lead vocalist with the Ray Ventura Orchestra, who had caused a stir by singing 'Maréchal nous voilà!', a personal hymn to the hated Pétain.

When Edith and Montand first became professionally involved, he was in the middle of an affair with Réda Caire (1908–63), who had begun his career partnering Mistinguett in a 1938 revue. Caire was of course sent packing, once Edith got her claws into Montand, yet she did later explain that there had been a great deal of difference between loving a handsome man and actually *liking* him.

His self-complacency narked me. I didn't understand what people saw in him – he sang badly, he could not dance and he had no timing. But once I had allowed myself to be pushed into taking him on, I realized at once that I would make something of him. The young are always the same when starting out. They think the world is going to be bowled over by their cynicism and wit. So I told him, 'Nobody's going to be bowled over by *you!*'

In fact, the feeling between the two artistes was decidedly mutual, for Montand at once branded her a *marchand de cafard* . . . a merchant of gloom! In spite of what she said, however, he did have a recommendable stage-presence, and his voice for one so young was curiously deep and resonant. Edith mercilessly criticized him for his choice of material, for his clothes, and for his 'dreadful' Marseillaise accent, though here she had a legitimate point – many years before, the revue star Gaby Deslys had been booed off the stage for her accent, and she had only become recognized by the general public once she had taken elocution lessons. The lessons offered by Edith were, to say the least, original. For several weeks she made him speak for hours on end with a pencil clenched between his teeth, and even so he never completely rid himself of his 'problem' – just as well, of course, considering that Piaf's own great quality was that she never lost her own Bellevilloise *argot*, which probably equates best to the English Cockney. The clothes she did remedy without too much fuss – Montand was advised to leave off his loud-checked jackets and sing in his shirt-sleeves, which certainly prevented him from perspiring half to death under the spotlight, and which also highlighted his superb silhouette, second only to Edith's until her successor, Barbara, took Paris by storm in the early sixties.

Edith's greatest trial came when she tried to stop Montand from singing the mock-cowboy songs written for him by the blind composer, Charles Humel. She convinced him that, with the Liberation just around the corner, his fake Americanisms would make him the butt of everyone's jokes once the real Americans arrived on the scene. With incredible nerve, she then asked Henri Contet to write him a complete repertoire of new songs – not a very wise thing to do, considering she was only stringing Henri along until finally convinced that Montand loved her as much as she adored him. This, of course, was the regular Piaf pattern – never to dump her current man until a replacement had been found. She also exacted immense pleasure from playing one man against the other, involving them in a potentially dangerous game of cat-and-mouse. Whenever she was with Henri Contet, she always made a point of getting a pal to call her at the 'crucial' moment so she could pretend that it was Montand on the line, and vice-versa. When the two men in her life began hating each other, despite their professional liaison, she then cheated on the pair of them by roping Yvon Jean-Claude back into her affections. This almost backfired on her when the young man was 'caught out' and forced to hide in a wardrobe for several hours before making his exit, stark naked, through a first-floor window! The crunch came when Edith thought she was two-timing Yves with Henri Contet, when all the time the singer was listening at the keyhole.

> I almost died of shame when I saw him standing there. His hand was bleeding from having crushed the glass that he had been holding, and he was livid. 'Don't ever do that to me again,' he said. 'You've got away with it this time, but next time I won't be responsible. I felt like killing you . . .'

Henri Contet provided Yves Montand with a handful of classic songs which he retained in his repertoire for the rest of his career. 'Gilet Raye', about an innkeeper who becomes a convict; 'Ce monsieur-là', about an inconsequential little man who evades the pressures of life by committing suicide; and 'Battling Joë', his most celebrated early song about the luckless boxer who goes blind. Edith also wrote him several songs which, though by no means technically or lyrically sound – her song-writing style would improve a few months later when offered a boost of confidence by passing her SACEM Socíete des Auteurs, Compositeurs et Musicians examination – have withstood the passage of time. These were 'Mais qu'est-ce que j'ai?', 'Il fait des . . .', 'Elle a des yeux', and 'La grande cité'.

Comme c'est drôle,
La vie perdue dans la cohue,
La sérénade des fauchés
Monte comme une mélopèe ...
Et le Bon Dieu qui est là-haut,
Doit trouver ça rigolo!

[How funny,
Life lost amongst the throng,
The serenade of reapers
Rises like a chant ...
And God on high must find this comical!]

Edith's season at the Moulin-Rouge was its usual sell-out, but if she received dozens of standing ovations every night, her protégé's reception was barely more than lukewarm. For this reason, Louis Barrier suggested dropping Montand from her forthcoming tour of France, something she vociferously opposed. Needless to say, from his point of view the tour grew increasingly more disastrous the further south he progressed. In his former stamping-ground of Lyons, Orléans and particularly Marseilles, the audiences felt so hostile towards his changed style that he was jeered. Some years later he said in an interview that he had only pulled through his ordeal because Edith had been standing in the wings every night, guiding his movements and encouraging him by alternately blowing him kisses and cursing him black-and-blue! Thus he became perhaps the only French male 'all-rounder', aside from Maurice Chevalier, to become a household name all over the world.

Of course, now that Edith had achieved her goal, her relationship with Yves Montand cooled somewhat. After the tour the pair returned to the Paris Étoile and the Alhambra. It was at the latter that she was introduced to the man she often referred to as her *génie-musicien*. Marc Bonel was a thirty-year-old accordionist who had recently accompanied Mistinguett in her revue, 'Paris-Paname', which was about to be revived. However, when Edith's regular accordionist, the Belgian Rudy Wharton, failed to turn up for the Alhambra premiere, the director Ray Plexon purloined Bonel, ostensibly for this one performance until a more permanent replacement could be found. Edith was so impressed that she told Bonel she would pay him twice the salary he had been getting from Mistinguett – a shrewd move, for La Miss was renowned for her stinginess, and had not been paying him much at all. This of course did not put Edith in a favourable light as far as Wharton was concerned – he threatened to sue her, dropped the case when he realized that *he* had been in the wrong, and soon afterwards he left for the United States, where he enjoyed a long career as a session musician at a number of recording studios. As for Mistinguett, she swore that if she ever came face to face with 'la petite salope en noir' she would scratch her eyes out. Fortunately, such a meeting never took place!

Although these Piaf-Montand recitals were immensely successful, they did cause a number of professional clashes. Firstly, Montand no longer considered himself *vedette-américaine* material, though his repertoire was probably not quite extensive enough to allow him star-billing. Secondly, now that he was a star, few establishments could afford the luxury of having him on the same bill as Piaf. Fortunately for Edith's entourage, who always suffered whenever she was between lovers, the parting of the ways took longer than expected on account of the film they made together.

Critics and admirers of Piaf alike have unanimously agreed that *Étoile sans lumière* was her best film, putting her in the same class as a Magnani, or even a Dietrich. It was directed by Marcel Blistène, whom Edith had befriended during the Occupation. A Jew, he had been hidden by Andrée Bigard at her farm, near Fréjus on the Côté d'Azur. Here, in comparative seclusion, he had completed his screenplay only with Edith in mind.

The story takes place in 1930. Stella Dora (Mila Parely), a famous star from the silent era, is desperate to make the transition to the newly-arrived talkies, but has failed her voice-test. Her agent takes her to his country home, where he hears the maid, Madeleine (Piaf), singing whilst about her chores, and decides to take advantage of her. He takes her to Paris where a technician (Serge Reggiani) feeds her hopes of becoming a famous chanteuse by inviting her to sing in front of a microphone. What Madeleine does not know is that her voice is being recorded to be dubbed over Stella's in a film. When she finally learns the truth during the film's premiere – Stella mimes to the superb 'Adieu mon coeur' whilst her character is chained to the wall in her prison cell – she is naturally upset, and the agent tries to make amends by offering her an engagement in a music-hall. Her favourite song is 'C'est merveilleux', which she has sung to Pierre, her lover (Montand) in the now infamous scene when the lovers are driving along a country road. Unfortunately, she dries up whilst trying to sing it in front of an audience, and collapses. Stella, filled with remorse over what she has done, commits suicide by driving off the road . . . whilst Madeleine returns to her village to be consoled by the man she loves.

The five songs for *Étoile sans lumière* were written by Henri Contet and Marguerite Monnot (the other three songs were 'C'était une histoire d'amour', 'Le chant du pirate' and 'Mariage'), and the film was a massive hit in France. In the United States, once Edith had become established there, it was an unexpected box-office sensation, playing in one New York cinema for fifty-two weeks. It also launched Serge Reggiani's enterprising film career – not long afterwards he and Montand scored a triumph in Marcel Carné's *Les portes de la nuit*.

To get over Piaf, Yves Montand embarked on another brief flirtation with Réda Caire. The greatest love of his life, however, would be the actress Simone Signoret, whom he married a few years later, though this never prevented him from expressing his profound admiration for Edith, and they remained close friends for the rest of her life.

On 3 April 1946, the day *Étoile sans lumière* was released, Edith signed a contract with French Pathé-Marconi which, barring two short breaks in 1947 and 1948 when she recorded ten songs for Decca with Raymond Legrand and his orchestra, would continue until her death. Three of the songs from the film featured in the first recording session of 23 April, one week before she was scheduled to embark on a tour of Alsace, organized by the Théâtre aux Armés. As Yves Montand now had other commitments, she was accompanied by a group of nine talented young singers who had started out as Les Compagnons de la Musique, but who had recently changed their name to Les Compagnons de la Chanson – they had appeared on the same bill as Edith the previous year, in a gala at the Comédie-Française that had been cut short by an air-raid. Impressed by their extraordinary vocal technique, Edith decided to take them under her wing:

Gérard, René, Albert, Hubert, Marc, Jo, Guy, Fred Mella their lead singer, and Jean-Louis Jaubert, the leader of the troupe who became her lover. The rehearsals for the tour coincided with Edith moving into a new apartment at 26 Rue de Berri – and to the amazement of the neighbours, all nine Compagnons moved in with her!

Back in 1944, when Edith and Yvon Jean-Claude had been appearing at Le Coup de Soleil in Lausanne, Switzerland, she had been introduced to Jean Villard, a middle-aged *chansonnier* better known in France by his pseudonym, Gilles. Edith was already familiar with his work, having recorded his 'Browning' and 'Le contrabandier' in 1937, though she had not met him then. Gilles had offered her 'Les trois cloches', in its original form more of a folk-song than the dramatic type of song that Edith preferred, which is why she had declined it. Now, however, she was incensed to hear the song on the radio, performed by a young singer named Edith Burger, and she telephoned Gilles, demanding to know why he had given *her* song to a 'wailer' who in her opinion possessed no talent whatsoever? The *chansonnier* attempted to explain that Burger had only been given the song because *she* had turned it down, but Edith would not listen. She told Gilles that she had decided to sing 'Les trois cloches' with Les Compagnons de la Chanson, and that it was now up to him to order Edith Burger to remove it from her repertoire – moreover, she also insisted that *she* be given another song that Gilles had composed for Burger, 'A l'enseigne de la fille sans coeur'. The man had no option but to agree. Being performed by Piaf was, after all, good for one's bank-balance!

When Edith adapted 'Les trois cloches' for herself and Les Compagnons de la Chanson, it became a true *chanson-réaliste*, telling the story in everyday words of the birth, marriage and death of one Jean-Francois Nicot in a small, provincial village. Nowadays it is frequently regarded as kitschy, and lampooned, but when the recording was released during the summer of 1946, in France it was hailed as a symbol of potent patriotism, a welcome antidote to the harsh ravages suffered by the country under the German Occupation.

> Village au fond de la vallée
> Loin des chemins, loin des humains,

Voici, qu'après dix-neuf années,
Coeur en émoi, Jean-François
Prend pour femme la douce Elise . . .

[A village, deep in the valley,
Far from roads and humans,
Here, after nineteen years,
Heart all-aflutter, Jean-François
Takes sweet Elise for his wife . . .]

'Les trois cloches', with absolutely no musical accompaniment, opens with Fred Mella singing the verse, and as this develops into a haunting crescendo Edith's voice is launched into the refrain. The first time it was performed on stage, she broke with her own tradition and wore a full-length, pale blue dress, a kind of 'prop' for the song which followed it on the bill, 'La fille en bleue', which was successful in Switzerland and Alsace, but never recorded commercially. The shellac recording of 'Les trois cloches' sold 60,000 copies within three weeks of its release in France – almost equalling Lucienne Boyer's 'Parlez-moi d'amour' of the previous decade. The English-speaking world got to know Jean-François Nicot as Jimmy Brown, and the song became Edith's ambassador in England and America. Ten years later she sang it alone, in English, as did Les Compagnons, and of the six songs they sang together, only this one made any great impression on the world. 'Piaf's voice is likened to an agate stream, flowing through their bronze and golden bell,' wrote her friend Cocteau.

All of a sudden, Les Compagnons de la Chanson were in demand everywhere, and quickly acquired a more definitive repertoire – though they still retained some of their former folk-songs and campfire ditties, such as 'Pérrine était servante', which appeared on the flipside of 'Les trois cloches'. Charles Trenet wrote them 'Mes jeunes années', they had a tremendous success worldwide with Georges Auric's theme from 'Moulin-Rouge', and Raymond Asso wrote them 'Comme un p'tit coquelicot'. Edith also gave them 'La Marie', which had been written for *her* by André Grassi, an unusual song for any woman to sing, let alone Edith Piaf.

T'en fais pas, la Marie, t'es jolie,
J'reviendrai . . .
Nous aurons du bonheur plein la vie,
T'en fais pas, Marie . . .

[Don't worry, Marie, you're lovely,
I'll be back . . .
We'll have a life full of happiness,
Don't worry, Marie . . .]

The song won the group the Grand Prix du Disque, but it was not included in the film which they made with Edith. Directed by Georges Freedland, *Neuf garçons et un coeur* was filmed over a period of just twelve days, and on a limited budget. It was a musical fantasy set one Christmas Eve. Christine [Piaf] is the leader of a group of hard-up singers who are waiting to find their own particular crock of gold at the end of the rainbow. First she falls asleep and dreams that she and her friends are in heaven, only to wake up to the harsh reality that for them all, the festive season will be a frugal time. Then, the true miracle occurs when they are hired by a kindly benefactor (Lucien Baroux) to perform in his club . . . Le Paradise.

Attached to this easy-going plot were five songs: 'C'est pour ça' and 'Les trois cloches' with Les Compagnons, and solo performances of the self-composed 'Un refrain courait dans la rue', 'Sophie', and one number which almost did not make it as far as the screen.

Quand il me prend dans ses bras,
Il me parle tout bas,
Je vois la vie en rose!
Il me dit des mots d'amour,
Des mots de tous les jours,
Et ça m'fait quelquechose!

[When he takes me in his arms,
He speaks low to me,
I see life in a rosy hue!
He says words of love,
Everyday words that do something to me!]

Edith had been sitting in a Parisian restaurant with a friend, the now-forgotten singer Marianne Michel, in May 1945 when an idea for a song had suddenly taken her senses 'by storm'. Unable to find any writing paper at a moment's notice, she had borrowed an eyebrow-pencil and had scribbled the words to 'Les choses en rose' on the tablecloth! Though against her character to 'mould' anyone she was not physically attracted to, she had offered the song to her friend, probably thinking that it was not much good anyhow, and Marianne had rebaptized it 'La vie en rose' because, she claimed, it had sounded better that way. The story would have ended there, had it not been for Edith's difficulties with the SACEM.

In those days in France, it was not possible for any artiste's composition to be performed in public or recorded unless he or she had passed their SACEM examination. Edith had already written a number of songs, but these had always been signed for by experienced songwriters. Marguerite Monnot would have nothing to do with 'La vie en rose', claiming that it sounded too much like the old Eugénie Buffet song, 'Les petits qui n'ont pas de nid', and Henri Contet dismissed it as 'rubbish'. Robert Chauvigny, who had signed one of her film songs and just become her orchestra leader, declared that he would only accept responsibility for this one as a last resort. Eventually it was signed by Louis Guglielmi, who under the pseudonym Louiguy had composed 'Le vagabond'. The song was then recorded by Marianne Michel, and a cover-version made by Roland Gerbeau, the charm-singer lover of Charles Trenet, who only succeeded in making it sound more syrupy than Edith could possibly have intended. 'Every time Gerbeau sings my song, I have to rush out and throw up,' she later told Marlene Dietrich, 'I wish I'd never written the accursed thing!' But if she never cared for the song, initially, public demand and her own conscience demanded that it be committed to shellac, and she recorded it in October 1946, whence it became the third biggest success of her career – after 'Hymne à l'amour' and 'Milord'.

Without waiting for the public release of *Neuf garçons et un coeur*, Edith and Les Compagnons signed independent contracts to appear in separate nightclubs in New York, and filled in the interim period with a tour of Greece. From everyone's point of view this was a disaster because the country was embroiled in a general election campaign. Again, now that her protégés had been etched on to the map of the music-hall, her ardour for Jean-Louis Jaubert had cooled somewhat, and after her Athens premiere she allowed herself to be swept off her feet by Takis Menelas, a struggling young actor who inadvertently gave her a taste for mean and moody Greek men.

Takis fell for Edith in a big way. In his early twenties, and undeniably handsome, he showed her the Acropolis by moonlight, and actually proposed marriage one evening within the shadow of the Parthenon, vowing to relinquish his career should she elect to stay with him in Greece . . . not that Edith would have given up her career for all the happiness in the world. Even so, she would have thought about his offer, married him and taken him back to Paris, had it not been for one small detail – Takis already *had* a wife! One week later, the pair parted reluctantly, but there was a coda to their story, as she explained in her memoirs,

> Four years later I saw Takis again, in Paris. He had just turned down fame and fortune, and a fabulous contract, on account of his being homesick. He told me, 'I know you no longer love me, but I haven't forgotten you. In memory of you I really *did* divorce my wife.'

Edith's brief affair with Takis Menelas gave her one of her most moving songs. After her return from Greece, she repeated the story of what had happened to Michel Emer, and in the space of twenty-four hours he gave her 'Si tu partais', the first of her songs to be translated into English, when it became 'If you go', a big hit for Peggy Lee.

> Si un jour tu partais sans retour,
> Les fleurs perdraient leur parfum,
> Et ce serait la fin de toute joie,
> Reste avec moi . . .
> J'en mourrais si tu partais.
>
> [If you left without returning,
> The flowers would lose their perfume,
> And it would be the end of all joy,

Stay with me . . .
I would die if you left.]

Edith now began planning the greatest challenge of her career
so far – her visit to the United States. As a part of the deal
negotiated between Louis Barrier and the New York entrepreneur Clifford Fischer, she was again accompanied by Les
Compagnons, but at the last moment – because Edith was terrified of flying – the entire group travelled by ship. The journey
was relatively calm: even so, when she arrived in New York
harbour in November 1947 several journalists reported her to
be suffering from 'what appeared to be fatigue'. In fact, they
were seeing Edith as she really was, not as some Parisian lovely
bedecked with jewels and expensive clothes, and little did they
know that once she stepped into the footlights she would not
look much different. All went well during her subsequent press
conference. When a young reporter asked her who, in America,
she would like to meet the most, she cracked, 'Einstein!' A few
days later this rendezvous was arranged by Clifford Fischer
and Jacques Bourgeat. When one of Les Compagnons was asked
'what the little lady looked like on the stage', the response was,
'Wait and see.' The ensuing trauma was almost as bad for the
Americans as it was for Edith.

She had been engaged 'on recommendation' by the Playhouse
on New York's 48th Street, but if the public were expecting
another Mistinguett, or Joséphine Baker, singing songs like 'Mon
homme' and 'J'ai deux amours', drenched in feathers and
wearing gowns by Chez Fath – they were to be sorely disappointed. What hit them for six was this dowdy little woman,
clad in black and singing songs about lost love and death in a
language which most of them did not even wish to understand.
Neither was she helped much by some of the critics. One,
without even referring to her obvious talents as a singer, wrote,
'Piaf wears far too much mascara, and there is so much lipstick
– she looks like she's dribbling tomato-juice!'

In order to cope with her failure – something she had not
had to deal with since the Leplée affair – Edith spent four hours
each day taking English lessons. With her astute memory she
did rather well, though her English teacher, Miss Davison, did
pick up just about every expletive in the Bellevilloise *argot*. The

first time Miss Davison met Marcel Cerdan, having been told the slang word for 'bruises', allegedly much-favoured by French boxers, she quite innocently asked him, 'Avez-vous des morpions?' ... 'Do you have crabs?'

Edith was helped somewhat by an article written on her behalf by the celebrated journalist, Nerin E Gun, who whilst also referring to the Marshall Aid Programme concluded a most complimentary article with, 'One can say she is the incarnation of the new European generation which is so worthy of our help.' This was followed by one of the most glowing accounts ever to have been penned in praise of a French entertainer – not by a particular lover of music-hall acts, but by the distinguished theatre critic and man-of-letters, Virgil Thompson. And this did not appear in any Arts column, but on the front page of the *Herald Tribune*.

> Miss Piaf presents the art of the *chansonnière* at its most classical. The vocalism is styled and powerful. Her diction is clarity itself. Her phrasing and gestures are of the simplest, save for a slight tendency to over-use the full-arm swing, with index finger pointed. She has literally no personal mannerisms. She stands in the middle of the bare stage in the classical black dress of medium length, her hair dyed red and tousled is equally classical. Yvette Guilbert, Polaire and Damia all wore it so. Her feet planted about six inches apart, she never moves except for the arms. Even with these her gestures are sparing and she uses them as much for abstractly rhetorical as for directly expressive purpose. There is apparently not a nerve in her body. Neither is there any pretext of relaxation. She is not tense, but intense. In no way spontaneous, just thoroughly concentrated and impersonal. Her power of dramatic projection is tremendous. She is a great artiste because she gives you a clear vision of the scene or subject she is depicting, with a minimum injection of personality. Such a concentration at once of professional authority and of personal modesty is no end impressive ...

It was largely due to this article that Edith was offered an eight-engagement contract with the Versailles, one of the city's most exclusive – and expensive – cabarets, situated at 151 East 50th Street. It was reported at the time that such was Clifford Fischer's confidence in Edith's abilities, *he* had signed a deal with the management offering to make good any losses they might have incurred. This did not prove necessary, though she still had quite a long way to go. When Edith opened at the Versailles, *she* predicted that she would be a failure because of the establishment's unlucky green curtains – following the premiere, and on each subsequent visit to the cabaret, these would be kept open so that she could not see them whilst singing.

At the Versailles, Edith was 'mounted' on a wooden platform to enable those at the back of the auditorium to see her. Initially, Clifford Fischer engaged a Master of Ceremonies who walked on to the stage before each song to explain what it was about. 'Je m'en fous pas mal' and 'Le petit homme' did not go down too well – it took the MC longer to spell them out than Edith took to sing them, and she soon realized that her recitals were beginning to lose all sense of continuity. Therefore, in the space of a single afternoon she wrote her own English words to 'La vie en rose', and 'Je m'en fous pas mal', thanks to a talented young admirer named Rick French, became 'I shouldn't care', though had she had her own way by insisting that it should be translated *literally* so as to show the Americans what the *chanson-réaliste* was all about, it would have been sung as 'I don't give a fuck'!

> I have to work for my living,
> I'm no Marie Antoinette . . .
> People who work for their living
> Can't run away to forget!

Edith proved so popular at the Versailles that her season was extended – to five months! And over the next twelve years the venue would act as her first port-of-call whenever she crossed the Atlantic. Here, she would meet many of the great American showbusiness legends: Sammy Davis, Judy Garland, Dean Martin, Orson Welles, Lena Horne, Rock Hudson, Danny Kaye and Bette Davis were all photographed congratulating her in her dressing-room after the show. What is amazing is that when one studies the obvious publicity shots, Edith appears un-Hollywood-like, natural, and wholly unaffected by the glamour she often admitted to loathing. Wearing no jewellery, little make-up, and almost always her black dress, she comes across as infinitely more glamorous and certainly more sincere than any of the 'posers' in the photographs.

Only one of these superstars touched her heart.

Marlene Dietrich.

Two women, on the face of it with little in common but the songs they shared: 'La vie en rose', 'When the world was young', and 'Un coin tout bleu', which Marlene sang but never recorded. Their backgrounds could not have been more different. Piaf, practically raised in the streets and apprenticed to life the hard way, taking her own and everyone else's share of its complexities, let-downs and knocks. Marlene, sophisticated, a daughter of the military, self-disciplined, and an acknowledged heroine of World War Two. Yet their friendship would remain rock-solid for the rest of Edith's life. She wrote in her autobiography,

> Marlene was so perfect, it was hard to believe that she actually ate. She is the most perfect woman that I have ever had the good fortune to meet. When she saw me downcast, worried, near breaking-point, she made it her duty to help and encourage me, taking care never to leave me alone with my thoughts. Because of her I was able to face up to my problems and overcome them. I have much to thank her for . . .

Edith's salary of $1,000 per week from the Versailles interested her far less than the new friend she had made, and in a rare but not unprecedented act of devotion Marlene gave Edith a precious gift – a tiny gold cross set with seven emeralds. With it was a piece of parchment upon which she had inscribed:

One must find God/ Marlene/ Rome/ Christmas

Marlene said little, over the ensuing years, about her friendship with Edith, though she did write two whole pages about their brief 'rupture', of which more later, in *Marlene D*, her autobiography of 1984. Then, in 1990, two years before her death, she opened up to me.

> Everybody thought Piaf was a fragile little bird, but such a thing could not have been further from the truth – though she wasn't at all like the horrible caricature in the play [Pam Gems' *Piaf*]. She and I spent a lot of time together at the beginning of 1948. I'd just finished making *Foreign Affair* and a film I don't care to remember [*Jigsaw*], so I had all the time in the world to help her with her American career. She was for ever calling herself ugly and insecure, yet such was her charisma that she could have had any man she wanted. One evening at the Versailles she made a play for John Garfield – now there was a man who really did have one hell of an over-inflated ego – and one night after one of her parties at the Waldorf Astoria I escorted her up to her room. And there he was, drunk and stark-naked on her bed. Edith didn't have much English in those days, but what she knew was very colourful, and after she'd given him a piece of her mind, we manhandled him out of the room and threw him right down the stairs. Ha – he was still there when I went up to her room the next morning!

When reporters tried to question Edith about the Garfield incident, she was unusually honest, adding via a reporter that only too often the man of the moment saw only the words 'EDITH PIAF' in big lights above the bed, and that in many instances once the man had attained a certain 'status' and come to the conclusion that she had outlived her usefulness, he had dumped her. Many years later, she would repeat this interview almost word-for-word for the magazine, *France-Dimanche*.

> My lifestyle was such in those days that I ended up being taken as an easy lay. Amongst my entourage I was the good time had by all. Men treated me like some territory which had to be conquered, even though deep inside I still felt pure and desperate – far different from my degrading image. Love has always run away from me. I have never kept the man of my life in my arms for very

long. Sometimes it is over nothing – a word out of place, or some unimportant lie and my lover vanishes. Then I pray that a miracle will lead me into other arms . . .

Although she did not know it at the time, that 'miracle' was waiting just around the corner . . .

Chapter Five

LOVE MAKES THE WORLD GO ROUND

Edith Piaf and the boxer Marcel Cerdan had first met at the Club des Cinq in December 1946, and at the time she is said not to have found him attractive. Nicknamed The Moroccan Bomber, he was a stocky man, not much above average height, with a tough face which, when he smiled to reveal a mouthful of gold fillings, gave him the 'lived-in' look. He was also the finest fighter his country ever had, and because of the legend linking his name to Piaf's is not likely to be superseded.

No one will ever be able to explain why Edith fell in love with Cerdan. He was the only one of her lovers who was her equal, and equally rare was the fact that he did not come from her music-hall side of the fence. She could do nothing to enhance or further his career other than love him, and this of course she did with every fibre in her being.

I loved Cerdan. More than this, I adored him like a god and would have done anything for him. Before him, I was nothing – morally, I was a lost cause. I believed life had no meaning, that all men were beasts, and that the best thing to do was to have fun and do silly things, whilst waiting for death to arrive as quickly as possible. Marcel taught me how to live again. He took away that sour taste of hopelessness which had poisoned me, body and soul. He enabled me to discover that sweetness, serenity and tenderness really did exist. He lit up my world!

Edith and Cerdan met again after one of her recitals at the

Versailles in December 1947, at a cocktail party attended by Charles Boyer, Marlene Dietrich and a number of others who were always homesick whenever away from Europe. The boxer had just arrived in New York to train for a fight, and had been given a hard time by his opponent's fans – something which would happen time and time again. Edith told a reporter, 'We're just a couple of bored, lonely French people who happen to be in New York. And we're just good *friends*. Marcel's a married man!' The next day, Cerdan rang Edith's suite at the Waldorf Astoria and invited her to dine with him – but instead of taking her to a fancy eatery they sat at the counter in a downtown drugstore and ate pastrami and boiled beef, followed by ice-cream and beer. Edith was amazed, and more than a little disappointed that the rumours of Cerdan's tight-fistedness were probably true. The following evening, the treat was on her and they ate at Le Gourmet, one of the most exclusive restaurants in New York, and it was here that they are said to have fallen in love.

Marcel Cerdan was closer to Edith's age than most of the others had been. He had been born on 22 July 1916 at Sidi-Bel-Abbès in Algeria, the eldest of five 'boxing-crazy' sons. His father had encouraged him to fight, and through him he had been introduced to the trainer Lucien Roupp, who ran a gymnasium. Henceforth, Cerdan's progress had astonished everyone. He had won every single one of his amateur fights, and every professional one too between 1933 and 1937. There was a little controversy in January 1939 when he fought Harry Craster in London and was disqualified for hitting below the belt, but he made up for this by winning the European Middle-weight Championship, later that year in Milan. During the war, whilst serving with the French navy, he fought successfully in Italy and Algeria. Of his final record of 113 fights, sixty-six were inside the distance wins, and 43 were won on points. He was disqualified twice, and lost just twice: once, it is thought, because he was fighting an older man who needed the lucky break.

Cerdan's entourage – Lucien Roupp in particular – strongly disapproved of his affair with Edith, claiming that she was bad for his 'family man' image. Indeed, it was Roupp who instructed him to tell the press that he and Edith were *not* sleeping together, and that he was madly in love with his wife, Marinette. Initially Marinette appears to have believed this – and even more astonishing was the fact that when she *did* learn the truth, this did nothing to prevent her and Edith from becoming lifelong friends. For the time being, however, because Lucien Roupp feared that Cerdan's reputation might be ruined should news of his adultery reach the ears of the then less liberal-minded American public, the press there were bribed into silence. Loupp actually gave Edith some credit for his protégé's well-being when, early in 1948, he beat Lavern Roach in New York after seven gruelling rounds, but when Cerdan lost to Cyrille Delannoit in Brussels in May 1948, the enmity began all over again. Edith, of course, ignored everyone, for incredible as it may seem, she did not even think that she was committing adultery, and neither did the thousands of her ardent admirers lapping up every one of the newspaper 'exclusives' back in France.

'Theirs is a unique, incomparable story of love,' one said, after Edith had paid nineteen-million francs for a town-house at 5 Rue de Gambetta, in the Bois de Boulogne, the first time she had actually owned a place of her own. It was a fortune she could ill afford, but she claimed that it would be worth every last franc because she truly believed that she had found the great love for which she had searched her whole life ... and that one day Cerdan *would* move in with her, even if it meant taking in his wife and three sons as well!

Edith moved her entire entourage into her town-house ... song-writers and musicians, her secretary and her Chinese cook, and Mômone, who within weeks would begin causing trouble, primarily because she was jealous of Edith's happiness, and wanted Cerdan for herself. In her famous book, she even confessed that he had an affair with her *before* the one with Edith, which was of course a blatant lie. In 1948, whilst the lovers were in New York, leaving the house in the 'capable' hands of Mômone, Edith's troublesome 'demon-spirit' broke into her writing-desk and stole a number of Cerdan's letters. First of all, she offered them for sale to Marinette, who was still living in Casablanca with her children. When this did not work, this spiteful woman threatened to write a number of 'exclusives' for an American newspaper. What is utterly remarkable is that she,

Edith and Cerdan posed for his pre-Championship publicity photographs after the couple had discovered the theft. One of these was printed in several of the New York dailies: whilst Edith smiles somewhat nervously, the best that Mômone can do, it appears, is frown. Afterwards, of course, when their story did leak to the Press and the Americans accepted them as lovers as opposed to adulterers, Mômone was sent packing. Even then, she persisted in causing trouble, taking the couple to court claiming that Cerdan had knocked her out before putting her on the plane for Paris. It then emerged during the subsequent hearing that Edith had hit her – and yet, after Mômone withdrew her allegation, she and Edith were photographed leaving the court-house, arm in arm and smiling radiantly as if nothing had happened!

Though she was happier than ever, the songs were sadder and more dramatic. Michel Emer arrived in New York, but Edith refused to have anything to do with him until he had written her a new song. In the space of twenty-four hours he came up with two. 'Bal dans ma rue' tells of the girl who meets her lover at a street-dance, introduces him to her best friend, only to lose him to her and suffer being asked to be witness to their wedding! 'Monsieur Lenoble' is a grim tale indeed, about a man who takes too much for granted, not least of all his wife, who leaves him for a younger lover. Thus, all that is left is suicide, and the song ends with Edith imitating the hissing of the gas-tap! And complementing these was the comic Francis Blanche's 'Le prisonnier de la tour', recounting a sorry story of unrequited love if ever there was one. The girl tells her grandmother why she cannot attend Mass: her lover, who has been locked up in the tower, has flung himself to his death, and her youth has died with him . . .

> Le prisonnier de la tour
> N'aura pas de linceul . . .
> Rien qu'un trou noir où s'engouffrent
> Les feuilles . . .
> Mais moi j'irai chaque jour
> Pleurer sous les tilleuls,
> Pas même le Roi n'empêchera mon deuil . . .

[The prisoner in the tower
Will not have a shroud, nothing
But a black hole which swallows up leaves . . .
Each day I will weep under the lime-trees,
And not even the King will prevent my grief . . .]

The biggest fight of Cerdan's career, the World Middleweight Championship against Tony Zale, was scheduled to take place on 2 September 1948 at the Roosevelt Stadium in New Jersey, and Cerdan's rigorous training programme coincided with Edith's new season at the Versailles. It is alleged that he had always hated training, and there were reports of Edith being smuggled into the camp at Loch Sheldrake in the boot of her car, because she could not bear being away from him. Fortunately, this was never proved, otherwise he almost certainly would have been 'disgraced' by the tabloids and disqualified by the boxing authority. He was also subjected to threats by some of Tony Zale's supporters, warning what would happen should he win the title, which none of them thought remotely possible. Zale himself was pictured in a series of poses: snarling at reporters, curling his lip, or just pretending to look angry. Cerdan's 'private' publicity agent – in other words, Edith – insisted on telling everyone that her boxer was not a violent man at all, but a teddy-bear who loved nothing more than to settle down in front of the fire with the latest Tarzan comic, or if it was fine to go to the cinema and see a Disney cartoon! Needless to say, his opponent regarded Cerdan as little more than a joke, especially when she told a young journalist that she was certain that Cerdan would win his fight, because Sainte Thérèse had told her so!

I was tying up my suitcases in preparation for my flight to New York. My friend Ginette was with me, and her husband Michel. Suddenly, we looked at each other in surprise. The room had become filled with the heady perfume of roses – it lasted but a few seconds. Ginette and Michel searched everywhere, assuming that a bottle of perfume had been broken. I knew otherwise. I knew that when Sainte Thérèse is about to grant a favour, she always sends a fragrance of roses . . .

During the late forties, Ginette Richer became Edith Piaf's *frangine* or soul-sister. She was so infatuated with her, in fact, that she eventually left her husband to accompany Edith on her travels. In those days, of course, there were never any questions posed about such a relationship, which incidentally was platonic, and their adventures, particularly amongst some of the more 'gullible' Americans – in other words, the ones who did not speak French too well – were legion. One of their 'songs' was the riotous 'Quand je bande', which they sometimes performed at private functions.

> Quand je bande
> Ça touche ma poitrine . . .
> Quand j'bande pas,
> Ça touche mes genoux!
>
> [When I get a hard-on
> It touches my chest . . .
> When I don't get a hard-on,
> It touches my knees!]

Marcel Cerdan drove himself to the fight, wearing what would later be hailed as the Piaf uniform: blue suit and tie, solid gold watch and chain, cuff-links and tie-pin from Cartier, and with the 'lucky' cigarette-lighter tucked away in a hip-pocket. Edith and Mômone were sitting in the back of the car, cowering as the vehicle was surrounded by Tony Zale's abusive admirers. The two women were photographed getting out of the car, and once Cerdan had left them some of her own fans began chanting.

This continued as she made her way to the ringside – if the crowd was for the better part anti-Cerdan, it certainly was not anti-Piaf!

The fight was a very tough one. By the end of Round One, the Frenchman was out of breath, and when the bell rang after the fourth, the American 'Man of Steel' had virtually walked away with the title. Then, Cerdan began fighting back, and halfway through Round Twelve Zale doubled up in agony and slumped to the canvas. Cerdan had won! A few days later he returned to France to be received like a hero. He was invited to the Elysée Palace and a private audience with President Auriol, and there followed a state drive through the streets of Paris in an open-topped car. Financially, however, he was not much better off – for reasons known only to the boxing fraternity, he had been informed that he would only receive his prize money providing he agreed to a return fight with the deposed champion!

As for Edith, she opened at the Versailles to rave reviews, though the adulation meant so little to her when the man she loved was getting more or less the same treatment but on the other side of the world. Matters were made considerably worse, too, when Mômone showed her several newspaper articles featuring photographs of Cerdan – taken at the family home in Casablanca . . . with Marinette and their sons.

Terrified that she might have lost Cerdan for ever – and she could hardly have complained, considering the fact that he *was* with his wife – Edith flung herself headlong into her work. She flew back to Paris and opened at once in a new season at the ABC – since his initial reluctance to have anything to do with her when pestered by Raymond Asso, Mitty Goldin had not changed his attitude. He still thought she was common, but could not deny the fact that she was very big money. Thus he did not argue when Edith insisted upon doing two shows nightly, as well as matinées on most days – around sixty songs a day, six days a week! On top of this, she also managed to fit in a 'command performance', at Chez Carrère on the Champs-Elysées. Princess Elizabeth and Prince Philip, on their first official visit to Paris, had asked to see her. Edith later said that this had been one of the proudest evenings of her life, and certainly her most nervous, though she could not have been too edgy to inform the royal couple's aide that the princess should speak to her in French, even though *her* command of English was more than passable!

Neither were Edith's songs specially selected. The distinguished gathering were treated not just to 'Les feuilles mortes' and 'La vie en rose', but to melodramatic pieces such as 'Le ciel est fermé', which tells of the catastrophe which will befall mankind should God go on strike – and 'Tous les amoureux chantent', a number which has to be heard to be believed, for it tells of a pair of young lovers who are mown down by a car on their wedding-day! On a lighter, more romantic note, she premiered 'Pour moi toute seule', penned by her friend Michel Philippe-Gérard, who would be responsible for so many of her later hits. Edith later sang it in English as 'I may be blue', but she never recorded it: the cover-version was by the British actress-comedienne, Dora Bryan. And, when Princess Elizabeth remarked that her father had a collection of her recordings at Buckingham Palace, Edith retorted, 'Then tell him not to bother buying any more. I'll start sending him them!'

In March 1949, Marcel Cerdan flew to London, where he fought and beat Dick Turpin at Earls Court. Edith accompanied him on what would be the first of her three brief visits to Britain – the others would be with each of her husbands – though she never gave any commercial concerts here, despite repeated requests and huge salary offers from some of the country's top impresarios. This visit, like the next one, would also be clandestine. The couple shared a room at the Mayfair Hotel, where Edith gave two short, private recitals, nothing more.

Nine months after winning his title, Cerdan returned to New York to defend it against Jake La Motta . . . and in Round Nine, the Moroccan Bomber lost to the Raging Bull. Lucien Roupp immediately arranged for a return fight to take place the following September – Roupp's last act as Cerdan's manager, for a few weeks later he handed over the reins to Joe Longmann. Cerdan trained rigorously, for once, in Edith's gymnasium, and needless to say she saw to it that there was a great deal of hype. However, when La Motta was injured during one of his training sessions, the fight was postponed until 2 December – ideal from Edith's point of view, for she had been engaged for a third tour of the United States which would coincide with this.

At around this time, Cerdan starred in the film, *L'homme aux mains d'argile*, said to have been loosely based on his life – an earlier excursion into the cinema had produced the Italianate *Diavolo la celebrita*. Though Edith did not actually appear in the film, she sang its theme: André Bernheim's 'Paris', an evocative ode to the intense joie-de-vivre which could only have been brought about by loving Marcel Cerdan.

> Un soir d'hiver, un frais visage,
> La Seine, un marchand des marrons,

Une chambre au cinquième étage,
Les cafés-crêmes du matin . . .

[A wintry evening, a fresh complexion,
The Seine, a chestnut-seller,
A room on the fifth floor,
The creamed coffees of a morning . . .]

In October 1949, Edith left for New York. Cerdan, who had never really conquered his fear of flying the way she had, made arrangements to follow on by ship. At the last moment, or so it seems, he changed his plans and on 27 October caught the evening flight from Orly. He was photographed at the airport, firstly with the violinist Ginette Neveu, admiring her Stradivarius – and secondly, boarding the plane, looking more than a little apprehensive, carrying his suitcase on his shoulder. Seven hours later, the craft crashed into Mount Rodonta in the Azores, killing all thirty-seven passengers and the crew of eleven. Cerdan was not the only celebrity to die: so too perished Ginette Neveu and her brother, who was to accompany her at Carnegie Hall in her highly-acclaimed rendition of Sibelius' Violin Concerto. The Americans had been touched to learn that, whilst recording the piece, she had been so determined to finish it in a single session that she had emerged from the studio trembling, her neck covered in blood.

It has been suggested that Cerdan took the plane because Edith had not been able to bear being alone longer than necessary – he had wanted to surprise her in her dressing room at the Versailles, before her performance. His widow, Marinette, told newspapers the next day how she had had a terrible premonition that the plane was going to crash, and that she had called him in Paris, begging him to travel by sea. The truth will never be known.

Marlene Dietrich remembered that awful day only too well:

Only two people were capable of breaking that kind of news to her – myself and her manager [Louis Barrier], who had time to get there only because Edith always slept in until the middle of the afternoon, then rehearsed or received friends until it was time to go on stage. Everyone else put on an act until he arrived. And, God above, she went *crazy* with grief. I was terrified of leaving her side for a moment. As an act of penance, she'd cut her hair – I still have the scissors – and she shut herself up in her room until she received a call saying he'd been buried. It was a terrible, terrible thing to have to watch her suffer.

Edith would not, however, allow Louis Barrier to cancel her performance that night. She wrote in her memoirs,

> The dreadful news knocked me senseless. I suffered a mar-
> tyrdom, on stage that night. I was like a corpse, a mortally
> wounded soul. Yet I hung on until the end, and I told them,
> 'Tonight I am singing for Marcel Cerdan. I am singing for
> him alone.'

Halfway through her performance, in what must have been one of the most heartrending scenes ever witnessed on an American stage, Edith collapsed. Still she would not allow the curtain to come down – she was helped to her feet, given a glass of water, and yelled at the audience, 'Please, let me sing!' Marlene was sitting in the wings, herself beyond tears, and Louis Barrier did not know quite what to do any more. Throughout the whole of the next day letters and telegrams poured into her suite at the Waldorf Astoria, offering messages of encouragement and sym-pathy. Andrée Bigard and Jacques Bourgeat, himself in poor health, flew in from Paris to be with her. Meanwhile, Cerdan's remains were flown back to Casablanca – he had been identified only because he had had a penchant for wearing a wristwatch on each hand – where, in a moving ceremony, the French Government posthumously awarded him the Légion d'honneur. So as not to offend Marinette, Edith did not send any flowers to his funeral – within a few months she would do better than this. For the time being her admirers understood her reasons for wishing to stay in the background, though they were absolutely horrified at what happened next.

In November 1949 Edith participated in one of the very first radio link-ups between New York and Paris, and she informed her fans back home that with Cerdan dead, she too wanted to die. The response to this was tremendous – thousands of people begging her with one voice not to do it. Even the radio announcer told her that she had no right to leave them in such a manner. Piaf belonged to the people! Piaf was a national monument! Edith then decided that she would *live* for Cerdan, though many of her close friends knew that henceforth it would be a living death.

> What I did for Marcel, afterwards, was worth infinitely more than killing myself. Our lives do not belong to us. Courage forces us to keep on until the end. Just speaking about Cerdan, today, makes me feel better . . .

Thus, over the next few days Edith spoke quietly about the greatest love in her life to her closest friends, and to a few privileged reporters. She told of how, exhausted between fights, he had signed up for dozens of exhibition matches simply so that he could raise money for a children's home, or for research into tuberculosis. She spoke of how he had once 'rebuked' her before dozens of fans because she had refused to sign autographs. She reminisced over the evening when Cerdan had taken her to the funfair at Coney Island, where they had been recognized – and when she had been compelled to sing 'La vie en rose', whilst the two of them had been whirling around on the cocks-and-hens. And she almost laughed when describing the big fight, when she had bashed the spectator sitting in front of her over the head in her excitement – far from being angry, the young man had offered her his hat as a keepsake, and she had rewarded him with a kiss.

Marcel Cerdan's tragic death clearly heralded the beginning of Edith's physical downfall, and she would never recover from it. Taking into consideration the pattern she had set for herself, it seems very likely that, had he lived, their relationship would have petered out like all the others, particularly as some of the leading boxing experts at the time had predicted that he would not have withstood the pace during the return fight with Jake La Motta – this, of course, would have 'demoted' his popular appeal, and unlike his famous mistress he would have found it impossible to move from strength to strength. Cerdan was also married – one fact which even the sometimes tyrannical little singer would not have been allowed to change, for he had told her on a number of occasions that for his sons' sakes he intended remaining so. So why, the cynics may ask, did he remain the greatest love of her life – more important than *both* of her husbands? The answer is so very simple: because he had died at the very zenith of their affair, without giving her the eventual opportunity of walking out on him, as she had all the others.

Immediately after her last performance at the Versailles, Edith returned to Paris, where she began a three-week season at the Copacabana, a Brazilian-style cabaret where she had given a one-off recital that April. She later confessed that she had struggled through each evening, hoping that she might drop dead on the stage, but that she had survived only because Cerdan had been watching over her like a guardian angel. At the Versailles she had been played on to the stage with either 'Y à pas de printemps' or 'La vie en rose', but as she was feeling anything but light-hearted she asked the musical director, Daniel White, to play something sombre and suggested 'Pour moi toute seule'. White refused to do this: the musicians struck up 'White Christmas' whilst she was making her way from her dressing-room to the stage, and she was introduced with 'Bal dans ma rue'. Edith sang this, along with White's own composition, 'C'est toujours la même histoire', and 'Les feuilles mortes' was performed for the first time in France. The song had been written for Marlene Dietrich by Jacques Prévert and Joseph Kosma in 1946, after seeing her opposite Jean Gabin in the film *Martin Roumagnac*. Marlene had *almost* recorded the song, but at the last moment had suggested that it would be better suited to Edith's style. Though Edith adored it, for reasons known only to herself she hardly ever sang it in France, and it became a big hit for Yves Montand and Juliette Gréco. 'La vie en rose' was also given its French premiere at the Copacabana – or at least the version with Edith's own English lyrics.

> You are dangerous, chéri,
> Too dangerous for me,
> I know I can't resist you . . .
> My heart tells me to beware,
> You're dangerous, chéri,
> But I don't care!

Edith later described this as 'a poor, over-sentimental version of an already out-dated song', and within days of adapting it set about locating an artiste who she hoped might sing it better than herself. Her first choice was Marie Dubas, but when Marie turned it down – and to be honest, even she would not have got away with performing a Piaf song – Edith chose 'the next best thing', Marie's British counterpart, Gracie Fields, whom she had first met in Athens in 1946 when she and Les Compagnons de La Chanson had participated in Gracie's concert for the RAF. Gracie had also been in the audience for Edith's ill-fated debut at the New York Playhouse the following year. When she remarked that she had very much admired one of the songs from that performance – Henri Contet and Paul Durand's 'Boléro' – Edith told her, 'Then you might as well have that one as well!' Edith would record 'Boléro' two years later, though so far as is known she only ever sang it once on the stage. Gracie had the song translated and it became 'All my love', sadly losing every vestige of originality, though with Edith there was no accounting for taste when trying to please the syrup-loving Americans . . . she liked Gracie's version of the song so much that she called her at her Capri home and asked for it back!

> The skies may fall, my love,
> But I will still be true . . .
> I can see, as I recall my life,
> I've waited all my life
> To give you all my love!

Gracie Fields always sang this song as a tribute to her husband, the film-director Monty Banks who in 1950 died in her arms whilst they were travelling by train through Italy. In memory of *her* dead champion, Edith would compose three beautiful songs, the last of which would be 'La belle histoire d'amour', of which more later. The first was 'Chanson bleue', for which Marguerite Monnot supplied the music, allowing her imagination to run wild. Usually, the addition of a choir had a weakening effect on Edith's voice – it was as if she deliberately held back for fear of 'drowning' everyone else. Not so with 'Chanson bleue'. For over a year she would have regular requiem masses sung for Cerdan at the church in Auteuil, and the ceremony always ended with this song. Such was the weight of its emotion that she did not record it until the summer of 1951, though she did sing it live during a French radio broadcast, breaking down at the end and saying, 'Of all the songs I have ever sung, "Chanson bleue" is my favourite, and I think that it will remain so for the rest of my life.'

> Je vais te faire une chanson bleue,
> Pour que tu aies des rêves d'enfant
> Où tes nuits n'auront plus de tourments.
> Tu viendras chanter dans les cieux . . .
> Chanson bleue!

> [I'm going to sing you a blue song,
> So that you might have a child's dreams
> Wherein your nights are no longer tormented.
> You will come to sing in the heavens . . .
> A blue song!]

The song sung in memory of Marcel Cerdan – and according to many, the most important song Piaf *ever* sang – was 'Hymne à l'amour'. She wrote the words in December 1949, and helped Marguerite Monnot to compose the music. Though premiered at the Salle Pleyel in Paris, in January 1950, Edith was too upset to record it until 2 May 1950, her first visit to the studio in ten months. It remains the quintessential Piaf – her personal testament of pure, unashamed love. Her recording of the song, in both French and English, has sold tens of millions of copies, and will go on selling until the end of time. There have been countless cover-versions, in dozens of languages, at their best but mediocre when compared to Edith's interpretation. No one has ever been able to sing it the way she did, and no one ever will.

> Si un jour la vie t'arrache à moi,
> Si tu meurs que tu sois loin de moi,
> Peu m'importe, si tu m'aimes,
> Car moi je mourrais aussi . . .
> Dans le ciel, plus de problèmes,
> Dieu réunit ceux qui s'aiment!

[If one day life snatches you from me,
If you die whilst far away from me,
It's not important, so long as you love me,
For I'd die too . . .
In heaven, no more problems,
God reunites those who love each other!]

Chapter Six

AFTERMATH: THE ROAD
TO CALVARY

In January 1950, immediately after launching 'Hymne à l'amour', Edith flew to Casablanca to 'explain her actions' to Cerdan's widow. She was accompanied by Mômone, who later reported that within a few hours the boxer's sons – René, Marcel and Paul – were being taken on a shopping spree and addressing their kindly benefactress as 'Tante Zizi'. What is astonishing is that although Edith *admitted* that she and Cerdan had had a very torrid affair, Marinette *still* would not believe that her husband had strayed away from the marital bed, a theory which she would cling to for the rest of her life. In 1970, she would attempt to sue Mômone for suggesting such a thing in her book – a legal process which not unexpectedly amounted to nothing, for the court decided that even if many of Mômone's 'revelations' *had* been little more than the workings of an over-ripe imagination, this particular episode in Piaf's life had been public knowledge for over twenty years.

Edith's visit to Casablanca must have been genuinely appreciated, for a few weeks later the entire Cerdan family returned with her to Paris, where they were pampered beyond belief at her town-house. Marinette was even given Edith's most prized possession, after Marlene's gold cross – the mink coat which her lover had bought her during their last outing to the shops in New York. Only *she* would have had the nerve to do such a thing and get away with it. But, as she recorded in her memoirs, she now had a *new* goal . . .

I had regained my will to live. I was saved, for soon I

would be caring for Marcel's sons! Some people may not understand this – the ones who have never loved and lost that love because death intervened. Those people content themselves with life's petty issues. As for Marinette and myself, a man had changed our lives! And then, six months after Cerdan's death, I allowed myself to fall straight into the deepest abyss . . .

There is little doubt that Cerdan's death temporarily unhinged Edith – even her closest friends have admitted this. Within weeks of the fatal crash she had been contacted by the mother of the dead violinist, Ginette Neveu, and informed that her daughter had been in touch 'from the other side'. Edith immediately went out and bought a *guéridon*, a kind of three-legged table used by mediums, and assisted by her secretary Andrée Bigard – and Mômone – séances were held and the table 'tapped'. Many sceptics at the time dismissed Edith's behaviour as 'incomprehensible', though it must be remembered that such was the intensity of her grief, her entourage would have allowed her to anything to find peace of mind. Andrée Bigard hoped that by 'rigging' the table, and telling her that Cerdan was well and always thinking about her, she might succeed in lifting Edith out of her depression. Unfortunately, things got out of hand whenever the secretary was not there – Mômone would always make a point of getting the table to ask for money, and this of course always had to be handed over to her for safe keeping. Even so, these séances did appear to help, and the table followed Edith everywhere over the next few years – even to America. Several things happened with it, however, which are, on the face of it, inexplicable. In 1956, when she was appearing in Chicago and due to fly to San Francisco, the table spelled out 'March 22nd . . . plane crashed . . . all dead!' Edith immediately asked Louis Barrier to check her itinerary, and sure enough she and her entourage had been booked on the flight. Barrier cancelled, and the plane did crash, killing sixty-seven people. The table, aided by her astrologer, also accurately forecast two of her car-crashes. Therefore she was not being morbid when she told a stunned American reporter, 'The only certainly about life is that we know it's going to end – and it isn't a bad thing, you know, because it reunites us with those we have loved. As far as I'm concerned, honey, death doesn't exist!'

Edith Piaf's superstitions formed an integral part of her own personal religious doctrine. Before going on stage she always performed the same 'ritual'. This involved kissing or touching the floorboards, kissing her medallion and making the sign of the Cross, and finally forming the little and forefinger of her right hand into the horns of her 'imaginary demon'. All this she took very seriously. Later in life, when her hands became crippled with rheumatism, she would put herself through any amount of pain to exorcise her demon, and absolutely no one was allowed to touch her medallion, or the cross given to her by Marlene. Days were also good or bad. Thursdays she deemed important because she had met Cerdan on a Thursday, and she would later marry on that day. Sundays she hated, and she would never discuss anything important to her career on this day, even if it meant losing out financially. She also had a fascination for birth-signs. If she hired a secretary or maid, she always tried to ensure that they had been born under Pisces – if not, then their name had to begin with the letters M or C. One only has to study the list of her friends to understand why. Marlene, Malleron, Marie Dubas, Monnot, Meurisse, Michel Emer, Moustaki, and her nurse, Margantin. And Contet, Carlès, Chauvigny, Cerdan and Constantine. Louis was another lucky name: the man who had discovered her, her impresario, the father of her child, her own father. The list seemed endless.

Another 'C' who managed to combine good fortune with the 'bad luck' which Sunday represented was Charles Aznavour, whom Edith had met some time before at Le Petit Club, an artistes meeting-place on Rue Panthieu. It would appear that Francis Blanche, the composer of 'Le prisonnier de la tour', had introduced them, and Aznavour – he was then one half of the Aznavour-Roche duo – was of course asked to supply her with a song. This was the somewhat maudlin 'Il pleut'. Shortly after Cerdan's death he turned up at her town-house with another song, 'Je hais les dimanches', which he had co-written with Florence Véran. Edith turned the song down, probably anticipating that Aznavour would simply go away and write something else. He did, eventually, though for the time being he gave 'Je hais les dimanches' to Juliette Gréco. The 'darling of existentialism' placed the song in her already exhaustive repertoire, scored a massive hit with it, and it is still there forty years on. Edith is said to have flown into a rage with Aznavour, though she was always outwardly kind towards Gréco, who also sang her 'Sous le ciel de Paris' with conviction. Therefore Edith was obliged to obey an edict of the French music-hall which in her formative years she had totally disregarded – that a new song should be performed by no one but the artiste who has introduced it for the first six months of its life, and she did not record it herself until the end of the following year.

> Tous les jours d'la semaine
> Sont vides et sonnent le creux,
> Mais pire qu'la semaine,
> Y a l'dimanche prétentieux . . .
> Je hais les dimanches!
>
> [Weekdays are empty and hollow,
> But worse than the week
> Is pretentious Sunday.
> I hate Sundays!]

Even though she was not interested in his song, Edith did recognize Aznavour's enormous potential, and she told him bluntly that his talents were wasted by singing in a duo. She also added that his profile was a mess on account of his crooked nose – not that this would pose a threat to his career for much longer, she concluded, for he would accompany her on her next trip to America and have it re-shaped!

Charles Aznavour has always maintained that he was madly in love with Edith for a week. She never fell for him at all – just for the nine songs he wrote for her whilst employed as her factotum: running errands, answering the telephone, driving her car, humping her luggage around, and even helping the stagehands. 'I adored every single moment of being Piaf's slave,' he told me, a few years ago. 'I could not possibly have had a better apprenticeship, believe me! And she made me work harder than I've ever worked in all the years since. She was a monster, and I adored her!'

Aznavour's songwriting phase for Edith Piaf lasted in effect less than three years – primarily because he was so phenomenally talented that he became a big star virtually overnight in his own country, and not much later elsewhere – but their friendship and close affinity lasted the rest of Edith's life. 'Il y avait', 'C'est un gars' and 'Plus bleu que tes yeux' are not as well-known outside France as they should be, though Aznavour's stunning adaptation of the Wayne Franklin song 'Jézèbel' – a worldwide hit for Frankie Laine, and a difficult one for Edith with its wide range – was almost as popular in America as the original. 'She always said that "Une enfant" was her favourite out of all the songs I wrote for her,' Aznavour told me. 'That's because someone died at the end, in this instance an errant child as opposed to the usual drowning, electricity, car-smash, gas or routine broken heart!' The music to the song was composed by Robert Chauvigny, and Aznavour was so taken up with the arrangement that he kept it for his own recording of 'Une enfant' a few years later.

> Une enfant de seize ans,
> Une enfant du printemps,
> Couchée sur le chemin . . . morte!
>
> [A child of sixteen.
> A child of Springtime,
> Lying on the road . . . dead!]

Edith now had another man in her life. A few weeks after Marinette Cerdan's return to Casablanca, Edith had opened at Paris's Baccara Club and one evening had been approached by a brash young American who told her that he had written English worlds to 'Hymne à l'amour'. His name was Eddie Constantine. Two months older than Edith, Constantine had won a prize for singing bass with the Vienna Conservatoire – not that this had done him much good, for over the next six months he had been forced to take any number of 'non-show-business' jobs to support his wife, Helen, and their daughter Tania. These included advertising chewing-gum, cleaning out horses on a ranch, and washing corpses in a funeral parlour. Paris, however, had acted like a magnet and he had eventually left his family – promising that he would only return to them once he had made a name for himself. For a while he had earned a pittance, doing the odd spot in the night-clubs around the Left Bank, until Lucienne Boyer had taken a shine to him and offered him a regular contract with her Club de l'Opéra.

When Constantine told Edith that he was working for 'La Dame en Bleue', as Boyer was affectionately known, without even asking to hear his voice Edith offered to double his current salary so long as he moved to her 'camp' . . . within minutes of meeting him, simply on account of 'Hymn to love', she had decided that he would become her lover!

Eddie Constantine quickly joined the ranks of 'Piaf's Boys', as Charles Aznavour called them: he was awarded the customary blue suit and all the trappings, and asked to move into her town-house. He is also supposed to have told her that their 'arrangement' was temporary, that he had every intention of returning to his wife and child. Like Marcel Cerdan, he was appealing to look at, though in a rugged way with a pock-marked face, deep-set eyes, a winning smile and an affable disposition. At 6 feet 5 inches he was also the tallest of her lovers, and because she was acutely aware of the vast difference in their heights Edith always tried her utmost not to be photographed standing next to him.

Such was Edith's now-expected tyranny that, though her English was good, she made her new lover learn French. She was also determined to make him a star, though in this respect he never had the potential of a Montand or Jaubert. Therefore, as she had recently been signed for another trip to the United States – preceded by a ten-week tour of France within which she would be in control of the other artistes on the bill – it was obvious that she would want her new protégé to be included. Aznavour had already been engaged to open the show.

The French tour was a triumph for Edith, but an ordeal beyond belief for everyone else. Constantine's French was so dreadful that the critics were merciless – yet it was Aznavour, who *had* been well-received, who was made to suffer the most when Edith decided at the last moment that he would not now be included in the American tour, because she did not think him good enough for his big break!

Aznavour beat Edith at her own game, however, for whilst she was in Ottawa she received a telegram informing her that her protégé had been interned on Ellis Island because he had travelled steerage-class, with little money and no work-permit. Edith was so impressed that she cabled him the $500 he needed to bail himself out, and a few days later Aznavour joined his partner, Pierre Roche, for a series of engagements in Montreal. These would be amongst their last: soon afterwards the pair split up, and Roche stayed on in Canada, where he married the singer, Agläé.

Edith, meanwhile, moved on to New York and another sensational season at the Versailles. This time she dined with General Eisenhower, who a few months later would be elected President. At his request she sang 'Les feuilles mortes', 'My merry-go-round' (the English version of 'Je n'en connais pas la fin', which would be retitled 'My lost melody' and become her signature tune in America), and 'Simply a waltz', an original composition and the only song she never sang in French. 'My favourite song of all time,' Eisenhower later declared.

> Simply a waltz that goes round
> And around in my brain,
> Like a merry-go-round in the spring,
> When the music's swaying,
> I start to dream . . .

Upon her return to Paris, Edith rested for several days at her town-house before flying to Casablanca to see Marinette Cerdan . . . the table had 'begged' her to do this. Then she began preparing her next venture, her first musical-comedy.

Some time before, Mitty Goldin of the ABC had commissioned Marcel Achard of the Comédie-Francaise to write a play which would combine witty dialogue with heartwrenching songs. Achard had immediately come up with a title, *La p'tite Lili*, and asked Edith to portray his heroine. The songs were no problem at all: most of them had already been written, so it was merely a case of them being vetted by Edith. 'Du matin jusqu'au soir', which she had written in French and English, had been in her repertoire for several years, and she had already sung 'C'est toi' as a duet with Eddie Constantine, for whom she had composed 'Petite si jolie' and 'Dans tes yeux'. She therefore insisted that both Constantine and Aznavour be

offered parts in the production: in anticipation, the latter supplied the tongue-twisting 'Rien de rien', roping in his ex-partner,
Pierre Roche, to provide the music. The remaining songs –
'Avant l'heure', 'Si, si, si' and 'L'homme que j'aimerais' were
written by Achard himself and set to music by Marguerite
Monnot . . . once the so-called 'bataille de l'ABC' had been
fought.

Edith and Mitty Goldin had never got along. Even when she
had appeared there as *vedette*, it had taken him all his time to
acknowledge her, and she had never gone out of her way to be
sociable with him. When Goldin learned that Piaf had been
engaged to play Lili, he told Marcel Achard that with her in it,
the piece would not be staged in his theatre. The tetchy little
Hungarian had acted in exactly the same way, thirteen years
previously, when Mistinguett had staged *Chansons de Paris*,
hailed by many as her best revue. Such had been the friction
between star and entrepreneur that she had actually *paid* the
theatre staff to prevent Goldin from entering the theatre. On
top of this, she had tried to sue him when a staircase commissioned by *her* had collapsed, injuring one of her million-
dollar legs. Therefore, when La Miss learned of the feud
between Goldin and Piaf, she sent one of her 'spies' to the
theatre and demanded that he report back to her anything that
he could about the actions of the man she loathed more than
any other. 'I was hoping that *la salope en noir* would get the old
**** so mad that he would have a heart-attack and drop dead,'
she told my godfather, Roger Normand, who was a friend of
both women.

Goldin was told, politely at first by Louis Barrier, not to upset
Edith because, at the end of the day, whether he liked her or
not her presence at the ABC would ensure record ticket-sales.
Edith, however, thwarted him by laying down conditions which
almost *would* give him a heart-attack: *La p'tite Lili* would be
produced by her friend Raymond Rouleau, and she insisted
that the sets be designed by Lila de Nobili, who a few years
later would work on the Callas-Visconti production of *La Trav-
iata*. Neither of these wanted to have anything to do with Mitty
Goldin *or* Raymond Rouleau, and not long before Rouleau had
come close to having a punch-up with Marcel Achard . . . who

on the eve of the first rehearsal very nearly sparked off a riot by announcing that he had not even begun *writing* the play!

The rehearsals for *La p'tite Lili* dragged on for six weeks, with everyone gathering in Achard's office each morning to read through what he had written the evening before. Each time Achard devised a new character, there would be a frantic search to find someone to play the part . . . and not even he had worked out the identity of the murderer until a few days before the premiere!

Typically, Edith had insisted that the central role of Spencer, the gangster, be given to Constantine, but his French was still so appalling – and, Raymond Rouleau declared, his acting even worse – that the producer cut out most of his lines and informed Mitty Goldin, via an intermediary, that Constantine was not worth one-tenth of the salary Edith had demanded. There were further problems over the casting of Mario, Lili's lover. Edith had given the part to Pierre Destailles, indifferent to everyone else's opinion, but he had walked out on account of the back-stage squabbles. She now suggested an up-and-coming young actor named Robert Lamoureux, declaring that if she *had* to kiss anyone on stage, then it might as well be a man who was tall, dark, and devilishly handsome!

Robert Lamoureux had visited Edith's town-house several times, on each occasion bringing songs which she had rejected as being 'too slushy'. Now, he was catapulted into the mêlée as his arrival on the scene coincided with Edith overhearing Constantine telling his wife over the telephone that they would soon be reunited . . . Edith immediately made a play for Lamoureux, hoping to make Constantine jealous, and Raymond Rouleau took advantage of *this* situation – assuming that she and Constantine were about to go their separate ways – by turning Spencer's part into a totally silent one! Edith immediately flew to Constantine's defence, telling Mitty Goldin that if this happened, she would leave the production, and when he threatened to sue her for breach of contract she took a leaf out of Mistinguett's book and told him to stay away from the ABC until the production had ended its run! This he did, and for the rest of his life Mitty Goldin would detest Edith. There was even a coda to the story when Mistinguett turned up unannounced for the dress-rehearsal. In spite of her own hatred of Goldin, La Miss, at seventy-six, had agreed to work for him one last time by embarking on a farewell tour of Canada and the United States. Delighted that Edith had got the better of her old enemy, she told her by way of a back-handed compliment, 'For sticking up to that old bastard, ma chérie, I *almost* admire you!'

La p'tite Lili opened on 15 February 1951, and took Paris by storm, proving more successful than anyone could have possibly anticipated and breaking only when Edith was injured in a car-crash. The plot was relatively straightforward. Lili works for one of the *grands couturiers*, and is in love with the porter, Mario. As the curtain rises we find her dressing Spencer's beautiful moll (the former mannequin, Praline), and singing 'Avant l'heure'. Later she dances the be-bop with Aznavour, is fired for singing too much and neglecting her work, and as a result of this meets Spencer, who has just been involved in a murder, and moves in with him. This does not work out. Spencer deserts her, so she decides to kill herself, though fortunately the pharmacist is 'tipped off' and sells her a fake poison which is actually a potion to make her fall in love again! Thus she and Mario are reunited and the ending, unlike those of most of her songs, is a happy one.

From Edith's point of view, the play was a personal triumph attributed to her extraordinary willpower and courage of conviction. Max Favalelli, writing in *Paris-Presse*, called it, 'Tender, rosy, grey and sweetened with the perfume of cornflowers', though what really got the play noticed – and its run extended – was the glowing review from the usually acerbic theatre-critic, Ribadeau-Dumas, which appeared in *Paris-Théâtre*:

Ten ravishing songs by Marguerite Monnot, a masterly production by Raymond Rouleau and an exquisite decor by Lila de Nobili, painted in dreamy colours on gauze fine as butterfly wings. A long time ago I considered Edith Piaf the greatest artist of our time. Her voice, grave and overwhelming, plunges me into an ice-bath and reaches my very core. Until now I had one small doubt. How would she face up to this new challenge? This is simple! From the very first moment Edith Piaf asserts herself as a marvellous actress. The music-hall decidedly is a famous *conservatoire*!

Besides her duets with Eddie Constantine, *La p'tite Lili* gave Edith a huge commercial success with the uncustomarily optimistic 'Demain il fera jour'.

> C'est quand tout est perdu
> Que tout commence!
> Demain, il fera jour!
> Après l'amour un autre amour commence!
> Tu vas sourire encore,
> Aimer encore, souffrir encore,
> Demain!
>
> [It's when all is lost
> That everything begins!
> Tomorrow will be another day!
> After love, another love begins!
> You're going to smile again,
> Love again, suffer again,
> Tomorrow!]

Both Robert Lamoureux and Eddie Constantine moved on to better things because of *La p'tite Lili*. The former became one of the country's leading actor-comedians. Constantine made a number of famous gangster films in Europe and America – his most celebrated role was that of Lemmy Caution, and he also starred in the highly successful *Alphaville* in 1965. Neither was he a bad singer once he had mastered the French language. One of his biggest hits was 'La schaphandrier', and he introduced the French version of 'Cigarettes, whisky and wild, wild women'. In his autobiography, *This man is not dangerous*, its title a contradiction of that of his most celebrated film, *Cet homme est dangereux*, he wrote:

Edith Piaf gave me confidence in myself when I had no confidence, the will to fight when I did not want to fight. For me to become someone, she made me believe that I *was* someone. She had a kind of genius for strengthening and affirming my personality. Time and time again she said, 'You've got class, Eddie! You're a future star!' Coming from her, a star of the highest order, that was enough! It gave me new life!

The production, however, was not without its touches of tragedy. On 21 February Edith's friend, the great singer Fréhel who had attended one of the earlier performances, was found dead in her Paris apartment of a suspected heart-attack – a little later Edith paid tribute to her by singing two of her songs, 'Dans les bars c'est la nuit', and 'Je n'attends plus rien'. The model Praline was then killed in an automobile accident . . . the day after Edith had ticked her off for turning up at the theatre in a green coat. And Edith's relationship with Eddie Constantine crumbled halfway through the run when his wife arrived in Paris.

Constantine's replacement in Edith's affections was not, however, Robert Lamoureux, as most people had anticipated, but the racing-cyclist André Pousse, whom she had met at the Versailles in 1949. Then, of course, romance had been out of the question on account of Cerdan. Pousse, the archetypal fitness fanatic, only made Edith aware of her own lethargy, and acting upon his advice she bought a small farm, Les Cérisiers, at Hallier, near Dreux. The venture cost her twenty-one million francs, and like the town-house would later be sold at a loss. She wrote in her memoirs:

I told myself that I wanted to breed cows. It was all the rage – all the artistes were going into breeding. But in four years I picked two kilos of green beans, a pound of strawberries, and some tomatoes. I bred two chickens, a rabbit, and all the cats in the neighbourhood. It cost me one and a half million francs for the central heating – and it never worked! Every time I wanted to take a bath my cook had to build a fire to boil the water! So I sold it for next to nothing and later on, when I was ill, I had no money left to pay my hospital bill . . .

Like Cerdan, André Pousse was essentially his own man – and a star in his own right. Edith nurtured ideas of turning him into a singer, and when this failed she planned a revival of *Le bel indifférent*. The stage did not interest Pousse, however, so she tried to persuade him to make a comeback on the racing circuit. This did not work either. Pousse refused to be manipulated, a clear indication that their affair would not last. In fact, it ended dramatically. On 24 July 1951, Charles Aznavour was at the wheel of Edith's Citroën when it crashed into a telegraph pole not far from her farm. Though the car was a complete write-off, no one was injured. Three weeks later, Pousse was driving her brand new car when it hit an oily patch and skidded off the road. Edith and Aznavour were asleep in the back, and this time she was not so lucky. She was dragged out of the wreckage and found to be suffering from two broken ribs and a fractured left arm. Rather than be transported all the way back to Paris, she was taken to a local clinic and patched up – rather badly, it would appear – and the doctor treating her prescribed morphine. The play was nearing the end of its run, but for Piaf of course it was a case of 'le spectacle doit continuer'. For several nights she performed with her arm in a sling, and the tight casing around her rib-cage caused her excruciating pain, particularly when she was singing – and she had to sing, otherwise life would have had no meaning. Thus the morphine injections continued, and she became increasingly dependent on the drug – so much so that within a few months she would be injecting herself through her clothes without even bothering to sterilize the needles. This, combined with the fact that she was still pining for Cerdan, increased her vulnerability, so that she became easy prey to the drug-peddlers and other leeches – especially Mômone – who made a fortune out of her.

Because he was terrified of something happening to her whilst under his wing, so to speak, Raymond Rouleau closed *La p'tite Lili* – perhaps the last thing he should have done, for with nothing to do Edith turned even more towards the needle for solace. Her true friends watched her carefully, but Edith outsmarted everyone by hiding drugs in places they would never have thought of looking. In her second autobiography, *Ma vie*, she cites her 'helper' as 'Janine', though to this day no one knows this woman's identity. One theory is that when Edith was dictating these memoirs for her pal Jean Noli to edit, she changed several names to avoid unnecessary repercussions, taking into consideration France's draconian laws on privacy –

and although nothing was ever proved, few would have put it past Mômone to actually supply Edith with drugs.

> Drugs scarred me for life, and it is perhaps because of my drug-taking that I will doubtless die before my time. Friends saw me foaming at the mouth, or clinging to the rails of my bed. They saw me inject myself through my skirt and stocking. Without drugs I would have been incapable of going on stage, let alone of singing – and not even the very worst of my despairs would have prevented me from singing.

This was Edith's second dark period, yet incredibly it produced some of her most amazing songs: the ingenious 'Télegramme' and 'La rue aux chansons' by Michel Emer, Marc Heyral's 'Le noël de la rue' and 'Notre-Dame de Paris' . . . and her biggest hit of 1951, Norbert Glanzberg's 'Padam, padam'.

> Cet air qui m'obsède jour et nuit,
> Cet air n'est pas né d'aujourd'hui,
> Il vient d'aussi loin que je viens,
> Traîné par cent mille musiciens!
>
> This tune haunts me day and night,
> This tune wasn't born today,
> It comes from as far back as I do,
> Dragged along by a hundred-thousand musicians!]

Born in Rohatyn, Poland, in 1910, Glanzberg had actually begun his career in Germany in 1930, firstly as an assistant voice-coach with the Berlin Opera, then composing scores for Max Ophuls and Billy Wilder. In 1933 he had escaped the Nazi persecution of Jews by fleeing to Paris, where for several years he had enjoyed a moderate success as a songwriter. During the Occupation, he had spent six months in a Nice prison, having been accused of being an enemy alien – the authorities there had refused to believe that he was Polish. Edith's friend, the actress Marie Bell, had secured his release just three days before he had been due to be deported, and he had remained in hiding in Antibes until the Liberation – Edith had provided him with a small monthly allowance, telling him, 'I expect to be repaid, but only in *songs*!' 'Sans y penser' had been the first of these, in 1946, a song which Edith had given to Lys Gauty, and this had been followed by the music for Edith's 'Sophie', from *Neuf garçons et un coeur*, which he had allegedly composed in less than an hour. 'Padam, padam', on the other hand, had taken eight *years* to see the light of day!

Glanzberg had first composed the music for his celebrated song in 1942, when he had played it to Charles Trenet. Within minutes, Trenet had supplied it with a lyric, of which the refrain had comprised the lines, 'Valsons, valsons, valsons, On oublie lorsqu'on danse la java!' [Let's waltz, let's waltz, let's waltz, One forgets whilst dancing the java!] ... which Edith had dismissed as 'sugar coated crap', In 1948, Raymond Asso of all people had come up with a lyric entitled 'New York-Paris-Berlin', which she had hated even more. Then, during the summer of 1950, when Glanzberg had presented her with the sexy 'Il fait bon t'aimer', she had asked him what had happened to his 'chanson sans mots', and he had told her – nothing! Edith had then instructed him to take the music to Henri Contet, and six months later, the 'miracle' had occurred!

> Padam, padam, padam!
> Il arrive en courant derrière moi ...
> Des 'je t'aime' de quatorze juillet ...
> Des 'toujours' qu'on achète au rabais ...
>
> [Padam, padam, padam!
> It comes running up behind me ...
> The 'I-love-yous' of 14 July ...
> The 'for-evers' one buys on the cheap ...]

Edith's car-crash brought about the end of her relationship with André Pousse. She told Marlene Dietrich how he had never once visited her in the hospital, and that even whilst she had been well he had been far too involved with his own ego to care about her. The cyclist himself said, some years later, 'I was never really in love with Piaf, only with her voice. The physical side of her only made my flesh creep!' His replacement was his best friend and fellow cycling champion, Louis 'Toto' Gérardin, who *had* made the effort to drop in on her whilst she had been recovering from the accident.

Much better-looking than Pousse, Toto had quickly won Edith over – her entourage thought *too* quickly, for when Edith returned to her town-house, Toto left his wife and children and moved in with her . . . he even boasted to friends that he would eventually become *Monsieur* Piaf. What Edith did not know was that during the first few weeks of their affair, Toto was two-timing him with Mistinguett, though how he had managed to become the lover of a difficult woman more than forty years his senior is not known. Suffice to say, when La Miss learned what he had done, she called Edith and thanked her for taking 'that prickless dreamer' off her hands, and named a pet monkey after him!

One very important difference between Mistinguett and Edith, however, was that though the older star was renowned for her meanness and tantrums, she had never insisted that her men choose between her and their partners, as Manouche explained:

> Miss and Piaf were both totally unreasonable where men were concerned, making all sorts of impossible demands. They both had a knack for choosing men who were already spoken for, or the ones who licked both sides of the stamp, like Gérardin. Miss, however, didn't mind *who* her men were screwing so long as they crawled into her bed every now and then. There were always plenty of other takers. Piaf, on the other hand, was so insanely *jealous*. If Toto went to the toilet on his own, she would start screaming that he'd been having it off with somebody in the bathroom! And in spite of his philandering, he was a gentle man, and a stupid one. There was Alice, his wife, who used to nag him and knock him around. Miss, who fussed around him like a mother-hen . . . and Piaf, who kept him on this invisible chain. Most of the time the poor boy didn't know whether he was coming or going! Is there any wonder he made a mistake?

The 'mistake' was revealed in December 1951, when Alice Gérardin hired a private detective and had the couple followed.

Alice was not particularly aggrieved by her husband's adultery – over the last few years she had become used to this – but with the fact that when Toto had moved in with Edith, he had taken most of the family valuables with him. The plain-clothes detectives who searched Edith's house from top to bottom found a veritable treasure trove of fine art, porcelain, antiques, jewellery, championship trophies, money and bonds hidden in cupboards and drawers – and eighteen gold ingots stashed behind the refrigerator!

Edith was accused of receiving stolen goods, and the story made the headlines across Europe. The police, who had been waiting to get even with her for 'copping out' during the Leplée affair, grilled her at the local commissariat for several hours just for the sheer hell of it. Manouche was able to verify this.

> The flics had questioned more than a dozen of her friends, and we all said the same thing. Wherever she lived, and no matter how long she'd lived there, Piaf's place always looked as though she'd just moved in. Apart from the living-room, every room was littered with boxes, packing cases and piles of this and that. There was so much junk in there that half the time even she didn't know *what* was hers. And there were so many free-loaders! Once a guy stayed for two weeks, and when he left, none of us knew who he'd been. Turned out he'd been the television repair-man, and every night a whole bunch of his mates had come to the house and feasted like kings! Piaf wouldn't have had anything in the house that was hot. That's why she flushed a million francs worth of jewels Toto had given her down the toilet, once she'd kicked him out into the street!

Manouche also explained another of Edith's characteristics which linked her with Mistinguett:

> Miss was proud of the fact that she lived in a house whose owner had ended up on the guillotine [Madame du Barry's, at Bougival], but it was run-down when she moved in, so she decided to add a few special touches. Firstly, she bought the gold and crystal bathroom that had belonged

to the Dolly Sisters, then she bought a huge, silver swan-shaped bed. The deal cost her millions of francs, but she still had one of us drag in the old tin tub from the back-yard, and slept in a moth-eaten bunk in the attic. Piaf was the same. She spent money she couldn't afford having the place done over by one of the most expensive interior designers in France, but as soon as she saw the blue satin bedroom, she was terrified of stepping inside it in case she dirtied it. And when she saw the rose-mosaic sunken bath, she filled it with goldfish!

Edith's goldfish, according to Mômone and a number of other more reliable sources, came to a decidedly unpleasant end whilst she was away on tour – Tchang, her Chinese cook, brought some of his friends home one night and, because there was no food in the house, served the goldfish on toast! Edith was furious, at first. However, when a medium friend told her that fish were *unlucky*, she became convinced that Marcel Cerdan had effected a miracle by entering Tchang's subconscious, com-pelling him to rid her of these 'demons in disguise'.

Soon afterwards, Edith decided that the house itself was unlucky, and she put it on the market. The sale lost her ten million francs. She then moved into a newly-refurbished but more affordable apartment on Boulevard Péreire . . . and it was from here that she began her swift, near-suicidal descent into hell.

Chapter Seven

JACQUES PILLS: THE YEARS OF HELL

In the midst of her monumental struggle, Edith married the popular singer, Jacques Pills. Some have claimed, rightfully one must now assume, that in doing so she made the greatest mistake of her life. Born René Victor Eugène Ducos, in Tulle, in 1906, Pills had trained as a pharmacist before moving to Paris and auditioning for a part in the 1933 revue, *Paris qui remue*, at the Casino. Here, he had begun a tempestuous affair with the star of the show, Joséphine Baker – they had recorded a famous song, 'Ram-pam-pam', and it was even rumoured at the time that they had secretly married.

Gracie Fields' stepdaughter, Irene Bevan, who spent some time as Joséphine's personal assistant, recalled how, many years after the event, the great star would still be 'ranting and raving' over the way Pills had treated her.

Pills was an opportunist, homosexual by inclination, whose *truc* was preying on famous women. He used Joséphine like a stepping-stone, then dropped her like a hot brick once his own career got under way. Her every move was vetted by him. He handled her bookings and contracts, and her money, much of which went into his own pocket. When he finally married Lucienne Boyer, he went around boasting that theirs was a marriage made in heaven, yet he was never faithful to her, and it ended in divorce. It's easy to understand how such a charlatan could have pulled the wool over Piaf's eyes. Like Joséphine she was astonishingly naive where men were concerned, though by the

time she got around to him she'd had more than her share
of men and ought to have known better.

Edith and Pills had first met in 1939 in the corridors of Radio-
Cité, the radio-station founded by Jacques Canetti. She had been
appearing at the ABC, and he was at the height of his career as
one half of the famous duo, Pills and Tabet – best known for
their interpretations of Mireille and Jean Nohain, and for one
song in particular, 'Couchés dans le foin', recorded in English
as 'Lazing in the hay' and covered by Bing Crosby. Most
recently, Edith and Pills had appeared on the same radio programme in New York. Very much impressed with his flashy
smile, casual manner and romantic interpretations of songs such
as 'Seul ce soir' and 'Cheveux dans le vent', the Americans had
dubbed him 'Monsieur Charm'.

   And in May 1952, Pills charmed Edith as many of his predecessors had done, by bringing her a song ... 'Je t'ai dans la
peau', set to music by his pianist, François Silly.

> Je t'ai dans la peau,
> Y'a rien à faire!
> Obstinément tu es là!
> J'ai beau chercher à m'en défaire,
> Tu es toujours près de moi!
>
> [I've got you under my skin,
> Nothing can be done!
> Stubbornly you're there!
> I've tried hard to rid myself of it,
> You're always close to me!]

This was such a *personal* lyric, hinting at one thing only, that
Edith accepted the song – and the man – without hesitation,
recording it just four weeks after Pills had presented it to her.
'I learned the song after hearing it twice,' she later confessed.
'The rest of the time we were together I spent gazing into
Jacques' eyes!'

   With the exception of her own 'Dany', which she had sung
in 1949, 'Je t'ai dans la peau' was the most suggestive number
Edith ever performed, a clear forerunner to the Gainsbourg-

Birkin duets of the early Seventies . . . one only has to observe her performing it in the film, *Boum sur Paris!*, to make the comparison. The song also resurrected Pills' flagging career in France, particularly when Edith took advantage of it being a Leap Year and asked him to marry her! Pills accepted, though most of Edith's friends believed that he was only interested in borrowing her name long enough to make a little more money as a 'top-of-the-bill curiosity', as opposed to the second-on that he had been demoted to.

It was also reported at the time that Pills had 'hesitated' before giving Edith his response, enabling him to call Joséphine Baker in New York with the ultimatum, 'Marry me, or I'll marry Piaf!' He also lied to Edith, as he had lied to most other people, about his age, and even then she did not see through him. In her autobiography Edith referred to him as her 'rock', but nothing could have been further from the truth.

At around this time, too, Raymond Asso entered Edith's life again, albeit briefly, to give her the very last song he wrote for her, 'Mon ami m'a donné'. It was a superb song which was neglected on account of Pills' song, for Edith recorded both during the same session. Had Asso in effect offered her more than a song, she might have avoided the many pitfalls and disasters of the years to come, for only he would have been strong enough to control or even stop her drug-taking and growing addiction to the bottle. One song which did not 'miss out' was a poem by Jacques Larue, beautifully set to music by Norbert Glanzberg. Called 'Au bal de la chance', though rarely performed on the stage, it was one of Edith's personal favourites, and used by her as the title of her first autobiography.

> Le vent tournant dans les feuilles des bosquets,
> Avec le chant des pinsons fait des bouquets . . .
> Mais elle n'écoute guère
> Que les mots de ce garçon,
> Des mots d'amour si vulgaires,
> Qu'ils font rire au ciel des pinsons . . .
> Danse, danse, au bal de la chance!
>
> [The turning wind within the leaves of the thickets,
> Makes posies with the finches' song . . .

But she barely listens to anything
Save this boy's words . . .
Words of love so vulgar
That they make the finches laugh in the sky . . .
Dance, dance, on the wheel of fortune!

The big difference between *Au bal de la chance* and *Ma vie* is that the former was ghosted in 1958 when Edith was worried about offending people – the latter was typed out exactly as she had dictated it when, in her own words, she was beyond redemption and close to death. She was therefore very cynical – deliberately misquoting the date – when discussing her marriage, ten years on, with a reporter from *France-Dimanche*.

I will always remember our New York wedding, which took place in October 1953. Bashfully, Jacques murmured that he had lied about his age. 'I told you I was thirty-nine, but the truth is, I'm forty-six!' In order to seduce me he had pretended to be younger than he really was. I had not been able to wear a white dress for my confirmation – at the time I had been working the streets with my father. Now I chose a pale blue dress – this did not cause much of a scandal, and it erased my sordid, unhappy past. I suppose I was trying to be romantic! And around my neck I wore the gold cross set with rubies, given to me by my chief witness, Marlene Dietrich. My wedding-day was the most beautiful day of my life . . .

The cross which Edith was referring to was the one set with *emeralds*, which Marlene had given her, but because she was intensely superstitious she often declared that they were rubies which had 'gone off'! Once, she actually blamed the cross for her later problems, both with Pills and her health, but her devotion towards Marlene compelled her never to remove it unless it came off of its own accord.

The couple had married in Paris, at the Mairie of the 16th arrondissement, on 29 July 1952. For Edith, however, no true wedding lacked church bells and a choir, and she absolutely refused to *wear* her wedding ring until it had been properly blessed. Therefore the 'real' ceremony took place in New York on 20 September at the Church of St-Vincent-de-Paul. The previous day, at the rehearsal, Edith had observed the notice on the door – 'Holy Hour, 5.15 to 6.15 Every Thursday' – and asked if this could be removed, telling a reporter, 'This is supposed to be a church, honey, not a bar!' On the morning of her wedding, though, the offending notice was still there.

Because Marlene was not a Catholic, Edith had to obtain a special dispensation for her to be a witness. Marlene also took a great deal of persuading to attend the ceremony, as she explained:

> The first time I met Jacques Pills, I took an immediate dislike to him. That man was too *charming* for his own good, and it was all put on. But, because she pleaded with me, because I loved her so very much, I gave in. That day I kept looking at her, hoping she would be capable of staying on her feet. She was very happy, but very sick also. I had arranged everything – her hair and her make-up, and the bunch of white roses which she carried. She seemed lost, like a little child. And I remember saying to myself, 'I hope this is going to work out for her,' though I knew that it never would.

Marlene also recalled a last-minute attack of nerves which was cured not by the syringe, as has been suggested, but by a couple of swigs from Marlene's hip-flask. Edith wore a long, pleated pale blue gown and a violet tulle hat – in the photographs, she declared, she would *look* as though she was in white. The ensemble, from Saks of Madison Avenue, cost $700 and represented Marlene's wedding-gift to Edith. 'I didn't buy him anything,' she added. 'Knowing him he probably would have sold it.'

Curiously, it was Pills who had chosen Edith's lipstick – even more so that he is alleged to have *inadvertently* chosen Elizabeth Arden's 'Victory Red', *the* colour worn by almost every one of the great gay icons. Tallulah Bankhead, Mae West, Judy Garland, Marilyn Monroe, Joan Crawford, Jayne Mansfield, Maria Callas – all of them were or would soon become 'addicted' to this vivid shade, and almost none of them bought it for themselves, as their gay fans invariably tossed sticks of it on to the stage whilst they were performing, or concealed it in stage-door bouquets. For the rest of her life Edith would consider her lashings of 'Victory Red' as essential a part of her stage apparel as her little black dress and crucifix.

The wedding reception was held at the Versailles – their wedding gift to Edith – and was followed by a luncheon at Le Pavillon, one of New York's most exclusive restaurants. Here, Marlene handled the Press, and one or two difficult gate-crashers. A lengthy tour of the United States constituted the honeymoon, with Edith and Pills almost always singing in different establishments. At the Sands Hotel in Las Vegas, Pills was allowed to attend Edith's show, but refused entrance to her dressing room afterwards because, the manager explained, 'Miss Piaf was otherwise engaged'. He later discovered that she had been holding a 'private audience' with Marcel Cerdan, whose dressing-gown and gloves from the World Championship fight had accompanied her almost everywhere since his death – one Chicago newspaper printed a photograph of them, hanging on the wall next to her dress.

In Las Vegas, the couple sang two duets on a television show. 'Et ça gueule ça madame' has Edith accused of being under her husband's thumb, something which never would have happened. 'Pour qu'elle soit jolie ma chanson' has them parodying several of their hits and harmonizing extremely well. Both songs were written by Edith – the first in collaboration with Francois Silly, still engaged as Pills' accompanist, though he would soon change his name to Gilbert Bécaud and take France, and eventually the world, by storm with a series of very individual songs, headed by 'What now my love?', 'The day the rains came', and 'Let it be me', a huge hit for the Everley Brothers.

Bécaud wrote two songs for Edith whilst she was touring America: 'Elle a dit', with words by her, tells the story of the man who ends it all after his lover leaves. 'Les croix', one of her most dramatic numbers and very appropriate at the time, was written by the poet, Louis Amade.

> J'ai ma croix dans la tête,
> Un immense croix de plomb,
> Vaste comme l'amour . . .
> Un mot y est gravé

Qui ressemble à 'SOUFFRIR',
Ce mot familier que mes lèvres répètent
Est si lourd à porter,
Que j'en pense mourir . . .

[I have my cross within my head,
An immense cross of lead,
Vast as love . . .
One word, 'SUFFERING' is engraved there.
This familiar word which my lips repeat
Is so heavy to carry,
That I think I will die from the effort . . .]

The highlight of Edith's honeymoon – an event which was not shared by her husband – was her meeting with Charlie Chaplin in Hollywood. She had first fallen in love with 'Charlot' in 1932, when Louis Dupont had taken her to see one of his films; since then she had developed a passion for the American cinema which can only be described as manic. Charles Aznavour remembered one trip to New York when she had been so impressed by Orson Welles' performance in *The third man* that she had made her entourage sit through it fifteen times in succession. Eddie Constantine remarked that the only means of catching up on one's sleep – taking into consideration her all-night rehearsal sessions – was to accompany her to a picture-show. Edith found Chaplin fascinating, and in her memoirs wrote about him with touching but wholly unnecessary over-reverence when one considers that she was as great in her particular field as he was in his. He invited her to stay at his home in Beverly Hills, and even promised to write her a song – a promise he could hardly keep, for Edith's highly dramatic style was not at all in keeping with his own.

At a party in Hollywood, Edith met the British singer Dorothy Squires, then married to the actor Roger Moore. During the late forties, Dorothy had had a number of massive hits with the songs of her then partner, the bandleader Billy Reid. Edith had imported some of her recordings from England, and had even considered adapting her 'I'll close my eyes' into French. Dorothy told me:

I was living in America at the time, and appearing in cabaret. I had no idea she was in the theatre, and that evening I sang her 'Hymne à l'amour' in English. When she walked into my dressing-room afterwards I was terrified, even more so when she told me she didn't care for my arrangement. Then, before I could offer my excuses she said, 'But you've got a lovely voice. Don't worry, I'll write an arrangement for you myself!' And that's exactly what she did. Nothing big-bandish, just a sincere, heartfelt arrangement which I recorded the following year. Then after her death I did my own arrangement of 'If you love me, really love me' and included it in the autograph sequence in my concerts, as a tribute to her. She really did hold the audience in the palm of her tiny hand.

Another singer who impressed Edith no end was Peggy Lee, who had recorded 'If you go', the English adaptation of 'Si tu partais'. Because the original had been recorded for Decca, between Edith's lengthy Polydor and Pathé-Marconi contracts, it had not been as widely distributed as her other material, and Peggy had recorded it knowing nothing of its background, as she explained:

Had I known it was Piaf's song, I would definitely have asked her permission to sing it. Then I heard on the grapevine that she was displeased with me, particularly as she had performed the song in English. I didn't know that either! So, I *asked* her if I could do 'All the apple trees' ['Le chevalier de Paris'] and she replied that if I did, it would be a great honour for her. Coming from a great lady like her, *I* was the one who felt honoured!

This delightful little piece by Michel Philippe-Gérard and Angèle Vannier had recently gained Edith the Grand Prix du Disque, a prize which had been presented by Edouard Herriot and Colette with considerable hype . . . yet Edith hardly ever sang it on the stage because, she said, the honour had 'over-commercialized' it. What is strange is that 'La chanson de Catherine' – a dramatic work telling the story of the woman who drowns herself on her wedding day because her new husband has been hanged! – which had won her the almost equally prestigious Concours de Deauville the previous year, was almost forgotten in 1952. Peggy Lee, however, was not the only big star to cover 'When the world was young', as it became known. During the early Seventies it became one of the 'property' songs of both Hildegarde Knef and Marlene Dietrich.

> It isn't by chance that I happen to be,
> A femme fatale, the toast of Paris,
> But over the noise, the talk and the smoke,
> I'm good for a laugh, a drink or a joke!
> 'Come sit over here!' somebody will call,
> 'A drink for the beauty, a drink for us all!'
> But I close my eyes as the past I recall . . .

Leaving Hollywood for the harsher but more welcoming reality of a Paris winter, Edith and Pills rented a new apartment at 67-bis Boulevard Lannes, an opulent quarter overlooking the Bois de Boulogne . . . she added the 'bis' because the two numbers totalled an unlucky thirteen, and *she* footed all the bills. The apartment would remain her home for the rest of her life, of which only a little over a decade remained. The most incredible thing of all was, however, that she never really moved in! There were nine rooms, but as far as Edith was concerned the only rooms of any importance were the kitchen, her bedroom, the bathroom, and the vast, ballroom-sized lounge which saw most of the action – endless rehearsals, parties, receptions. She installed a huge grand piano, a number of tables which were constantly cluttered with glasses, bottles and manuscripts, and dozens of armchairs and divans were scattered about the apartment for those members of her entourage who could not keep up with her to flop into. Her clothes and other effects were kept in trunks and chests – as Edith was always on the move, she saw little point in unpacking them. Marcel Blistène, who directed two of her best films, told me, 'We were once touring the Midi when we bumped into an old pal. Edith told him, "I haven't seen you for ages. Where are you living right now?" Then he told her, "At your place, in one of the spare rooms. I've been there these last two weeks!" '

Professionally, now that they were back in Paris, Edith and

her husband were totally incompatible, and he very quickly found himself incapable of keeping up with her. Edith had always had an enormous zest for life and was utterly indefatigable, even towards the end. Before a show or tour she would fling herself heart and soul into her work, caring little for the creature comforts of her fellows – if she could do it, then there was no compromise for them and absolutely no escaping her tyranny. New songs were rehearsed or rehashed with fervour. Edith was known to work solidly from dusk until dawn perfecting a single song – she would even wake up a lyricist in the middle of the night (once during an actual *wedding* night!) and instruct him or her to rush over to Boulevard Lannes just because one or two particular words did not sound quite right. Because she was a perfectionist, she demanded nothing less from those who worked with her. Marguerite Monnot, Michel Emer, Henri Contet and Jean Dréjac were just a few of the composers who adapted their lives to please her – and the rewards, of course, were so tremendous that no one ever complained.

The Piaf-Pills union was doomed from the start. Edith, since leaving her father, had been perpetually in search of that security which had always evaded her, had drifted uncompromisingly from one man to the next, and each relationship had been more intense than the last. This of course was the secret of her success: had her personal life been less complicated, there would have been fewer good songs, for much of her work bespoke her own experiences. Pills, with his too-casual manner and sycophantic charm, might have made a better husband had he been more persuasive, as Marlene confirmed:

> Edith needed an iron hand to guide her back on to the rails, a man who genuinely cared about her, and not for what he was getting out of her. Pills knew that his career was over, but he hung on because of the money. Afterwards, Edith told me that she had told him that she was taking drugs on account of her rheumatism, and that he had believed her. Now, that man was anything but stupid! He knew what she was doing, and he did *nothing* to stop her because his own career was over and she was paying

for everything. I told her, 'Get rid of that son-of-a-bitch and find yourself a *real* husband!'

As far as Edith's drink problem was concerned, Pills was more of a companion than a moderator. Some of their binges were almost as notorious as the ones with Yvonne de Bray, and one was described by Edith herself to *France-Dimanche*:

> The first time I *really* drank was after coming away from the cemetery. They had just put my kid in a hole, and I realized that as well as enabling me to forget, alcohol allevi-ated my suffering. It was another miracle – but one sent by the devil! Jacques Pills and I once went into a bistro in Lyons, after our show – intentionally, just for one glass of beer. At eight the next morning we were still propping up the bar, in a dreadful state. Then suddenly, we decided to go off and have breakfast in Valence. When we arrived at our hotel there, he ordered eggs and white wine. Then he asked who had driven us there, and like an idiot I laughed. I thought it was funny . . .

And yet there must have been *some* genuinely contented moments. During the summer of 1970, just weeks before his death, Pills was interviewed for the BBC film-documentary, *I regret nothing*. He spoke cheerfully of how he had been proud to be Edith's husband, even if he had never become 'Monsieur Piaf' . . .

The professional problems which Edith and Pills encountered on home ground were pretty much the same as they had been in America – few theatres could afford to have them both on the same bill, even though Edith refused to appear anywhere without him. Ignoring her friends and Louis Barrier, who insisted that such a project would not be viable, she signed for a series of 'sandwich' recitals which would prove the biggest financial disaster of her career and almost put paid to her repu-tation as the greatest *chanteuse-réaliste* of this century. The first part of the show would have Piaf and Pills singing duets. After the interval, there would be a revival of *Le bel indifférent*, with Pills playing the role of Emile . . . and after this, the couple would sing more duets, but of *Edith's* songs.

(*Above*) *Écoute, peuple de Paris!* Looking perplexed, hours before her first one-woman show at the Bobino in 1938.

(*Below*) 'If Piaf dies, part of me will die too.' Reading the script of *Le bel indifférent*, 1940. Piaf and Jean Cocteau died on the same day.

J'ai dansé avec l'amour . . . From the 1941 film *Montmarte-sur-Seine*, singing '*Un coin tout bleu*'.

(*Above*) *Car c'est Noël à Paradis*. With Lucien Baroux in the 1947 film *Neuf garçons et un coeur*.

(*Below*) *Le diable est près de moi*. With Mômone, 1952, the woman who later told the world that she was Piaf's sister.

(*Above*) *Je veux te faire une chanson bleue.* With Marlene Dietrich, on her 45th birthday, during the 'suicide' tour.

(*Left*) *Dieu réunit ceux qui s'aiment!* A few days after the death of Marcel Cerdan, for whom Edith cut her hair as a penance.

Avante l'heure. 1951, during rehearsals for *La petite Lili,* with Robert Lamoureux.

En écoutant tinter les muguets . . . Pictured in 1952, after being awarded the Grand Prix du Disque.

Non, la vie n'est pas triste! Montreal, 1956, surrounded by the essential Piaf accoutrements – the Bible, flowers, and the statue of Ste Thérèse.

C'est un homme terrible! With Felix Marten, during Olympia '58.

(*Above*) *La foule!* Being congratulated after Olympia '58.

(*Top right*) *Devant un téléphone qui ne sonnera pas* . . . 20 February 1959, in her suite at New York's Waldorf Astoria, only hours before she collapsed and almost died.

(*Bottom right*) *On cherche un Auguste.* Théo walks offstage after turning Piaf to face her audience during Olympia '62.

Le chant d'amour. On stage at the Bobino, with Théo in March 1963, her last Paris season.

Barrier told Pills that the part would not suit him: though there was no dialogue, Paul Meurisse's success had had quite a lot to do with his arrogant, surly mannerisms on and off the stage. Even so, Pills persisted with his theory that he could act as well as the next man, and Edith gave instructions for the production to go ahead. First of all, however, she declared that she would rid herself of her dependency on drugs.

The detoxification affected her badly. The doctors at the clinic began by administering the number of injections she had become addicted to – as many as eight each day. Day by day these doses diminished until they ceased altogether, and Edith almost went insane with the pains which racked her fragile body. She lost weight – not that she had ever had any to spare – but after just three weeks Pills came to collect her and drove her back to Boulevard Lannes. Her physician, Doctor Migot, forewarned her of the depression which would be certain to follow the cure – in order to cope with this, she began injecting herself with cortisone again. For the first time ever, her public questioned her credibility. Gilbert Bécaud's 'Les croix' almost became her theme-song, for she was indeed struggling beneath an immense, leaden cross. Sometimes she was not even strong enough to stay on her feet throughout a full performance, and she would fake curtain calls after just ten songs so that she could rush off the stage to inject herself. The problem became so distressing that some theatre managers refused to accept responsibility for her during the gala shows running up to her new venture. Much worse than this, no one at all would stage the double shows with Pills – not that this bothered Edith, for she resolved the problem by personally booking the Théâtre Marigny, at the bottom of the Champs-Elysées.

Edith lavished millions of francs on the project – money she could ill afford. Two mandolinists were imported from Florence though these were put to some good use, accompanying her o her May 1953 recording of the semi-operatic 'Les amants Venise'. Other new songs included Michel Emer's 'Soeur An and 'Et moi', and two new ways of dying were found for 'T va pas Manuel' (drowning) and 'Jean et Martine' (motor-c crash). Apart from these, all the dramatic songs had removed from her repertoire, and the result was a 'syrupy despaired of by the critics and her baffled admirer

problem, of course, was too tough for Edith to deal with – the drugs saw to that. The critics hammered her, and the fans booed Pills, who proved hopeless in the play, even in a silent role. The production closed after less than a month, much to everyone's relief.

Rather than take a well-needed rest, Edith at once embarked on a tour of the provinces, and in order to cope with the self-inflicted pressure she began drinking heavily. This affected her performances. In Lyons, she was whistled at and left the stage in tears. On another occasion she was too drunk to stand: the curtain came down after the fifth song. At Royat she was jeered because she forgot the words to 'Le chant du pirate', and as the manager rushed to her aid whilst she was tottering pronounced the infamous line, 'Get your fucking hands off me!', which some years later would open the stage-play which Marlene loathed so much.

After the tour, there was another visit to the drying-out clinic, but Edith discharged herself after just three days to prepare for a gruelling ninety-day tour with the Super-Circus. Pills accompanied her, and each evening she performed in a huge marquee, not unlike the set-up for the 1981 recitals at Pantin by her successor, Barbara. By this time the greater part of her earnings was being doled out to drug-peddlers, and she was constantly hounded by the Press, who threatened to expose her 'deplorable' way of life. To make ends meet, she sold her farm, several valuable oil paintings, and her jewellery collection – the latter had never been of any use to her, for hardly any photographs exist of Piaf adorned with anything more than her talisman, Marlene's cross, and her 'lucky' rabbit's foot. She wrote in her memoirs:

It was May 1954. I will never forget the ninety days which followed – my ninety-day trip to Calvary, moving from one place to the next and seeing nothing, not one town, not a single face. And was there any wonder? I was little more than a broken-down puppet. Each engagement began with my secretary dragging me into her car. Each night, after the show, I was hoisted in clammy somnolence up to my room and put to bed. Here I would wait for Janine to come out from Paris with my drugs ration. I was in such

a state that my musicians had to work wonders to keep up with me . . .

The Super-Circus tour ended at Cholet, where Edith's final song was 'Bravo pour le clown', by Louiguy, perhaps the biggest hit he ever wrote – discounting 'La vie en rose', which in actual fact was all Edith's own work. Despised by his son and nagged by his dreadful wife, the unfortunate clown murders her and ends up in a lunatic asylum. It is an extremely melodramatic piece, both to listen to and to watch. On stage, Edith actually became 'mad', lolling her head to one side and outstretching her arms as if in a trance, her hands dangling limply.

> Je suis roi et je règne! Bravo!
> J'ai des rires qui saignent . . .
> Venez, que l'on m'acclâme,
> J'ai fait mon numéro,
> Tout en jetant ma femme
> Du haut du chapiteau! Bravo!
>
> [I am king and I rule! Bravo!
> I have jokes which bleed . . .
> Come, let me be acclaimed,
> I've done my bit
> In throwing my wife
> From the top of the tent! Bravo!]

As a last resort, Louis Barrier stepped in and whisked Edith off to a clinic – it was an act of pure devotion, from the heart. Edith was putty in his hands because at this stage in her life she trusted him more than anyone else. Her circle of close friends had started to diminish, and for a while even Marlene appeared to have turned her back on her. 'It was like banging my head against a brick wall,' she later wrote. 'My love for her stayed intact, but it had become useless. I abandoned her like a lost child.'

These words, which appeared in Marlene's 1984 autobiography, had actually been penned *thirty* years previously, as she explained:

I never really *abandoned* Piaf. I wrote that, I know. The truth is, Edith's husband asked me to stay away from her, and that's what I did. And we *always* kept in touch on the telephone, or I would drop in at her apartment when Pills was not around. She always sounded or *looked* so strong and I thought she'd gotten over her problems. Obviously, she hadn't, and there were always plenty of hangers-on to complicate matters. One in particular . . .

Marlene was referring to Edith's second 'demon-spirit', one who was almost as bad an influence as Mômone. Charles Aznavour, well on the road towards international stardom, had been replaced as factotum by a young man called Claude Figus.

Today, Figus would be described as a 'groupie', a stage-door Johnny who had more or less pestered his way into Edith's life, and who would stay there because of his unselfish devotion and an extraordinary commitment to a woman he had idolized since childhood. He was also a tremendous liability. During the worst part of her alcoholism Figus had helped her to hide bottles and cans all over the apartment, and he had always refused to participate in the 'booze-searches' organized by her friends. More than this, Figus would wait until the household was asleep, then sneak her out to an all-night bar or club. Figus had begun his 'career' as a rent-boy at the age of fourteen and now, seven years later, he still plied his trade in Edith's presence. Even her eyes are said to have been opened by some of the 'monuments' he brought back to Boulevard Lannes. 'He was only a couple of inches taller than Piaf, handsome as the day was long, sweet as sugar and an absolute creep,' recalled Roger Normand, a frequent visitor to the apartment.

Some years later, Figus boasted to friends that he had enjoyed a brief spell as Edith's lover during these dark, drugs and drink-induced days, a fact which even she denied. He did however spend a lot of time with her at the clinic, and on neutral territory his presence was certainly more beneficial than that of Jacques Pills, whose importance in Edith's existence was rapidly diminishing.

Edith pulled no punches when describing her last day at the detoxification clinic.

It was the longest, most horrible day of my life. From eleven in the morning until five in the afternoon I bawled like a lunatic. I chewed the curtains. I foamed at the mouth and writhed on my bed in agony, insane with my hideous urge for drugs. Doctor Migot found me clawing the floorboards with my fingernails, and asked me if I still wanted one last shot ... then a presence saved me, *in extremis* of myself, as my mother's face swam before my eyes. The mother who had abandoned me, whom I had four times tried to disintoxicate, only to watch her fall back on her vices. Seeing *her* lifted me out of the pit. That and my little girl, Marcelle, who appeared to me in my sleep. She was crying, and I told myself that it was I, her mother, who had made her cry.

Again, Edith was 'stretching' the truth, for she had never tried to cure her mother of drug-addiction.

Edith emerged from the clinic almost cured – almost, for when Doctor Migot prescribed a healthy diet comprising lots of white meat and fruit, Edith rendered the latter more palatable and very soon became addicted to melons in port, strawberries in kirsch, and her personal favourite, pineapples in brandy. The drug-peddlers also hung around her door, though this time she was sensible enough to send them, and Mômone, packing.

At around this time, Edith and Jacques Pills appeared in her *Là joie de vivre*, French television's near-equivalent of *This is your life*. There were contributions from many of her friends, including Gilbert Bécaud, Marguerite Monnot, Suzanne Flon, Charles Aznavour, Les Compagnons de la Chanson ... and Damia. The great *chanteuse* was now sixty-five, but her voice had lost none of its power over the years. She sang 'Les croix', still refusing to use the microphone, and Edith was *so* impressed by Damia's interpretation of the song that she never sang it again.

During her 'years of hell', Edith also played cameo roles in three films. *Si Versailles m'était conté* was directed by Sacha Guitry, the acknowledged genius of the French cinema. Some years before, Edith had attended one of his famous 'jumble-sales' when he had demanded that everyone take off an article of clothing or jewellery so that it could be auctioned for the needy. Because she had yelled at the would-be purchasers for being 'tight-fisted', the event had raised millions of francs, and it was on her insistence that some of the proceeds from the film were donated to the Versailles restoration programme currently in operation. Guitry's idea, which worked tremendously well, was that the major roles in his film should be played by unknowns, an idea which is said to have been inspired by the 'Hollywood Canteen' movies he had seen in America during the forties, and that the big names be assigned to cameos. Thus, Guitry himself played Louis XIV, Gérard Philipe was d'Artagnan, and Tino Rossi – whom Edith still refused to speak to – played a gondolier. Edith herself played 'une fille du peuple' complete with mop-cap and apron – in her scene she is carried on the shoulders of her fellow revolutionaries and scales the ladder which leans against the palace gates, from which she incites the rabble into action by singing 'La carmagnole'. Guitry later admitted that though the first take had been adequate, as with most of Edith's recordings, he had asked for the scene to be shot several times because he had been so enthralled by watching her work!

In Jean Renoir's *French Can-Can*, a highly-fictionalized account of the birth of the Moulin-Rouge, Edith interpreted the role of Eugénie Buffet, the Algerian-born *revanchardiste* who had begun her career as a camp-follower, traipsing across the North African desert after *légionnaires*. Part of her story had been used for the film *Morocco*, starring Marlene Dietrich and Gary Cooper. In *French Can-Can*, Edith sang her most famous song, 'La sérénade du pavé'.

Finally, *Boum sur Paris!* was a musical extravaganza, now more important for its distinguished cast of music-hall artistes than for its flimsy plot – the search amongst the night-clubs of Paris for bottles of perfume, one of which contains an explosive. The songs were 'Pour qu'elle soit jolie ma chanson' and 'Je t'ai dans la peau', and the other stars included Mouloudji, Juliette Gréco, Charles Trenet, Lucienne Delyle . . . and Gregory Peck!

Arguably the biggest song of 1954 – and, at just two minutes, one of Edith's shortest – was René Rouzaud's and Marguerite Monnot's 'La goualante du pauvre Jean', described by one critic as 'the perfect *symphonie-en-miniature* of morality and wit', and by Edith herself as 'a direct descendent of *The Threepenny Opera.*'

This tale of the Beau Brummel-type character who takes everyone for granted and only uses women was written in slang, and like much of Edith's earlier work is virtually untranslatable.

Poor Jean spends all his time in ladies' chambers, he dresses only in the finest clothes, no scam is too much for him, yet at the end of the day he achieves nothing because no one really loves him. And the song ends with a message for the youth of today:

> Esgourdez bien, jeunes gens,
> Profitez de vos vingt ans,
> On ne les a qu'une fois . . .
> Et n'oubliez pas!
> Qu'on soit riche ou sans un sou,
> Sans amour on est rien du tout!
>
> [Harken well, young people,
> Make the best of your twenties,
> You only have them once . . .
> And don't forget!
> Whether you're rich or penniless,
> Without love you're nothing at all!

Edith always refused to sing 'La goualante du pauvre Jean' in English: the first adaptation she received, 'The ballad of poor John', caused hoots of laughter amongst her American entourage – due to the fact that 'john' was their slang-word for 'toilet'. The song eventually became world-famous as an instrumental, 'The poor people of Paris', and was a big hit for Winifred Atwell, though without words its 'old-world' magic was lost.

By the end of 1954, Edith's career was more settled than it had been for some time, though she still had some way to go before ridding herself completely of her drink and drugs problem. And then, quite out of the view, she attained previously undreamed-of heights when Louis Barrier secured her a contract with the most famous of all the French music-halls, the Paris Olympia.

This time, Edith declared, there would be *no* stopping her, and her entourage were delighted when she announced that Jacques Pills would *not* be included on the bill. More than this, she had written a song, 'Un grand amour qui s'achève', celebrating being rid of him!

> Quand tu m'disais que tu m'aimais,
> Mon amour, tu le croyait . . .
> Peut-être un jour tu reviendras,
> Mais moi je ne serais plus là,
> Et toi tout seul tu pleureras . . .
> On y peut rien, c'est la vie!
>
> [When you said you loved me,
> My love, you believed it . . .
> Perhaps you'll come back some day,
> But I won't be there,
> And you'll cry alone
> Nothing can be done, that's life!]

Chapter Eight

SUDDENLY THERE'S A VALLEY!

The Olympia had a long, chequered history. In 1893, the height of *la belle époque*, it had been baptized Les Fantaisies Oller, in honour of its founder, Joseph Oller. Its heyday, however, between 1915 and 1928, had witnessed the greatest names of the *café-concert* era: Grock, Fréhel, Yvonne George, Mayol and of course, Damia. Then it had ingloriously been converted into a cinema, reverting to its former glory only in 1954 when taken over by Bruno Coquatrix, the former director of Chez Odette and the man responsible for Edith's famous black dress. Since their last professional encounter, Coquatrix too had moved up in the world: not only was he now Lucienne Boyer's impresario, he had also written a number of hugely successful songs, including Jacques Pills' 'Cheveux dans le vent' and Pierre Dudan's 'Clopin-clopant'.

The Olympia was – and to a certain extent still is – the most prestigious music-hall in France, and its audiences were notoriously difficult to please. Until Coquatrix's death in April 1979, its billboards boasted a galaxy of international superstars, sadly no longer with us: Jacques Brel, Georges Brassens, Barbara, Léo Ferré, Judy Garland, Marlene Dietrich and Joséphine Baker. However, when the entrepreneur had been preparing his first programme, early in 1954, he had *refused* to have Edith in his theatre, declaring that in the light of her recent disastrous tour and on account of her drinking and drug-taking, she was too much of a risk. Consequently he had engaged Lucienne Delyle, a young singer of great charm who was married to the bandleader, Aimé Barelli. Until Delyle's death from leukaemia in 1962, Edith would despise her.

Lucienne Delyle's *vedette-américaine* at the Olympia was Gilbert Bécaud, and his presence caused more problems for Coquatrix than he could possibly have imagined. Bécaud was France's very first *idole des jeunes*, and thousands of francs worth of damage was caused when his crazed fans began ripping the seats apart!

Louis Barrier, however, was as persistent with Coquatrix as Raymond Asso had been with Mitty Goldin of the ABC, and Edith was eventually signed up for one month – a better deal than Barrier had anticipated, for this was twice the length of a normal contract. She opened on 27 January 1955, after 'trying out' her new songs at a *générale* in Lausanne . . . and very quickly proved beyond doubt that she was the hottest property in France.

The Olympia recitals incorporated many Piaf classics, perfectly blended with exciting new material from the pens of Contet, Monnot and René Rouzaud. Her opening number was 'Heureuse', which at its inception had been inspired by her marriage and its holy vows – now, of course, the public was well aware that the union was a sham, that her only *true* happiness was gleaned from an audience. There were revivals of 'Je n'en connais pas la fin', where everyone joined in with the refrain, and 'L'accordéoniste', with the applause edited out, was released on a 45rpm record, its popularity quickly surpassing the already outdated original version. Edith championed whores in 'C'est à Hambourg', and Jesus in 'Soeur Anne'. She confessed her sins in 'Mea Culpa', declaring that for love she would commit them all again. And she brought the house down with Jacques Larue's 'Miséricorde', a rare political statement for her about a woman who has lost her lover to the horrors of war.

> Les beaux rêves sont gratuits,
> Moi, le seul qui me reste
> C'est l'odeur de sa veste,
> Quand j'dansais avec lui . . .
> Et la vie est si moche,
> Que même ca je l'oublierai . . .

[Beautiful dreams are free,
For me, all that remains
Is the odour of his jacket
When I danced with him . . .
But life is so lousy,
That I'll forget even that . . .]

Olympia '55 also produced one of Edith's most disturbing songs – 'Légende' was so disturbing, in fact, that she never recorded it in the studio. With her own very poetic lyrics set to Gilbert Bécaud's music, the narrator speaks from beyond the grave about his love, who is lost for ever.

Dieu n'a jamais permis
De supprimer sa vie,
Elle est morte pour moi,
Et je suis mort pour elle . . .
C'est en vain que j'appelle,
Chaque nuit je l'entends pleurer
Seule, dans son éternité.
Christine, je t'aime!

[God never allowed her
To deprive herself of life,
She died for me, I for her.
I call out for her in vain,
Each night I hear her crying,
Alone in her eternity.
Christine, I love you!]

It was during the Olympia run that Bruno Coquatrix hit upon the idea of measuring the success of his stars – literally. Since its re-opening, the theatre had been selling records in the foyer, so Coquatrix put up a list of how many 'centimetres of micro-sillon' each artist had sold on the evening of their respective premieres. Jacques Pills and Lucienne Delyle were at the bottom of the list: their piles of records measured barely 15 centimetres, which only delighted Edith, and former protégés Les Compagnons de la Chanson and Eddie Constantine attained 35 and

85 centimetres respectively. Edith topped the poll . . . with an astonishing 1 metre 28 centimetres.

After the Olympia, Edith was offered a two-week contract with Her Majesty's Theatre, in Montreal. There was, however, a sizeable hitch. Her American agent, Clifford Fisher, who had arranged the tour, had recently retired through ill-health and his replacement, Eddie Lewis – a close friend of Jacques Pills – now tried to insist that she would not receive any further engagements in French-speaking Canada unless Pills was included on the bill. She was furious: this was exactly what she had been trying to avoid, but for the time being she relented and the couple opened in Montreal on 9 May.

Revenge was swift, however, for Edith went behind Lewis' back and personally negotiated a contract – though not her fee – with a young businessman, Gérard Thibault, who owned two cabarets in the heart of Quebec – Chez Gérard and À La Porte St-Jean – knowing full well that Pills would not be appearing with her because he was due to leave for London to prepare for his first British musical-comedy, *Romance by candlelight*. Eddie Lewis did not argue with her, particularly when Thibault informed him that if Pills set foot in either of his establishments, the deal would be called off. Lewis therefore had no option but to deliver the news to Pills – who behind *Edith's* back had arranged a two-week stay of rehearsal with his London producer – that he had *already* been replaced. The singer is reported to have threatened to punch Lewis on the nose.

Gérard Thibault and his wife Simone had first seen Edith at the Versailles in 1952, since which time he had committed himself to presenting her, even if it meant losing out financially. For her two-week stint at Her Majesty's Theatre she had been paid $30,000 and the wily Eddie Lewis demanded a pro rata fee for each of her performances in Quebec, which Thibault could not afford unless he *tripled* his ticket prices. Again, Edith solved the problem, telling him, 'Just pay me what you can afford, and make sure that I open on a Thursday. *That's* more important than any money!' Thibault suggested $700 a performance, she immediately agreed, so the premiere was set for 26 May 1955 – a Thursday, one of her 'lucky' days.

Thibault booked Edith and her entourage into the Hôtel Château-Frontenac, and had her dressing-room redecorated.

When she turned up for her first rehearsal and found this filled with flowers – a gift from the Local Ladies' Circle, for whose tea-dance she had also been engaged – she turned to Thibault and asked, 'Where's the coffin? The place is like a funeral parlour!' He later said that it had been impossible to discern exactly when Piaf had been acting sarcastically or genuinely pulling his leg when she had demanded 'two-thousand smackers' for the American choir she had hired to accompany her on her English songs. When he told her that such a luxury was entirely out of his price-range, she merely shrugged her shoulders and told him that the bill had been 'taken care of'.

The comparatively small (363-seat) but extremely snobbish À La Porte St-Jean had never seen anything quite like Edith, and to be perfectly honest was extremely lucky to have secured her in the first place. The Versailles aside, she had never liked 'singing to money' because, she said, being out of her depth frequently affected her performances. One only has to compare the recorded Quebec concerts with her more famous ones at the Olympia and even in Lausanne to observe this. Her shows in Quebec were also short, rarely more than fifteen songs, though they did spring a few pleasant surprises. In French-speaking Canada her songs from the thirties were just as popular as the later classics. Raymond Asso's 'C'est toi le plus fort' was spoken all the way through and 'Browning' brought its usual titters of amusement, though one young American woman sitting at a table next to the stage clearly did not appreciate it. Leaping to her feet, she cried, 'Why don't you sing something that we *all* know, such as "La Marseillaise"?' The laughs were on her, however, when Edith retorted, 'If you know it so well, honey, why don't *you* sing it?'

Having attended a rehearsal, Gérard Thibault had advised Edith *not* to risk shocking her audiences by singing 'Elle fré-quentait la rue Pigalle' or Michel Emer's 'Qu'as-tu fait John?', the disturbing story of the Negro slave who is hanged for raping the plantation boss's daughter. This almost led to her backing out of her contract: she told Thibault that, as Princess Elizabeth had not objected to the song, neither should the 'fuddy-duddies' of Quebec, and the song ended with her emul-ating a corpse dangling from the end of a rope, twitching until one of her musicians brought his hands together to represent the snapping of the prisoner's neck! But if many of her audience were appalled by such unaccustomed reality, there was worse to come when she announced the equally harrowing 'Tous les amoureux chantent', saying, 'Et maintenant, la triste histoire de deux gosses!' – 'And now, the sad story of two kids!' . . . completely forgetting that in this part of the world, 'gosses' meant 'bollocks'!

The journalist Renaude Lapointe witnessed several of Edith's shows in Canada, though for her the performances which took place in the intimacy of the St-Jean were the best ever. Writing for *Le Soleil*, she said:

> In the semi-darkness of a smoke-filled room, Piaf's spell may not be analyzed. So too the voice, an evocative force which defies the norm, is without equal. It was as if we were living through a film mirroring our own lives. Piaf sang marvellously, taking possession of her congregation and not letting go, putting her soul out to pasture whilst embodying every one of us with her immortal sentiment. Her hands speak every language whilst her face expresses every joy and sorrow of the pityful buffoon, the cocky gangster and the obsessive lover. Piaf is unique!

The next day, Edith and her new secretary Danielle Bonel went to see Gérard Thibault and explained that she was not too happy with her hotel arrangements – the Château Frontenac was far too snobbish for her liking, she declared, and too public. By the next morning she and her entourage had been installed in a house on the fashionable Murray Avenue: the owner, a Doctor Larochelle who was away on vacation, had called Thibault with the message that he would be proud to allow Edith full use of his house and its possessions. Edith showed her gratitude by singing for another ladies' tea-dance and waiving the fee. A few days later, she was guest-of-honour at a reception given by the French Consul. She told her gathering, 'I love Quebec *so* much. If you hadn't *asked* me to come here, I would have come of my own accord – to sing in the streets like I did in Paris in the old days!'

The Quebec recitals also set another important precedent, when she 'fell in love' with the establishment's translucent, powder-blue backdrop curtains. Designed by the local Maison Irène Auger, these almost totally concealed her musicians and backing singers from public view, and were particularly effective during her final song, 'Hymne à l'amour' – during the crescendo which leads to the last line, 'Dieu réunit ceux qui s'aiment', they opened slowly to reveal her musicians, who simultaneously rose to their feet. One critic wrote, 'Piaf now sings in an *éspace céleste*', and when she read this, Edith informed Eddie Lewis that she wanted an identical backdrop for every one of her future venues in North America – a matter of some forty-five different theatres! Needless to say, in the wake of the Jacques Pills fiasco – and finally aware of Edith's pulling-power – the impresario did as he was asked.

From Quebec, Edith moved around the United States with limitless energy, still a little shaky at times after her detoxification. Doctor Migot had warned her of the impending perils of the third, sixth and eighteenth months after her cure, and though she had rid herself of tiresome leeches such as Mômone and Claude Figus for the time being, she was still aware of her vulnerability. Even so, she never slipped up on stage, and every packed performance received only the most scintillating reviews. First stop on the road was Hollywood, where after spending an evening catching up on all the latest gossip from Marlene Dietrich, she accepted another invitation to visit Chaplin's house. Then she performed in Washington, Las Vegas, Miami, Chicago and Texas, flying on to Cuba for two shows in Havana, before the start of another record-breaking twenty-week season at the Versailles.

On 4 January 1956, Edith appeared at Carnegie Hall, the first time that a popular singer had performed in this, the most famous concert-hall in America. It was her first legitimate one-woman show, within which she was the only artiste on the bill, with an interval dividing the twenty-seven songs. The recital is said to have been taped, though if this is so it has yet to come to light – an enormous tragedy, for eight of the songs were sung in English including 'If you go', 'All my love', 'Suddenly there's a valley', and 'Allentown Jail'.

It was in New York, early in 1956, that Edith first publicly expressed her disapproval of the *chanteuse* Patachou, who had just recorded cover-versions of several of her songs, including

'La goualante du pauvre Jean' and 'Padam padam'. The same thing had happened not so long before with Jacqueline Francois, but this had not perturbed Edith because, she said, no one in their right mind would have termed Francois a singer! Patachou, however, she had always admired. Born Henriette Ragon in 1918, this tremendously gifted and much-loved entertainer had been launched by Maurice Chevalier, who for a time had been her lover. This earnt her the somewhat incongruous nickname, 'Patamerde' [Patashit] from his ex-mistress, Mistinguett... and 'Patafoutre', which was infinitely more insulting, when she had covered the older star's signature-tune, 'Mon homme'. Edith could never be quite so vengeful, though she did see red when she learned that Patachou had *also* 'purloined' 'Avec ce soleil', a brand-new protest song composed for *her* by Jacques Larue and Michel Philipe-Gérard ... for this very individual number represented Edith's personal message to the world's youth, a message which she declared could not come from a woman who had spent half her life wrapped in cottonwool. Patachou was *ordered* to remove the song from her repertoire, which she did for a little while, though one has to confess that her interpretation is just as definitive as Piaf's.

In 'Avec ce soleil', Edith proclaims that present-day children are only taught how to grow up tough, cynical, and incapable of dreams and laughter. 'When people criticize the youth of today,' she told the audience at her Versailles premiere, 'they all too often forget that not so very long ago, they too were young.' And the song ends portentously, with these youngsters being compared to wild flowers.

> Et ce jour encore, le long du talus,
> Les coquelicots avec les bleuets,
> En vain attendirent une main cruelle
> Qui les cueillerait ...

> [And today still, along the slopes,
> Poppies and cornflowers,
> In vain await a cruel hand
> Which would pluck them ...

Edith was still drinking heavily between recitals, though this, incredibly, was kept out of the American press, who in those days were far less tolerant than their French counterparts. Joséphine Baker, Gaby Deslys and Mistinguett had all been criticized for their personal lives, and whilst working in America Edith always tried her utmost to be on her best behaviour. There were two reported incidents – potentially scandalous at the time, but hilarious in retrospect.

Edith would never forget how she and Marlene Dietrich had ejected a drunken, naked John Garfield out of her bedroom – rarely one to bear grudges, she had sent flowers to his funeral in 1952 – and now, once again at the Waldorf Astoria, she was propositioned by a man who she declared was almost Garfield's double, a young bit-part player named John Glendale. One evening, Edith and Marlene were invited to participate in a game of Blind Man's Buff during which those caught had to forfeit a $100 bill. Much to the amusement of his friends, Glendale allowed Edith to grab him, but instead of the banknote, he took out his penis and pressed this into her hand. The joke backfired, however, and the actor fled from the room red-faced when she cracked, 'Honey, that must be the smallest dick I've *ever* handled!'

The second incident concerned Raymond Asso's 'Mon légionnaire', which Edith and Marlene had 'rearranged' to perform at a Hollywood party. The result of this collaboration – which according to Marlene was taped – was that the line, 'Il m'a aimé toute la nuit' became 'Il m'a *foutré* toute la nuit'. 'And that was the *cleanest* line in the song!' Marlene concluded, adding that after their performance, Edith had fallen on to the floor and begun crossing the room on all fours, 'barking' at her astonished audience and shouting in English, 'I am a dog!' . . . at which Marlene had borrowed a belt from one of the waiters, placed it around her neck and scolded, 'Don't you *dare* bite anyone, you vicious little beast!'

In her memoirs, Edith confessed that she had had an affair with Glendale, which Marlene assumed could not have been more than a one-night stand, and she attempted to save Marlene's blushes by naming the 'dog-handler' as Ginette Richer, a *frangine* not unlike Mômone though considerably less demanding on her purse, who sometimes accompanied her on her travels. It is a terrible pity that the tape-recording of 'Les feuilles mortes' which Edith and Marlene made at the time, in the same studio where Marlene recorded her famous duets with Rosemary Clooney, does not appear to have survived.

Edith returned to the Paris Olympia in May 1956 when her *vedette-américaine* was a twenty-seven-year-old *fantaisiste* named Marcel Amont. He became a friend, and later recorded two of her lesser-known songs, 'Va danser' and 'Les bleuets d'azur'. This time Edith was engaged for three months, breaking every conceivable attendance record – the theatre even contravened fire-regulations by setting up folding seats in the aisles, and on the opening night she took twenty curtain calls. The recording of the premiere sold 20,000 copies in Paris on the day of its release, and 500,000 nationwide by the end of the Olympia run.

Edith's new songs included Jacques Larue's 'Marie la Fran-caise', about the girl from Paname who becomes a whore in Sydney – only her mother, attending her funeral, still believes the story that she left to find a rich husband. 'Toi qui sais' and 'Une dame' were both from the pen of Michel Emer. In the former, a lover who has been dumped pleads with his replace-ment to put in a good word for him, whilst in the latter a woman is sent to prison for exacting her revenge on the man who has abandoned her.

There were also two quite phenomenal numbers from Jean Dréjac, a young composer Edith had first encountered during the war. Dréjac had offered her several songs over the years, but she had dismissed them as too sugary: he had gone on to write 'Le petit vin blanc' for Lina Margy, and 'Le p'tit bal du samedi soir' for Georges Guétary. On the eve of her trip to Canada he had offered Edith 'Allume tes lampions', which she had also rejected – telling him sarcastically, 'Better take it to Patachou. It's about time she sang something original!' ... hardly expecting him to take her at her word, or that Patachou would score a big hit with the song! Peeved, therefore, Edith had asked Dréjac to join her in America, promising to reimburse his expenses should he provide her with a song worth singing.

Dréjac certainly had not disappointed her again. 'Soudain une vallée', an adaptation of an American song superbly orches-trated by Robert Chauvigny was, Dréjac said in 1994, 'the perfect expression of Piaf's Rosicrucian spirit': it is so easy to travel around the world and believe that one has found nothing, then, suddenly there is a valley where hope and love begins. Dréjac also adapted an American *rock*-song, 'Black denim trousers and motorcycle boots'. Inspired by the Marlon Brando film, *The wild one*, it became 'L'homme à la moto', and was such a massive hit for Edith that the original was quickly forgotten. Again, it recounted an 'important' death – that of the leather-clad demon who terrorizes the neighbourhood with his infernal machine, until he and his girlfriend Marie-Lou attempt and fail to out-race the Southern Express.

> Jamais il ne se coiffait, jamais il ne se lavait,
> Les ongles pleins de cambouis,
> Mais sur le biceps il avait
> Un tatouage avec un coeur bleu sur la peau blême,
> Et juste à l'intérieur on lisait, 'Maman je t'aime' . . .

> [He never combed his hair or washed,
> Fingernails caked in grease,
> But on his biceps there was a tattoo:
> A blue heart above the pale skin, inside which
> One read, 'Mum, I love you' . . .]

Edith's *greatest* success at Olympia '56, however, related a suicide which is so sensitively portrayed that the tragedy becomes an event of considerable romanticism and beauty. 'Les amants d'un jour' is arguably one of the finest *chansons-poèmes* ever written, and certainly the best Piaf ever sang. One is instantly reminded of those little French tourist-class hotels with never-ending spiral staircases, sagging beds, cracked sinks and peeling wallpaper, yet with unmistakable qualities of their own. The woman is at the back of the café, washing glasses, when something happens which transforms her life . . .

> Ils sont arrivés se tenant par la main,
> L'air émerveillé de deux chérubins.
> Portant le soleil, ils ont demandés
> D'une voix tranquille,
> Un coin pour s'aimer . . .

> [They arrived hand in hand,
> The wondrous aura of two cherubs.

Bringing sunshine, they asked calmly
For a corner to love in . . .]

Not unexpectedly, the songs ends with a tragedy, and with a shattered glass dropped on to the stage – the only time Edith ever performed with a 'prop'. Outside the café, the sign says Rooms to Let, and the woman is still washing glasses though her eyes fill with tears when she remembers:

On les a trouvés se tenant par la main,
Les yeux refermés, vers d'autres matins.
Remplis de soleil, on les a couchés
Unis et tranquilles, dans un lit creusé . . .

[They found them hand in hand,
Their eyes closed towards other mornings.
In the sunshine, they laid them to rest
Peacefully together, in a hollow bed . . .]

Several other songs, each in a class of its own though not included in the Olympia programme, appeared at around this time. Jean Dréjac's surrealist 'Le chemin des forains' was set to the music of the classical composer, Henri Sauget, originally scripted for Roland Petit's first ballet of 1945. There was an excellent cover-version by Colette Renard which Edith approved of: for her, the *chanteuse* could do no wrong because she was Damia's 'fille-spirituelle' and a close friend of Marie Dubas. Her own interpretation was issued in France on a hard-to-come-by extended-play recording, ESRF 1036, along with another 'classical' piece. 'L'homme au piano' was an adaptation of Henning and Terningsöhn's 'Mein klavier'. Also on this EP was 'Retour', a moving anti-war song which Edith never once sang on the stage, though every one of these songs was over-looked by disc-jockeys and critics in favour of the title-track, Marguerite Monnot's 'C'est à Hambourg', another cherished theme telling of a whore's quest for sailors in ports around the world. The lyrics to this song were *certified* Piaf's private prop-erty in France during her lifetime – when Catherine Sauvage and her old foe, Renée Lebas, recorded cover-versions, they were compelled to sing words which were not only inferior to the originals, but considerably tamer. To the English-speaking world, the song became an instrumental, 'On the quayside', thereby losing much of its effect.

During the Olympia run, Edith was inundated with offers to sing in Britain. Again the response was the same, though there did appear to be some hope that she would change her mind in the near future. She said, 'The British know nothing about love, so I'll record them a few songs and see where we go from there!' This she did, and on 11 July 1956 she entered the Pathé-Marconi studios and cut ten record sides, all in almost flawless English. 'La vie en rose' was given a new arrangement – when Edith had recorded the first English-language version in 1950, she had been displeased with the way the drums had almost drowned her. Lyrically, these songs were not as exciting in English as they had been in their original French, and today most of them sound old-fashioned and un-Piaf-like. Rick French's 'One little man' and 'Heaven have mercy', his adaptation of 'Miséricorde', were notable exceptions: the latter was certainly the most disturbing song she had ever sung in English.

> Now he's gone, why be brave?
> Why should I live like this?
> Should I wait by the grave
> For my lost lover's kiss?
> Why should I live in hell?
> Lord above, let me die . . .

Curiously, these songs were *not* released in Britain during her lifetime – instead, they were issued on an American album when the sleeve notes wrongfully declared that Edith had recorded them in New York.

In October 1956, Edith flew to New York, and after her first port-of-call at the Versailles began a lengthy tour of the United States and Canada. On 16 November she returned to A La Porte St-Jean in Quebec, and two of her ten performances were taped by a fan. 'Les amants d'un jour' brought the house down and the emotion was so intense that several people were reported to have actually fainted in the auditorium. Edith also sang two songs unique to her Canadian audiences: sadly, 'Pleine de la nostalgie' and 'Une jeune apatride' seem to have disappeared without trace, as has 'Just across the way', Christopher Hassall's masterful adaptation of 'De l'autre côté de la rue' which Edith is at least reported to have taped – possibly during her brief visit to Britain with Marcel Cerdan, when she sang it for her privileged audiences at the Mayfair Hotel.

> Close by the fish-and-chip shop
> Smart people never use,
> Step through a sort of hoarding,
> Turn down a sort of mews.
> Stop by the yellow doorway,
> Start climbing up the stairs,
> Try not to kick the dustbins,
> Three flights and then you're there!

Raymond Asso's 'Browning' was performed once more in Quebec, but with a slight amendment: Edith had been asked to remove the line which referred to Greta Garbo's fondness for being photographed with gangsters! Also, the dramatic intensity of 'Hymne à l'amour' became too much for her – she broke down during the last refrain and ended it without the choral reprise, leaving her musicians in a quandary over what to do next, then rushing off the stage after just eleven songs without taking a curtain-call. This prompted an announcement from Gérard Thibault, who later said that he had been talking off the top of his head by telling the audience, 'Miss Piaf's says she's had enough. And if you want to hear any of the songs you've missed this evening, well, that's too bad because all the seats have been sold for tomorrow's performance. So, I guess you'll have to be content with listening to her records!' Such a gabbled statement caused a minor panic, and Edith was forced to hold an impromptu press-conference to prove to everyone that she was not ill. The next evening, of course, the show went without any hitch and she took ten curtain-calls!

1957 dawned with Edith's greatest personal triumph: another concert at New York's Carnegie Hall, no more important than its predecessor, but one which has survived on tape thanks to a thoughtful radio technician. Stephen F Temmer had negotiated with the CBS network, hoping to record an earlier Piaf performance in Chicago, and broadcast it simultaneously on 230 radio stations across the North American continent. The deal, however, had fallen through, so Temmer taped this one – 13 January, a curious date for Edith, with her superstitious nature – just in case he could secure another deal, but without her knowledge. Edith was furious when she found out what he had done, claiming that had she been aware of his actions she would have selected a more varied repertoire, and sung more songs in English. Even so, the recording, released on a double album in 1977, is an invaluable item in the Piaf catalogue, and as such is her only recorded complete American recital that has been found to date.

Edith's fans had queued for hours in sub-zero temperatures to buy tickets, many of which had been snapped up by racketeers and sold on the black market for many times their value. Prior to this, the students of New York's Columbia University had had little difficulty persuading her to sing 'La vie en rose' and 'L'accordéoniste' on New Year's Day, whilst standing under the Statue of Liberty, muffled against the freezing cold.

Carnegie Hall seated just under four thousand people, in those days a sizeable audience for a music-hall recital. Such was the demand for tickets that Edith could have filled it several times over. One critic wrote that New York had claimed her as its very own Joan of Arc – so far as the Americans were concerned she could do no wrong.

As before, Edith sang twenty-seven songs, opening with 'C'est pour ca', the song she had introduced with Les Compagnons de la Chanson. It was a difficult number, even for her, and she had to struggle to meet its wide range. She was also put off considerably by some of the audience – the management had stupidly placed over a hundred seats on the platform itself, and the fidgeting of these spectators irritated her so much that after her opening number Edith asked for the microphone stand to be moved further forwards towards the edge of the stage. But if at first Edith sounded a little tremulous and off-key, this was soon put to rights – her heart-rending 'Lovers for a day' defied even the most hard-bitten listener to remain dry-eyed.

> So why must I keep the ribbon she wore?
> The smile on his face when I closed the door?
> Sleep still, children, still,

> Your shadows may start
> The tears in my eyes, the tears in my heart . . .

Besides the Rick French songs from her first American album, many other songs were sung in English, including 'Je t'ai dans la peau', 'Heureuse', 'Autumn leaves' and 'The highway', Edith's own English adaptation of Raymond Asso's 'Un jeune homme chantait'. There was also Edith's first performance of the better-known translation of 'Hymne à l'amour' – 'If you love me, really love me', and superb revivals of 'La fête continue' and 'Monsieur Saint-Pierre'. 'Les grognards', by Hubert Giraud and Pierre Delanoë, was given its debut at Carnegie Hall. It is a wonderful piece, opening with the marching of feet and a spoken verse: 'The Grumblers have no guns, no grenades, no shoes. They are the ghosts of Napoléon's soldiers who are haunting Paris because, in life, they never got to see it, yet now the city's streets are audaciously named after their famous battles!' The song builds up to a tremendous crescendo, with the rolling of drums and Edith's voice practically raising the roof. Then it subsides and dies with the retreating footsteps – a masterpiece!

> Wagram, Iéna, Eylau, Arcole, Marengo . . .
> Quelles jolies batailles!
> Tout ce travail c'était pas pour rien!
> Il y a eu tant et tant de soldats,
> Mais cette nuit vous nous verrez!
>
> [Wagram, Jena, Eylau, Arcole, Marengo . . .
> What fine battles!
> All that work wasn't for nothing!
> There've been lots and lots of soldiers,
> But tonight you're going to see us!]

Edith was now the highest-paid female entertainer in the world – in fact, only Frank Sinatra and Bing Crosby were earning more than she at this time. Sadly, she was forced to admit to herself what her friends had been saying all along: her marriage to Jacques Pills, hardly ever more than a joke, was finally over.

On the eve of our marriage I had made him swear never to remove his wedding ring – it was bad luck! Then, whilst we were shooting a film at Vichy his dresser came in to tell him to take his ring off. I closed my eyes to conceal my tears. We were heading towards catastrophe, and two months later we were divorced. Once again the love of two stars had died, unable to cope with showbusiness pressures, and bad memories surfaced, like bubbles on the surface of a pool. Once again I was alone, making the same mistakes I had made after Cerdan's death. I was searching for consolation by reverting to my former weaknesses . . .

The pair were divorced on 15 May 1957. There were no bad feelings, even if some of the scars inflicted during those four tortured years would never heal, though henceforth Edith would never be able to give her love to one man in particular. Her public would have to come first.

Carnegie Hall was the turning-point in Edith's career, for in America as well as in France she had become a living legend – a 'sacred monster'. Even the Soviet Union, one country which had no chance whatsoever of seeing her, thought there was no one like her. Once again Australia, Great Britain and New Zealand came up with offers that no one in their right mind could have refused. Australasia was too far away to take the risk, she declared. As for the British, she was still convinced that they had never understood her.

And, after the triumph at Carnegie Hall?

In California the Texan millionaire, Ed Murrow, hired El Mocambo – the state's most exclusive nightclub – for what he predicted would be 'the party of the century'. Depositing $45,000 with the management for the entertainment alone, he asked them to engage the best female artiste they could think of. They chose Edith, and after a knockout performance of twenty songs the film mogul, Darryl Zanuck, rushed across to her table and offered her $500,000 for the film-rights to her life story. Zanuck told her that the film would be called *Little Miss Courage*, and that it would follow along the lines of *With a song in my heart*, the biopic which had featured Susan Hayward as the American singer, Jane Froman, who had fought her way back to health after being crippled in an air-crash during the war. Edith, however, was not interested. She told Zanuck, 'If the public want to know anything about my life, honey, all they have to do is listen to my songs!'

Edith's American tour lasted almost a year. There were tremendous successes in Las Vegas and at Chicago's Selwyn Theatre – here, she linked up with Marguerite Monnot, who from the stage of the Paris Olympia accompanied her on several songs, including 'La goualante du pauvre Jean'. What is remarkable is that, in spite of the feedback, she did not once go off key! And in San Francisco, the captain of the French battleship, *Jeanne d'Arc*, invited her aboard his vessel to review the French Navy. Edith had always adored men in uniform, and of course the 'inspection' ended with a song!

The tour also took in South America, with engagements in Buenos Aires, São Paolo and Rio de Janeiro. Here, Edith's drinking caused a problem when, after an argument with her pianist, Jacques Liebrard, she ordered a crate of beer and shut herself in her room until it was all gone – ordering Liebrard to do the same, and prove which of them was the biggest 'man'. Edith emerged from her boozing session without so much as a headache: not so Liebrard, who had to miss the next day's matinee performance. In Lima, Peru, her *vedette américaine* was a young Spanish singer named Camilla, whose 'Amore di mes amores' was currently riding high in the hit-parade. Edith arranged to meet the composer, Angèl Cabral, and asked his permission to borrow the music. A little later, her friend Michel Rivgauche would provide her with a lyric, and as with 'L'homme à la moto' the song, which became 'La foule', would quickly be forgotten in its original form.

'La foule' tells the story, relived in the present tense whilst it is happening, of a holiday crowd. It is reminiscent of the final scene in Marcel Carné's famous film, *Les enfants du paradis*, when the mime, Baptiste, loses his beloved Garance to the hustle-bustle of the carnival throng. A bewildered girl finds momentary joy when she is swept into a young man's arms – but her happiness is short-lived when he is just as quickly dragged away from her . . .

> Je lutte et je me débats . . .
> Et je crispe mes poings,

Maudissant la foule qui me vole
L'homme qu'elle m'avait donné,
Que je n'ai jamais retrouvé . . .

[I fight, struggle and clench my fists,
Cursing the crowd which steals
The man it gave me,
Whom I never found again . . .]

The same recording session, 25 November 1957, would produce no fewer than five Piaf classics. 'Les grognards' has been mentioned. 'Les prisons du roi', one of the handful of Edith's songs not especially written for her, had been translated from the original 'Allentown Jail' by Michel Rivgauche – an eccentric-looking character with a little moustache, untidy hair and long, thin eyebrows – Edith once described him as 'looking like the baddie in a silent movie'. His reworking of the song stuck close to the original theme: the young woman's lover has been thrown into prison for stealing jewels which he believes will make her look prettier than all the other ladies at court, and now she pleads with the king to put her in prison with him, for she too is a thief, having stolen his heart. Thus, a schmaltzy, over-sentimental ballad was wonderfully transformed into a *chanson-dramatique*, complete with choir.

'Salle d'attente', about the goings-on in a provincial railway-station waiting-room, was another Rivgauche poem, set to an alarmingly difficult composition by Marguerite Monnot. So far as is known, no one has ever *attempted* to sing it in the same key as Edith, whose range had seemingly doubled overnight.

The final song from the session was 'Opinion publique', lyrically one of Edith's most complicated works and virtually a *chanson-parlée* in the Marianne Oswald tradition. Wherever he goes, the man is pursued by rumour – in the street, in cafés and bars. He finds his reputation advertised in the town hall and market place – until one Sunday he stands in the Square and yells, 'It isn't true!' Now he is a famous man, but the rumours are the same . . .

On dit qu'il a, on dit qu'il est,
On dit qu'il a fait,

A fait ceci, a fait cela!
Non, il a dit ça? Oui, il a dit ça!

[They say he's got . . . they say he's . . .
They say he's done . . .
He's done this, he's done that!
No, he said *that*? *Yes*, he said that!]

Edith's lengthy spell in North America made her homesick for
for France, particularly when she gave a series of recitals at the
St-Jean in Quebec, now almost as regular and important a port
of call as the Versailles. Neither was she interested in sight-
seeing, when away from the music-hall environment. On a trip
to Niagara Falls, she dismissed it as 'just a lot of water'. In an
interview she confessed that her favourite country air was that
of a Paris park, and that her favourite mountain was Montmartre! As a true *enfant du faubourg*, she was not ashamed of
admitting, when invited back to Hollywood for a last series
of shows before heading back to her beloved Olympia, 'Not for
the moment, honey! The artificial glamour there bores me. I'm
looking forward to getting back to a place which is real and
where the people are real.'

Chapter Nine

'THE MOST AMAZING NINETY-SEVEN POUNDS IN SHOWBUSINESS!'

During Edith's absence from Paris, Marguerite Monnot had collaborated with the singer Colette Renard and between them they had produced the highly successful stage musical *Irma la douce*. Whilst apart the two friends had kept in touch, either by link-up or by telephone – it is estimated that as much as one third of Edith's earnings went on telephone calls alone, often as much as $500 a day whilst she was in America. Now, she was welcomed at Orly airport like a queen. There was also a new song. To make up for lost time, Marguerite Monnot had written 'Comme moi'.

> Peut-être bien qu'ailleurs
> Une femme a l'coeur éperdu de bonheur,
> Comme moi . . .
> Elle attend son amour,
> Les yeux de son amour,
> Les bras de son amour comme moi!
>
> [Perhaps elsewhere
> A woman has a heart mad with happiness,
> Like myself . . .
> She is waiting for her love,
> The eyes of her love,
> The arms of her love like myself!]

The song was perhaps a little too optimistic, for at the time there was no man in Edith's life – one of the reasons, of course, why her American tour had been so successful was because there had been no distractions. On the other hand, this lack of stimulus had produced fewer songs, with sixteen months separating her last two visits to the recording studio. However, now that she was back on terra firma, all this would change.

By November 1957, rehearsals were well under way for Olympia '58. Marguerite Monnot, Norbert Glanzberg and Michel Rivgauche had been commissioned to write new songs, and before the premiere the customary provincial tour had been arranged: Louis Barrier had discussed the venues with Edith over the telephone whilst she had been in New York. When Barrier had brought up the subject of her *vedette-américaine*, however, she had told him, 'Leave that to Coquatrix. You know how much I trust his judgement. Even if he hired a deaf mute to sing *Tosca*, it'd be fine by me!' The director of the Olympia did not go quite this far – he engaged Félix Marten, a thirty-eight years old German-born singer who had recently scored a big hit with his recording of 'La Marie-vision', itself perhaps not a good sign because Edith had already complained to friends that she was sick to death of hearing it on the radio.

At 6 feet 5 inches, Marten was one of the tallest of the Piaf Boys, and a good deal more handsome than the last few. He was talented and, according to the people who had worked with him at the time, knew it. He even committed the 'carnal sin' of barging into Edith's dressing-room, without knocking, and announcing, 'Hi, Edith. I'm Félix Marten!' ... to which came the response, 'Hi, Félix. I'm Edith Piaf. Fuck off!' A few days later, however, when she was passing *his* dressing-room and saw him with his shirt off, she was incapable of preventing herself from falling in love with him. And when he presented her with a song, 'Je me souviens d'une chanson', she immediately made up her mind to knock him into shape. Marten, however, would prove her toughest 'customer' to date.

First of all, Edith tried to convince herself that Marten had a fine singing voice which would adapt well to some of the love songs she had in mind. This was only partly true: Marten possessed a distinct nasal quality which suited the numbers he was preparing for the Olympia – 'T'as une belle cravate' and 'Fais-moi un cheque' were cynical, but melodious, with a speedy delivery, but whenever he slowed down the tempo, he tended to go off-key. His stance was also very wooden, as Montand's had been in his early days and, conscious of his great height, he would stoop over the microphone, arms akimbo like some gigantic bird of prey.

Edith promised herself that she would rectify all of Marten's faults. Halfway through the French tour, tired of listening to him 'wailing', she called the Monnot-Contet-Rivgauche team and asked them to meet her at Nevers, the next stop on the road. Here, they were told that they had just forty-eight hours to supply her new discovery with a romantic repertoire. They obeyed – how could they possibly refuse? – and over the next forty-eight hours worked without a break. Marten was also made to commit himself to his cause by making himself available around the clock – in other words, by leaving his wife. This was the most vital condition of all. 'Wives have a habit of getting in the way,' she said, which in her case had always been the case. And of course, the coup paid off. Marten was given several new songs, though there would only be one sizeable hit, 'Je t'aime mon amour'.

Louis Barrier had fixed Edith's Olympia premiere for 17 February 1958, wholly unaware of the date's significance. On 17 February 1936 she had appeared in her very first gala at the Cirque Médrano, fourteen years to the day later she had met Marinette Cerdan . . . and five years hence, she would have her final Paris premiere. Her season ran for four months, allowing her to break all her previous records there: the drink-drugs era may have taken a severe toll on her health, but her voice and stage-presence were more powerful than ever. Her subject range was also wider – from 'Comme moi' and 'Les grognards', which her French admirers were able to hear for the first time – to the unusually strident and optimistic 'Le ballet des coeurs' and 'Mon manège à moi', both by Norbert Glanzberg, who later reflected on the latter, 'The first time Piaf heard it, she said it was shit, but she accepted it all the same!'

> Tu me fais tourner la tête,
> Mon manège à moi, c'est toi!

Je suis toujours à la fête,
Quand tu me prends dans tes bras!

[You set my head reeling,
You're my very own merry-go-round!
I'm always at the fair,
When you take me in your arms!]

On the personal side, Félix Marten was a not unexpected failure. She had upset him the first evening he had sung 'Je t'aime mon amour', shouting from the wings, 'Give it your best shot, and play to the gallery. You'll even have the men coming in their underpants!' Then, in Marseilles, the pair had had a blazing row in a restaurant when Marten had accused her of being stupid for paying for forty dinners, when only twelve guests had been invited. She had screamed at the top of her voice, 'What the fuck has it got to do with you? It's *my* money!' 'I felt just like crawling straight under the table,' Marten later said.

In Paris, things went from bad to worse. Edith accused Marten of being too arrogant, sarcastic and sure of himself – characteristics which have been since verified by others who knew him – and she told him that unless he knocked the chip off his shoulder, he would have to step down as her *vedette-amèricaine*. He retaliated by telling a reporter who broached the subject of his adultery, 'You don't think for one moment that I could ever love a woman like Piaf in the *carnal* sense, do you? God help me, she's just one of those women a man *has* to sleep with to get on in life!' For Edith, this was the last straw. Ordering her entourage, Marten, and the entire staff of the Olympia to a meeting behind the famous red curtain, she told him, 'You've just played your last ace, Félix. You may be famous for your lack of talent and your big prick, but to me you're just one more little cunt!'

Edith's friends were stunned. Marten had been awarded the full Piaf honours – on account of his size, the suit had taken longer to tailor, so she had ordered two – and he had been her first man since her divorce. She had struggled to get back to the top, and in his own selfish way, Marten had helped. Now she was alone again.

Marcel Blistène, her old film director pal, inadvertently came to the rescue. For years he had been searching for an appropriate vehicle for her, a film which would naturally have a few songs in it, but a story hopefully more credible and melodramatic than the others she had made. His first choice was opposite Marguerite Moreno in *Macadam* – Edith would play the elderly actress' on-screen daughter – but Moreno had been taken ill, and been replaced by Francoise Rosay, herself not much older than Edith. Blistène's alternative therefore was *Les amants de demain*, a superb work scripted by an undisputed *monstre sacré* of the French cinema, Pierre Brasseur. It also boasted a fine supporting cast, headed by Armand Mestral, Raymond Souplex, Mona Goya (in her last role), and Francis Blanche. But oh, what a woeful tale!

The story could have been the setting for one of Edith's more harrowing songs. Like *Neuf garçons et un coeur*, it begins one Christmas Eve, though the ensuing events are a far cry from any fantasy. Pierre (Michel Auclair), a composer, is on the run after murdering his wife – we are not told how, or why. His car breaks down and he seeks shelter at Les Géraniums, a provincial hôtel-restaurant which contains the oddest assortment of characters one can imagine. Here, he is ejected headlong into an even more dreadful situation when he meets the hotel owner (Mestral) and his drunken, dogsbody wife Simone (Piaf), who for years has been the butt of everyone's jokes and bad moods. The husband turns out to be a horrible thug who cheats on his wife and beats her, hence her addiction to alcohol. Pierre stays the night. He hears Simone singing, and the pair fall in love. The husband finds out and tries to kill Pierre, only to be shot dead by Simone. Thus the film ends with the lovers, having fulfilled their destiny, descending a seemingly endless succession of flights of stairs to the waiting police van – past her husband's spiteful, spitting cronies, whilst Piaf's voice soars over the proceedings singing the title song. It is an intensely moving moment, which does not fail to bring a lump to the throat, and after which the director said, 'Piaf really is another Magnani!'

The soundtrack for the film was composed by Marguerite Monnot. 'Tant qu'il y aura des jours' and the haunting 'Fais comme si' had lyrics by Michel Rivgauche. Henri Contet wrote the stirring title track, and the sublime 'Les neiges de Finlande', surely one of the most poignant lullabies of all time.

> Le Méchant Loup est un archange,
> Les ogres mangent des oranges,
> Cendrillon file la laine
> Pour habiller l'Croque-Mitaine,
> Et je le crois!
> Alors je dors sur des légendes,
> Et je peux voir dans mon grenier,
> Tomber les neiges de Finlande . . .

> [The Big Bad Wolf is an archangel,
> Ogres eat oranges,
> Cinderella spins wool
> To clothe the Bogey-Man,
> And I believe it!
> Thus I sleep on legends,
> And in my loft I can see
> The falling snows of Finland . . .]

'Les neiges de Finlande', at 96 seconds, is the shortest song Edith ever sang, and in France acts as a 'two-minutes' silence' when friends and admirers celebrate her birthday and the anniversary of her death. More than other songs it also confirms her childlike belief in fairy-tales, superstition and mythology: the fact that with the precognitive dream, all will turn out well in the end so long as one believes that it will. It was this naivety, incredible but undeniably effective, which saw her through some of the worst traumas of her life, and which ultimately helped her to face the inevitable. 'I have to ask for signs from across the other side,' she confessed, shortly before she died. 'I'm not a good believer, and I don't give in to the moral requirements of any religion in particular. And yet my faith is so much stronger than anything which exists in *this* world!' In some of her other songs, such as 'Chanson bleue' and 'Le ciel est fermé', this naivety is especially poignant.

Edith's first autobiography, *Au bal de la chance* (English version, *The wheel of fortune*) was ghosted and published in 1958, though it was nowhere near as controversial as most people anticipated. The fabled lovers were there – Albert the pimp, and the *légionnaire*, who could effectively have been anybody until they were verified in 1963 – but her relationships with Montand, Meurisse, Jaubert and Contet were kept in a minor key, and Cerdan accorded just two paragraphs. Mômone, and Edith's alleged half-brother and sister, were not mentioned at all, and much of what she wrote about Louis Gassion and Line Marsa was pure invention. The idea that, having spent so little time together, she had had them buried together in Père Lachaise so that she could pray quietly at the side of their grave, was frankly laughable. What *was* extremely interesting was Edith's unpretentious philosophizing; she knew what she was writing about, quite simply because she had *been* there.

Au bal de la chance contained a lengthy preface by Cocteau, taken from his 1947 tome, *Le foyer des artistes*. In it, in his own inimitable surrealist style, he praised Edith's 'Napoleonic forehead' and 'lizardous hands', and compared her voice with that of the nightingale which toils, hesitates, rasps and chokes, rises and falls before reaching its zenith. He concluded:

Edith Piaf, like the invisible nightingale installed on her branch, becomes herself invisible. Nothing is left of her but her eyes, her pallid hands, her waxen forehead reflecting the light, and that voice which swells, which mounts, which little by little replaces her. The soul of the street filters into every room of the town. It is no longer Madame Edith Piaf who sings. It is the rain that falls, the wind that blows – the moonlight which spreads its mantle of light!

Edith's autobiography ended with the phrase, 'Better to live than to vegetate'. She had adopted it from someone else who had fought constantly against ill-health: her friend, President Eisenhower. In fact, the phrase could just as easily have been her own as far as it came to getting over Félix Marten, for within days of their break-up he had been replaced by a handsome young man. As far as her career was concerned, he would be regarded as the most important lover since Henri Contet, but who from a personal angle would probably cause her more anguish than all the others combined. She told a reporter from *France-Dimanche*:

This man caused me so much pain that I don't even want
to mention his name. He was young, talented, and spirited.
I was going through a very lonely phase in my life, and I
thought I had found the perfect companion. My astrologer
warned me about him, but I took no notice even though
when I looked at my lover I saw that, in spite of his velvety
gaze and tender smile he was a hard, cynical, dislikeable
boy . . .

Georges Moustaki was a budding singer-songwriter who was
then appearing at the College Inn, a students' meeting-place in
the heart of Montparnasse. Born Joseph Mustacchi in Alexandria
in 1934, but brought up in Greece, he had arrived in Paris with
empty pockets and a head brimming with ideas and hopes for
a showbusiness-orientated future. He could not possibly have
imagined that by the age of twenty-four he would have
achieved a success beyond his wildest dreams. Before going on
stage to sing and play his guitar for the students, Moustaki
always made a point of going to see Edith's show at the
Olympia. Back in 1936 Edith had appeared on Radio-Cité
singing 'La fille et le chien', accompanied by the great gypsy
guitarist Django Reinhardt, and some years later a photograph
had appeared in *Paris-Match* of her examining his injured
fingers. Reinhardt had died in 1953, shortly after introducing
her to his cousin, Henri Crolla, and Edith had at once persuaded her orchestra leader Robert Chauvigny to take him on.
Crolla's best improvisations may be heard in her recordings of
'Tatave' and 'Cri de coeur', which he composed. Though a much
better musician than Moustaki, he was nowhere near as good
looking, and when he arranged a meeting between the two in
Edith's dressing-room he could not have known that he was
about to kiss his career as her personal guitarist goodbye.

Moustaki has never disclosed their subsequent conversation.
Needless to say, that same evening she accompanied him to the
College Inn, 'in his battered old wreck of a car'. The next day he
was invited to Boulevard Lannes, though according to Marlene
Dietrich and another friend, the actress Catherine Jan, Edith
flatly refused to have him anywhere near her until he had taken
a bath. 'The irony was that Moustaki slipped on the wet tiles
and dislocated his shoulder,' Jan explained, 'so out of motherly

pity, Edith took him in. Henri Crolla was then returned to the ranks of the session musicians, and Moustaki became her personal guitarist – and the new boss at Boulevard Lannes. And this one was apparently *so* special that the cuff-links, tie-pin and cigarette lighter were all made of platinum!'

Moustaki's bohemian spirit was very much in keeping with Edith's own, so her unusual lifestyle did not put him off. Several years later he would work with another great *chanteuse*, Barbara, who like himself and Piaf was basically a noctambulist who preferred to live each day as it came. 'Moustaki never minded slaving over the same song for hours on end,' Barbara told me. 'He tolerated the snatched meals and cat-naps because, he claimed, he was but a gypsy at heart. But despite his immense, immense talent, he was not always an agreeable man, and he had a very nasty, unpredictable streak.'

Both Marlene Dietrich and Roger Normand confirmed the fact that there were frequent brawls within the Piaf household whenever Moustaki was around. Roger told me:

Edith was one of those women who genuinely believed that to get to a man's heart, you had to feel the force of his fist. During the years that I knew her, I saw her with some real shiners! She confided in me, 'He beats the shit out of me, but when he's asleep in my arms, it's like nursing a child. Isn't it wonderful? Now I know that I've got a man who *really* loves me!' And it's true. During her 'Greek summer', as she called it, she was happier than I'd seen her in years.

Edith repeated the story of her tempestuous relationship with Moustaki to a songwriter friend, Jean-Pierre Moulin, as a result of which she was presented with 'C'est un homme terrible', though Edith insisted that the narrator's words be changed to the third person so that Moustaki would not think she was referring to him. Barbara too sang the song, immediately after her Moustaki period.

> Il me prend pour cible . . .
> Il me fait pleurer avec un regard,
> Il me passe au crible,

Il me met en croix . . .
C'est un homme terrible!

[He uses me as a target . . .
With one glance he makes me cry,
He monitors my movements,
He crucifies me . . .
He's a dreadful man!]

Louis Barrier was planning Edith's next trip to America. She
had already signed a four-week contract, not with the Versailles
this time, but with the Empire Room at New York's Waldorf
Astoria, and her departure had been scheduled for 18 September
1958. She had naturally decided to take her new 'discovery'
with her, but only if he supplied her with a new song. Moustaki
wrote her four: the folksy 'Eden blues', the simplistic 'Les orgues
de barbarie', 'Un étranger', his duet with Edith which was based
on his own harsh experiences as an immigrant (ten years later
he would endear himself to an entire generation with 'Le
métèque', a variation on the same theme) – and the song which
Edith's friends have described as Moustaki's confirmation that
the events detailed in 'C'est un homme terrible' were indeed
true – the intensely passionate, 'Le gitan et la fille.'

Le gitan a dit à la fille:
'Qu'importe le prix de l'amour?
Pour toi j'irai finir mes jours
Derrière les grilles.
J'irai tuer ceux qui te regardent' . . .

[The gypsy told the girl;
'Who cares about the price of love?
For you, I'll end my days behind bars.
I'll kill those who look at you!']

After the Olympia, Edith and Moustaki toured France. The
critics had a field-day, drawing attention to the fact that she
was old enough to be his mother – her reaction to this was, 'I
only wish I was, but then I'd be arrested for incest!' They did,
however, look remarkably good together on stage, and in the
photograph that appeared on the cover of the EP, 'Edith Piaf

chante Jo Moustaki', and she never appeared to 'mother' him in public. Her hectic schedule and way of life, though, had sapped her strength and her doctors advised her to rest up in the country before leaving for America.

Knowing that she would probably fight him every inch of the way, Louis Barrier rented her a house at Condé-sur-Vésgre, in the Seine-et-Oise department. Surprisingly, considering her hatred of the open air, Edith agreed to go there, though she refused to cut down on rehearsals. Her entourage was also augmented by Marcel Cerdan Jnr, the favourite of her self-appointed godsons who, a quarter of a century later, would portray his father in the bio-pic, *Edith et Marcel*, the glossy, unconvincing account of what some of her most zealous admirers called 'the love affair of the century'.

On 7 September Marcel was due to fly home to his family in Casablanca, and Edith decided to accompany him to Orly airport. Moustaki was driving her DS19, and she was sitting next to him. Marcel and his girlfriend were sitting in the back. It had been raining heavily most of the night, and the road into Rambouillet was in an atrocious state. As they were passing the A La Grâce de Dieu transport café, the car skidded suddenly and somersaulted off the road. Moustaki and the girl were unhurt. Marcel suffered cuts and bruises, and was later treated for shock. Edith was not so lucky. When the ambulance arrived she was stretched out at the edge of the road, clutching Marlene Dietrich's gold cross with its seven emeralds. In his panic, Moustaki had rushed into the transport café, yelling to all and sundry that Edith Piaf was dying in the middle of the road. One of the truck drivers had administered emergency treatment on the spot – he later told a reporter that for many years he had dreamed of holding 'the most important woman in France' in his arms, though never like this. When advised by one of the paramedics to remove and burn his bloodstained pullover because could have been infected, he had quipped, 'But that's Piaf's blood. It's holy!' This man, who has never been named, was one of her first visitors at the hospital in Rambouillet. She had a four-inch gash across her forehead, severed tendons in her left hand, and severe facial abrasions including a split lip. The car, a total write-off, was towed into a garage near Dreux

– amazingly, when one looks at the pictures of the wreckage, one wonders how anyone could have been pulled out of it alive.

Most of Edith's injuries were patched up, though her doctors were concerned that the gash across her forehead would leave a scar – unthinkable, under stage lights, and with the American tour so imminent. Edith was not bothered about this, though she was worried about her split lip, for this impeded her speech and made singing virtually impossible. Louis Barrier advised her to cancel the tour; she was so angry over this that they almost fell out for good. There had been difficulties before, she declared, and she had always overcome them. She could let herself and her agent down – her public, *never*! During the next few weeks she subjected herself to a series of agonizing facial massages – even Moustaki kept his distance – and the scars were gradually smoothed away, but at a cost because in order to cope with the pain she had begun taking morphine again. Thankfully, the doses were low and the course of 'medication' did not last long. Edith arrived in New York one month late, but to an ecstatic reception. One of her first engagements was when she topped the bill on *The Ed Sullivan Show*. She sang several songs, but the one which really hit the audience for six was 'Gypsy', the English language version of 'Le gitan et la fille'. After hearing this, Sullivan announced to the American nation, 'This little lady is the most amazing ninety-seven pounds in showbusiness!'

> When a gypsy's in love with a lady,
> No price is ever too high.
> I'd rather hear death's lullaby
> Than never hold you!
> I'd die for one taste of your love!

However, if the Piaf voice was in immaculate fettle – indeed, after each relapse in her health it only seemed to increase in depth of feeling – the Piaf body was not. A few days later she complained of feeling unwell, but when someone suggested sending for a doctor she said that it was merely fatigue. She was able to make several test recordings for what would have been her very first concept album: twelve songs which would be recorded in both French and English – the French versions to be recorded in New York, and the English ones at the Pathé-Marconi studios. The first two, taped during the afternoon of 24 February, were Julien Bouquet's 'Je sais comment', with an effective piano arrangement by Jacques Liebrard – and Moustaki's stirring 'Madame la Vierge Marie', for which he accompanied her on the guitar.

> Madame la Vierge Marie,
> Si j'ai volée, si j'ai mentie,
> Pardonnez-moi, je vous en prie,
> J'ai déjà tant et tant souffert,
> N'm'envoyez pas en enfer . . .
>
> Madame Virgin Mary,
> If I've stolen and lied,
> Forgive me, I beg you,
> I've already suffered so much,
> Don't send me to hell . . .]

There were two more Moustaki songs, both with prostitutes as a central theme: 'T'es beau tu sais', which tells of the blind girl who reminds the customer how beautiful he is by tracing his features with her fingertips – and 'Milord', of which more later. All these songs had been premiered at the Waldorf Astoria on 26 January 1959, and it was here, on 20 February, whilst she was halfway through 'Milord' that Edith collapsed. In the wings she vomited blood, and was at once rushed to the Presbyterian Hospital on 168th Street. A team of surgeons, headed by a Professor George Humphreys, fought to save her life, and she only just managed to pull through – a perforated stomach ulcer had been diagnosed, and during the four-hour operation she was given several blood transfusions. For more than a week, hospital bulletins described her condition as critical.

The Americans were stunned. They had thought her invincible, and with the shadow of death hanging over her sent her so many flowers that these overflowed into the corridor outside her room. The hospital switchboard was jammed by calls from fans and well-wishers, the most faithful of whom kept all-night vigils out in the street, praying and humming her songs. There were telegrams from colleagues around the world, and her first visitors were Marlene Dietrich and Maurice Chevalier: both currently working in Hollywood, they had flown across America in the middle of the night to be with her.

When Edith came to after her operation, however, Moustaki was no longer there. The couple had begun experiencing difficulties the moment they had arrived in New York, though it has to be said that Moustaki's attitude towards her now that she was ill – regardless of whether they were still lovers or not – left a great deal to be desired, as she herself recalled.

When I went into the hospital, I asked him if he loved me. Without even looking at me he said, 'You don't mean anything to me any more. Fucking well leave me alone!' I was stunned, and hoped that I might die on the operating table. Even so, after my operation I telephoned him every day – he had left me so that he could amuse himself on the beach in Florida. Then he added sarcastically, 'The sun's shining here, and *I'm* in excellent health! There are *girls* here!'

Moustaki had replaced Félix Marten overnight. Now, he received his come-uppance for taking advantage of Edith's illness and leaving her in the lurch. She told the press that henceforth all of his songs would be removed from her repertoire and even broke with her own tradition – keeping one man hanging on by a slender thread until she had found another – and allowed herself to fall in love, on account of a superstitious whim, with a man who was as far removed from her world as anyone could have been.

Douglas Davies was a twenty-three-year-old American painter, and, dreaming of holding an exhibition of his work in New York, he had gone to see his idol at the Waldorf Astoria, hoping to meet her and pluck up the courage to ask her to sit for him – it is now known that he had been sitting in the audience when she had collapsed, hence his great concern. During her illness, rather than buy her huge bouquets and baskets like some of her other fans, he had brought her simple bunches of violets, wholly unaware of her foibles and superstitions. This, and the fact that he spent two hours every day on the New York subway bringing them to her, touched her heart – along with the fact that 'Douggie', as she christened him, had been being born at around the time that the aviator Jean Mermoz had given her her first violets after her Gerny's premiere. Quite obviously, the friendship could only have gone in one direction! Later, she wrote:

> Faced with Doug's naive expression and cordial smile, I knew that I had been given the will to live again. One afternoon he brought me five gaily coloured balloons – he gave them to me because I had told him that balloons had been my childhood dream, and that my father had never wanted to buy me any. Then I kissed him for the first time . . .

Edith and Douglas' affair, however, was not regarded as a fairy-tale romance by the entire American media. Many people considered him far too young for her, and an opportunist. He was nothing of the kind, and promised to rectify the accusation by seeking Moustaki and 'punching his lights out' – something which impressed Edith, because apart from this one outburst of temper he was a shy, reserved man. It was also just as well for all concerned that Edith's entourage prevented her two 'champions' from meeting, for the gentle, willowy Douglas would not have been any match for the tough, sinewy Greek. It is also a great pity that her relationship with Moustaki could not have endured just a little longer, for there doubtless would have been more songs from one of the most acerbic poets of his generation.

On 25 March, just days after Douglas had collected Edith from the hospital, she collapsed again and had to be readmitted with an intestinal blockage. This time, when she came to after her operation, she was not alone. The room was filled with violets and Douglas was holding her hand. Again, he had brought her balloons, and a photographer was on hand to record the happy event, and the result was immensely touching. Two months later she left the hospital, clutching Douglas' hand and looking so emaciated that when the photographs were wired back to France, one newspaper began writing an obituary.

For Piaf, of course, the show had to go on, and even Louis Barrier was afraid of arguing with her. She guested again on *The Ed Sullivan Show*, ostensibly to prove to the American public that she could still stand on her feet, and her musical-director Robert Chauvigny stayed on the stage with her, as opposed to positioning himself behind the backdrop. She had been scheduled to sing 'Hymne à l'amour' and 'Mon manège à moi', but Sullivan asked her to sing his personal favourite – 'Lovers of one day' – and despite her earlier oath that she would never sing Moustaki again, when Douglas requested 'Milord', she could not hurt his feelings by refusing. Rick French, her young American friend who had translated several of her songs, had already supplied her with an English prologue to this one – this would do her, he said, until he had completed the full text. The lyrics caused some consternation amongst Sullivan's fickle viewers and the moral majority, who thus far had turned a blind eye to 'Piaf's championing of the oldest profession' because, so far, this had been restricted to a foreign language.

> Ah, come on, Milord!
> Sit down at my table!
> Look at me, Milord!
> You can afford me, you've got the time!
> Here's my apartment,
> It's so warm inside . . .

Two evenings later, Edith returned to the Waldorf Astoria and bravely carried on from where she had left off. The Americans had been good to her, she said – she wanted to leave them with happy memories. They reciprocated, as if aware that they would never see her again. The huge playbills outside the Empire Room depicted a playing card containing her portrait – above was the slogan, 'Edith Piaf, Queen of Hearts'. After New York, there was a week-long engagement in Washington: she was paid $40,000, but gave every cent to her entourage, who had passed a frugal winter during her illness, accepting work wherever it could be found, which was not often. Such was the devotion of her musicians, however, that when she offered to pay to send them home to be with their families, not one would leave her.

On 25 March 1959, Edith sang for the last time in the United States – at Carnegie Hall. The performance was no less subdued than her others here: tickets still sold at an astonishing $100 each on the black market, but this time there were only seventeen songs, and no interval. This time, too, twelve of the songs were performed in English, including 'When the world was young' and 'Milord' ... though she announced the latter as a Rick French and Marguerite Monnot collaboration, and actually told a journalist afterwards that she had never *heard* of Georges Moustaki! And, unusually perhaps, the recital ended not with 'Hymne à l'amour', as she had planned, but with 'Les neiges de Finlande'.

In the late spring, Edith embarked on a tour of French-speaking Canada, but for once Louis Barrier put his foot down. She would no longer perform in small venues such as Chez Gérard – so long as her health continued to deteriorate, the concerts would be fewer and the establishments as large as possible. In Montreal, she played four weeks at the Casino Bellevue, and it was here in May 1959 that she met the composer, Claude Léveillé, of whom she would say, upon her return to France, 'There have been four milestones in my search for *good* songwriters – Contet and Monnot, Norbert Glanzberg, and Léveillé. The others, compared with this distinguished quartet, are just so-so.' She was perhaps being just a little unfair, as Roger Normand pointed out, 'With Edith, every new songwriter was the best she'd ever had, and when she made such comments she had no idea how hurt some of the others felt, particularly as Glanzberg and Léveillé only wrote her a handful of songs, whereas Asso wrote dozens.'

This remarkably talented young man had been born in Montreal in October 1932. A student of sociology, he had left the university in 1956 to pursue a showbusiness career, and for several years he had enjoyed success as the children's entertainer Clo-Clo. In May 1959, however, he decided to branch out. A favourite meeting place for the Montreal showbusiness fraternity was the Café des Artistes, just down the road from Radio-Canada. Here he had become friendly with the songwriters Raymond Levesque, Hervé Brousseau, Jean-Pierre Ferland and Jacques Blanchet – the latter had just won the Prix Canadienne for his song 'Le ciel se marie avec la mer', which Edith is said to have admired. With a pianist named André Gagnon, these five had formed the group Les Bozos and they had opened their own club, La Boîte des Bozos, an establishment similar to those which had sprung up in Paris during the dawn of Existentialism in the late forties. Hoping to drum up a little free publicity for his venture, Jean-Pierre Ferland sent a message to Edith's dressing-room inviting her to 'drop in' at his club – hardly expecting her to honour the invitation, taking into consideration her health and still hectic schedule.

What Ferland did not count on was Edith's fondness for these clubs – Jean Villard, Eddie Constantine, Francis Blanche, Roméo Carlès and Charles Aznavour had all entered her life because of them, and now there would be another. Claude Léveillé remembers how one evening he was singing a song called 'Les vieux pianos', almost nonchalantly whilst accompanying himself at the piano – and unusually with his back to the audience – and after he had finished, remarking that the silence was glacial. Turning around, he saw Edith and her entourage sitting at a table near the stage, obviously the focus of everyone's attention because no one expected seeing an artiste of her magnitude 'drinking in a downtown bar'. Then, quite suddenly she stood up and started off a round of applause which within seconds became deafening, and which lasted several minutes. The next day one newspaper ran the headline: 'Edith Piaf beams the spotlight on the Bozos.' The article then went on to describe how she had asked the group to prepare a private *mini-spectacle* for that afternoon, though even then she had made it very clear that she was only interested in Léveillé, whom she invited to her show at the Casino Bellevue. Here, he was given the official command – she would expect him in Paris, by August at the latest, and with as many songs as he could muster at such short notice. 'It all went so fast, and I was quite disturbed,' he said, later. 'It's as if I never had the *choice* to go to war! I was ordered to 'get out there and dig that trench! And I at once realized that a new chapter was beginning, that life would never be the same any more!'

As a 'down-payment', Edith accepted 'Les vieux pianos', arguing that she would be able to present it better than Léveillé had at his club. She did, however, express some disapproval at the lyrics, and asked Henri Contet to rewrite them so that only *two* of the original lines remained, and the work was retitled 'Le vieux piano'. This act of 'sacrilege' did not endear her to the other members of Les Bozos, and when Léveillé left the group soon afterwards it was with considerable ill feeling. A year or so later he attempted to make up for his 'indiscretion' – not that he should have reproached himself, for he had done nothing whatsoever untoward – by recording 'Les vieux pianos' with its original lyrics, and it was a smash-hit in Canada.

Ce sont vos pianos mécaniques
Que vous avez remplacés
Par des boîtes à musique,
Qui pour trente sous vous tirent deux disques,
Coup sur coup pourvu qu'ça joue!
Nous on s'en fout . . .

[These are the mechanical pianos
You have replaced with juke-boxes,
Which give you two records for thirty sous,
In rapid succession, provided they play!
They don't give a fuck about us . . .

There were the inevitable rumours, of course, that Léveillé might have been considerably more than Piaf's *compositeur du moment* – rumours which were very quickly quashed by Douglas Davies who, during his stay in Montreal, had been pushed into the ranks of her entourage. The reasons for this were obvious. Like Cerdan, Pousse and Toto Gérardin, he was not interested in showbusiness, apart from listening to her sing. Unlike them, he was not a regular 'he-man' and apart from the incident when he had threatened Moustaki he lacked *le fluide* which she had always expected in her men. Maybe she hoped that she might find a replacement before leaving Canada. Some of the journalists who followed her around tended to think so, particularly as Douglas also had an American boyfriend, and one commented that the young painter was 'little more than a convenient crutch for Piaf's self-inflicted manic depression'. Lysanne Coupal, her personal assistant during this Canadian tour, admitted, 'Piaf would be so unbelievably and wildly gay when happy, then in a flash, for no reason at all sink into hopeless despair. That's when we would hide the bottles and the pills. Most of the time she didn't even *know* what she was looking for in life.'

Edith had left Paris with one man, and when she arrived at Orly on 21 June 1959 it was on the arm of another – her American painter. Newsreel pictures show her being lifted from the steps of the plane by Bruno Coquatrix, smiling radiantly and gradually being swallowed up by the loving arms of her Parisian friends, whilst Douglas is being pushed more and more into the crowd of reporters and journalists. Then, as one cynic put it 'as though remembering she had left something behind on the plane', she turned around and began searching amongst the sea of faces for her lover, who by this time was looking decidedly embarrassed. Eventually, he was introduced to everyone, and in English. 'His name is Davies!' she said. 'You must remember how to pronounce his name – not Davis, but Davies!' Throughout their brief but not uneventful relationship she never missed out on an opportunity to remind everyone how to pronounce his name, yet in her memoirs she herself referred to him as *Davis*!

Edith would never forget her debt to Douglas Davies, and despite some of their very public differences of opinion, henceforth there would be few photographs or newsreel clips of her where she did *not* look gloriously happy. The intensity and drama of her songs aside, like Damia and Fréhel before her and like her successor, Barbara, she was by no means a morbid woman. In an article for the magazine *Paris-Match*, written to mark the twentieth anniversary of her death in 1983, Alexandre Astrue wrote, unfairly, that she had only searched for happiness and joy within her songs. This is not true, as many of her surviving friends have confirmed. 'When Piaf laughed, everyone had to laugh,' said Catherine Jan. 'That was one of the rules of the household, but Piaf's laugh was very genuine, and so loud it would have demolished a building from two hundred metres!' Marlene Dietrich and Michel Emer also spoke of her practical jokes – such as 'spiking' the coffee with Epsom salts, or emptying shampoo into the lavatory cistern. And once, to get her own back on Félix Marten for some misdemeanour, she had hidden a dead fish inside his car engine!

At Boulevard Lannes there was a second welcoming committee – headed by Marguerite Monnot and Georges Moustaki. The scene was shown later that evening on television, and of course Edith had to appear outwardly friendly towards her former lover. When the group gathered around the piano to sing 'Milord' – the first time anyone in France had ever heard the song – she pushed them laughingly aside, told them how they were ruining it by singing off key, and sang it herself. All the while Douglas Davies was skulking around out of camera, levelling obscene remarks at the man he only ever referred to as 'that Greek motherfucker'.

In Paris, suddenly propelled into the mêlée of Piaf's ultra-bohemian existence, Douglas Davies was decidedly out of his depth. He was an artist, albeit not a well-known one, and he was in the cultural centre of his world. Paris was waiting to be explored and committed to canvas. There were galleries and museums galore. Typically tyrannical, Edith refused to let him out of her sight for a single moment. She also had the habit of of having the central-heating on full-blast, which in the middle of June must have been distressing for everyone. She did, however, allow him to open his paintbox: the four portraits he did of her are striking because they depict a Piaf hitherto unseen by the media. Mômone described them, quite aptly, as 'the Piaf that the people carry around in their hearts'. Three of them achieved world fame on record covers: who has not been almost moved to tears, studying these whilst listening to the superb Piaf voice?

During Edith's absence, manuscripts had piled up on top of her piano – they were always left there, along with her mail, because the household staff were terrified of touching them. Within her personal portfolio was the sheet-music of 'Milord' and a number of other Moustaki songs, and again these were put aside. Though they would remain reasonably good friends for the rest of her life, she would never forgive him. Her debts, too, had mounted during her absence – the rent for the apartment, the bills for the electricity had not been paid for almost a year. Yet once again fate was on her side, for amongst the cheques in her mail was one amounting to ten million francs in royalties from Pathé-Marconi. For the moment she had been saved. Contracts too had poured in, and she had every intention of fulfilling them all. She began rehearsals for a forthcoming tour of France, ignoring the pleas of her doctors and friends, who feared a relapse . . . and even death itself.

In July 1959 she paid another visit to her clairvoyant. Though her *guéridon* had 'mysteriously' disappeared whilst she had been ill in America, she was still convinced that the answers to most of her problems could be found in the other world. She had even set up a meeting with her long-dead father, scrubbing out one of the spare rooms at Boulevard Lannes, and spending the night there surrounded by his personal effects. The results of the meeting are not recorded, other than the event scared the living daylights out of Douglas Davies, who by now was wondering what he had let himself in for. The clairvoyant was not optimistic. He told her, 'At the moment you are going through a period of well-being, but in a few months there will be long months of suffering. I have never seen death as close to you as I do now.'

Chapter Ten

JE ME FOUS
DU PASSÉ!

In August 1959, Claude Léveillé arrived in Paris for a visit, and of course he moved straight into Edith's apartment. Over the next few weeks she praised him beyond belief, even though he had brought her no songs. This was remedied, naturally, as soon as he had met her 'regulars' – Monnot, Contet and Michel Rivgauche, with whom he wrote his first official song for Edith, 'Boulevard du crime'. This was in every sense a miniature symphony which Léveillé himself sang exceedingly well in his husky, Brel-like tones a few years later. Curiously, the song was not properly released in France until 1973, though it did appear on the best-selling British album, 'C'est la Piaf', in 1962.

> Sur le Boulevard du Crime,
> Pour voir la pantomime ce soir
> On se bouscule au Théâtre des Funambules.
> Masques sans bergamasques,
> Pour les danses fantasques,
> Et la foule coasse au milieu
> Du Carnival des Grimaces . . .
>
> [On the Boulevard of Crime,
> To see the pantomime tonight,
> They jostle at the Funambules.
> Mummers without masks for whimsical dances,
> And the crowd croaks in the middle
> Of the Carnival of Grimaces . . .]

Léveillé is alleged to have based what many believe to have been his greatest work on life at Boulevard Lannes – if this is so, then his study was an accurate one. He wrote around a dozen songs for Edith, but largely due to the ups and downs not just in her private life but in her health, she only got around to recording three: the others never progressed beyond the acetate or tape-recording stage. Unlike most of her other song-writers, Léveillé was also different in that he never allowed her way of life to interfere too much with his own. Edith is said to have been shocked to learn of his 'secret' marriage, which may suggest that she was keeping him conveniently waiting in the wings whilst deciding what to do with Douglas Davies – she had been informed, no doubt by the errant Mômone, that the latter was 'just another opportunist and a closet homosexual'. The news of Léveillé's marriage actually reached her ears by way of a telephone call from his father, telling him that his wife had given birth to a son. The marriage ended soon afterwards, and a few years later the boy died – inspiring him to write the song 'Le pierrot lunaire', a fine piece which would have suited Edith down to the ground. Léveillé also directed his own club in Montreal, Le Chat Noir, named after the more famous one in Paris, and when this opened in 1960 Edith sent a recorded message.

> Amongst composers, Claude Léveillé is a great revelation. Only rarely in my recitals have I included several songs by the same composer, unless it was Marguerite Monnot. In my next tour leading up to the Olympia I shall be having five of his songs, for I'm sure that he will have a massive influence over the future of the *chanson*. I've never been wrong before, and I don't think that I'm wrong now!

Because Douglas Davies distrusted driving 'foreign' cars, Edith bought him an expensive customized Chevrolet. He was at the wheel on the first day of her provincial tour when it shot off the road just outside Divonne and hit a crash barrier. The car was not badly wrecked this time, and Douglas was unhurt. Michel Rivgauche, travelling in the back, was badly bruised. Edith had three broken ribs.

There was absolutely no question of cancelling the tour, of

course, and in order to sing that night Edith was given just one morphine injection. This time it was for her own good – indeed, just as it had been back in 1951 – only this time she did not become addicted. She was, however, still having cortisone injections for her rheumatism which was steadily getting worse, so much so that sometimes she could hardly manipulate her hands, and each time she reached for the high register, excruciating pains shot through her body, necessitating fake curtain-calls so that she could leave the stage for more shots. The cortisone bloated her features. On the stage her audiences saw a pathetic little Piaf doll in a black dress, her make-up smudged on anyhow, and her stockings creased. Only the voice had changed for the better.

Edith and Douglas spent a short time in Cannes, where they rented a suite at the Hôtel Majestic. They argued one day when he turned out wearing just a pair of swimming-shorts, for Edith was jealous of the other women on the beach staring at his fine, athletic body. To prove that he had eyes for her alone – which was not specifically true, for by way of Claude Figus he was almost immediately accepted into the coterie of Riviera homosexuals headed by the American pianist, Ned Rorem, and Edith's old ally, the critic Virgil Thompson – he fitted Edith out with a modest bathing costume, and began giving her swimming lessons! Such was Edith's naivety that she broke her own cast-iron rule and rose early each morning to suffer long hours in the sea, just to watch the other bathers' faces, and of course she always drew a sizeable crowd. One of these episodes even gave her an idea for a song – whilst staying at the Hôtel Majestic she wrote the words to 'T'es l'homme qu'il me faut', though as yet there was no music to go with it.

Cannes, of course, offered Douglas a once-in-a-lifetime chance to meet his idol, Picasso – a meeting which was arranged by Edith, under considerable pressure. He also visited those localities associated with Cézanne and Van Gogh, which to a certain extent she tolerated. When she found out that he was 'hob-nobbing' with the Rorem clique, she was furious – there was a tremendous bust-up at the Hôtel Majestic, which ended with Edith flinging a teapot at her errant lover. They made up afterwards, only to fall out again when the tour reached Bordeaux. Having offered her the ultimate 'proof' of his love – a slap across the face – Douglas walked out on her in the middle of the night, and the ensuing scene was such classic Piaf that it was later turned into a song, 'C'est peut-être ça'. Throwing a coat over her nightdress, Edith ran after him, but as she arrived at the railway station, the train was pulling out. Once more she was alone.

At around the time she had recorded the tests for 'Milord' and 'Gypsy', Edith had made a poor quality recording of Moustaki's 'Faut pas qu'il se figure', with lyrics by Michel Rivgauche. This was one song which could not possibly be sung adequately in English, though the Canadian star Libby Morris later made a good attempt in her acclaimed stage production of 1977, *Edith Piaf, je vous aime!*: 'He mustn't work out that I'm so throw myself into his arms as soon as he comes near me! But he's late! There's the lift again. First . . . second . . . third floor! Now he rings! And yet he must never know that I'm so happy when he's there, so lost when he's not!'

Edith had sung the song in New York, and on French television, but she stopped singing it now. It reminded her of Douglas, she said, and of her excitement in the Presbyterian Hospital when she had lived only for the sound of the elevator outside her room. Subsequently she entered the studio just the once, that year, during the afternoon of 5 August when she recorded 'T'es beau tu sais' and the French version of 'Milord'.

The prostitute works the dockland beat, where she meets an aristocratic gentleman with a long, flowing silk scarf – his description in the song is said to have been inspired by newsreel footage of the Duke of Windsor leaving a London hotel. The girl has seen him the day before on the arm of a beautiful woman, and now she understands how sad he feels, for his sweetheart's ship has sailed away and his heart is broken. She tells him,

> L'amour ça fait pleurer,
> Comme quoi l'existence,
> Ça vous donne toutes les chances,
> Pour les reprendre après . . .
>
> [Love makes you cry,
> Life's like that,

It gives you all the opportunities,
Only to snatch them back again . . .]

For some reason, Rick French's excellent translation of 'Milord' was overlooked, and the song was given English words by Bunny Lewis, a British impresario who once again invited her to London. This time, she said, she was too ill to travel far, though later she confessed that the *only* reason she had declined Lewis' offer was because he had ruined one of her most beautiful songs. She loathed the cover-version by Frankie Vaughan, telling Marlene Dietrich, 'It's a *woman's* song, for God's sake. What the hell does *he* know about being a whore? If that's all the respect the British have for my work, I'm *never* going there!' Her own version of the song reached Number 17 in the British charts, in those days extremely unusual for a song performed in a foreign language.

Immediately after her French tour, Edith left for a series of engagements in Sweden. A previous visit to this country had left her feeling so homesick that she had chartered an aircraft to fly her and an entourage of seven back to Paris for a single meal – extravagant even by her standards. Louis Barrier had secured her an engagement with the Stockholm Bernsbee, then the country's most important music-hall, and she was singing 'Mon manège à moi' in front of 5,000 people when she collapsed. The audience applauded, thinking it a part of her act: she even looked up, grimaced, and quipped, 'It's okay – I'm still here!' Even so, it was serious, and terrified of dying in a foreign country she made her impresario charter a plane to fly her back to the American hospital at Neuilly – the only one available at a moment's notice was an immense forty-five seater DC4, and the venture cost her almost three-million *ancien francs* – where she underwent an emergency operation for pancreatitis. Because of the delay she almost died on the operating table, and after her discharge Louis Barrier decided that he would take no more chances. He drove her to his house at Richebourg, accompanied only by her nurse, Mamie, and by the ubiquitous Claude Figus.

Edith was now suffering from acute agoraphobia, and so crippled with rheumatism that she was unable to walk unaided. During this debilitating period she took great comfort from Jean Cocteau, who visited her regularly and helped her with her studies in Rosicructianism, a doctrine he had long practised, and whose members were alleged to possess magical powers and the secrets of alchemy. Just how far Edith became involved with the movement is not known, though she did spend several hours of each day in deep meditation, and her beliefs were expressed in profound *chansons* such as 'Je sais comment'.

Je sais comment sauter les verrous
Entre la liberté et nous . . .
Comment faire tomber en poussière
Ce mur énorme d'énormes pierres . . .
Comment briser de nos mains nues
Toutes ces entraves sans être vus . . .

[I know how to leap over the barriers
Between freedom and us . . .
How to reduce to dust that enormous wall
Of enormous stones . . .
How to break all those shackles
With our bare hands, without being seen . . .]

Edith's doctor also prescribed her the best, but of course most expensive, chiropractor in France. His name was Lucien Vaimber, and she later sang a song about him – one of the rare occasions when she did not sing about love. She suffered excruciating pain as Vaimber unknotted her joints and spine. She recovered, and a few days later had the entire Barrier household in uproar when she awoke screaming after a nightmare in which she had seen an ambulance. The nurse simply prescribed a sedative, but Claude Figus, who seems to have shared her avid interest in 'supernatural presences', called the hospital. Two hours later, Edith underwent an operation for intestinal adhesions, after which she lapsed into a hepatic coma from which few expected her to emerge.

Incredibly, by 13 May 1960 she was back in the studio, working on a new album, 'Huit chansons nouvelles'. Such was her professionalism that by 20 May the album was ready for release: every song had been recorded with a single take. 'T'es beau tu sais' and 'Le vieux piano' have already been mentioned. 'Ouragan', by Léveillé and Rivgauche, is an inspired but brief piece in which Edith's voice really does lash out like a hurricane. Julien Bouquet's 'Je suis à toi' was a surreal study of lost love: once, the springtime repainted the grey walls of Paris, and this reflected in the lovers' eyes ... but now those days are gone, and life will ever be grey unless you return and tell me, 'I am yours!' Robert Gall's and Florence Véran's 'Les amants merveilleux' tells of the lovers who pass by in the deserted street, eyes half-closed and oblivious to the world ... the narrator is afraid of witnessing such happiness, until she runs into the arms of *her* lover and realizes how lucky she is! 'Cri du coeur', a poem by Prévert set to music by Henri Crolla, was a rare, self-indulgent study of Piaf *by* Piaf: without pity she has walked over her tears and never made them public, and if the landscape was too ugly, she merely waited for beauty to reappear ... though she has hardly seen love's face, should she meet it again she will recognize it all the same.

The one song, however, which rode high over its contemporaries was 'C'est l'amour', with words by Edith herself – her final collaboration with Marguerite Monnot. 'I know all there is to know about love,' she told a young British reporter who witnessed the song being recorded. 'And I also know how much it costs.'

> Dans l'amour il faut des larmes,
> Dans l'amour il faut donner ...
> Et ceux qui n'ont pas de larmes,
> Ne pourront jamais aimer!
> J'ai pleuré pour mieux t'aimer,
> J'ai payé de tant de larmes,
> Pour toujours le droit d'aimer!

> [In love there must be tears,
> In love there must be giving,
> And the ones who don't have tears,
> May never love!
> To love you better, I've cried,
> I've paid with so many tears,
> For the eternal right to love!]

On 27 May, Edith recorded 'Boulevard du crime', but the

limited-edition EP of the song missed out commercially on account of the staggering success of 'Milord', which was still topping the French hit-parade when it was released: it would remain elusive until ten years after Edith's death.

These recording sessions behind her, Edith began rehearsing for a 15-venue tour of the provinces, to be followed by a season at the Olympia. This was sheer madness. Her friends – even those such as her musicians who relied on her for an income – *begged* her not to do it, but she ploughed on relentlessly, knowing only too well that she was slowly killing herself.

And then, a miracle! On 5 October 1960, Michel Vaucaire effected a meeting with a young composer who would not only help resurrect her faith in herself . . . he would also inadvertently offer her three more years of life. His name was Charles Dumont.

Dumont, at thirty-one, had already contributed to the *chanson*, having written for performers as diverse as Tino Rossi and Cora Vaucaire, Michel Vaucaire's wife who had provided the theme for *French Can-Can*. He had approached Edith several times by way of mutual acquaintances, but she had always refused to have anything to do with him. It has even been suggested that she disliked him. Dumont told me of their first meeting:

I was invited into her vast, cluttered living-room. Before leaving home I had received a telegram saying that she was too ill to see me, but assuming this was just another of her excuses, I pretended not to have seen it. She yelled out from another room that seeing as I was there, she might as well see me, and said she would be out in a minute. Then she kept me standing there for over an hour – I wasn't even offered a chair. When Piaf came into the room, she looked a fright – she was wearing a nightdress several sizes too big for her, odd carpet slippers, and she hardly had any hair. And she was *so* rude, telling me to play my song, then get out!

Edith herself recounted *her* first impression to Mômone, saying, 'He was dressed like a civil servant, and couldn't stop staring at his shoes. If he'd have been a travelling salesman he wouldn't have made a single sale, not even with God on his side.'

Thus, feeling decidedly ill at ease, Dumont sat at Edith's piano and played the music he had composed to Michel Vaucaire's simple, but devastatingly effective lyric.

> Non, rien de rien!
> Non, je ne regrette rien!
> Ni le bien qu'on m'a fait,
> Ni le mal!
> Tout ca m'est bien égal!
>
> [Nothing whatsoever!
> No, I regret nothing!
> Neither the good done to me,
> Nor the bad!
> It's all the same to me!]

The rest is, of course, an essential part of the Piaf legend, and Dumont explained her reaction:

> She had stood hunched over the piano, her head on one side, and as I finished the song I half-expected her to bring the piano lid down on my fingers. Then she straightened up, and asked, 'Did you *really* write that?' When I told her that I had, she exclaimed, 'But it's *wonderful!*' ... and as if by magic, all the lines of illness seemed to drop off her face, and her attitude towards me changed alarmingly. Then it was as if we'd been friends her whole life!

'Non je ne regrette rien' became Edith's biggest international hit, and of all her songs will always be the one most associated with her. It would be translated into a dozen languages, including Japanese, and Edith herself also sang it in English and German. As far as its composers were concerned, they never looked back. Michel Vaucaire wrote dozens of hits for other artistes, and Charles Dumont later became a *chanteur* of considerable acclaim: his great successes on the Continent include 'Une femme' and 'Une chanson'. By the end of 1960 he would be regarded as Piaf's principal composer – replacing even the stalwart Marguerite Monnot. In all he would write the music for thirty of her songs, almost all of them million-sellers, and she repaid him by writing a song for him: 'La fille qui pleurait dans la rue'.

Edith's 'suicide-tour', as it was baptized by the media and in particular by those journalists who hounded her everywhere she went – she labelled them her 'vultures', waiting to pluck the flesh from her bones before she died – began on 14 October 1960 at Rheims. Here, 'Non je ne regrette rien' proved so popular that she was made to sing it three times. The tour, however, robbed her of what little strength she had left. For two months she lived on a diet of pep-pills, steadfastly refusing the needle, though for once in her life this would have done her some good. Several theatres were so terrified of her dying on them that they cruelly cancelled her contracts. Edith later admitted that she was so ill and confused that she never knew what was happening at the time, otherwise they would have suffered severe retribution. This was perfectly true. The film footage of these performances shows her singing magnificently, but mechanically. She scarcely moves away from the microphone, her gestures are more sparing than usual, and she stares fixedly in front of her. And if she had rejected several Marguerite Monnot songs in favour of Charles Dumont, so too did she stop singing many of her classics: 'La vie en rose', 'L'accordéoniste', 'La goualante de pauvre Jean' and even 'Hymne à l'amour' were all dropped. Edith also told a journalist, when he asked her what she thought of the town she was singing in, that in order to answer that question she would have to check the posters outside the theatre – and she was not joking.

At Maubeuge the audience were informed, ten minutes before her performance was due to start, that she was far too sick to sing. Edith, waiting in the wings when the announcement was given out, refused to be beaten. The last straw came when Robert Chauvigny, himself not in the best of health, told her that he would not direct the orchestra. Edith seized the baton, walked on to the stage and drew back the curtain which would separate her from her musicians, and ordered them all to move forward so that she could direct them herself. This would have caused monstrous problems for all and sundry, and fortunately Chauvigny allowed her to have her way. The performance went without any further hiccups, and one of the newspaper headlines read: PIAF'S SHOW NOT JUST ANOTHER MIRACLE

BUT A SPLENDID EXAMPLE OF COURAGE, LOVE AND THE WILL TO LIVE!

At Nancy and Chaumont she sang with a raging fever and had to be carried on and off the stage – her state of well-being was not helped at the latter venue when she introduced a song called 'Les blouses blanches', of which more later. On 19 December, her forty-fifth birthday, she sang at Thionville to scenes of incredible mass hysteria – this was one of the theatres that had cancelled her contract, but which at the last moment had suffered a twinge of conscience. This spurred her on, but at the Caméo de Béthune the standing ovation she received when walking on to the stage lasted so long that halfway through her opening number, Norbert Glanzberg's 'Le ballet des coeurs', she ran out of breath and told the orchestra to stop. After a drink of water, she continued – the show was being listened to by an estimated ten million fans on the French radio and the commentator, Claude Lableau, observed – as did the entire audience – that it was astonishing how she could manipulate her crippled hands on the stage, particularly during 'La foule', one song which she had refused to leave out of her recitals.

Edith managed to complete her performance that evening, but she was absolutely worn out when Lableau interviewed her afterwards in her dressing-room. His questions were representative of the whole of France – and beyond.

LABLEAU: Madame, many people ask the question: why, in spite of your illness, do you keep on singing?
PIAF: It's an accidental illness, nothing to do with my general state of health, which is quite good.
LABLEAU: You would like to reassure our listeners of that?
PIAF: I'm very well. I really want to sing. I've never needed to sing as much as I do now. It's necessary for my health!
LABLEAU: But don't you feel tired?
PIAF: Absolutely not! Singing isn't weariness and hard work! It's a pleasure!

The tour ended abruptly on 13 December at Dreux, a town which Edith later denounced as 'unlucky', for it was near here that her car had crashed in 1951. She was filmed entering the theatre on the arm of Charles Dumont, and looked so appallingly ill that many wondered how she could stay on her feet long enough to announce her first song. Most of the front row was taken up with journalists and photographers, and the media had made no secret of the fact all along that they were waiting for the best exclusive of them all – the spectacle of Edith Piaf dropping dead on the stage. Louis Barrier and Charles Dumont had carried her from her dressing-room to the wings. Her only wish, she declared, was that she should die on the stage with the applause still ringing in her ears. Barrier knew, of course, that if this gruesome event did ever take place, then it would have to be in the Paris that had given her the inspiration to sing in the first place. Even so, no one tried to stop her, and when she walked on to the stage, she faced the storm of Press and put any such morbid thought out of her mind. She even looked one photographer in the eye and mouthed, 'If you're expecting *that*, it won't happen tonight!'

The pictures taken during the performance by Hughes Vassal are heart-breaking. Vassal, who worked for *France-Dimanche*, a *torchon-scandale* not unlike our own *News of the World*, had actually been *ordered* to photograph her in her most distressing moments, as he later confessed:

> She told me to photograph absolutely everything – even her face when she was going into or coming out of a coma. Her every conceivable image had to be shared with her public, and some of those pictures made me feel ill and ashamed. I was only twenty-four, and didn't know how to disobey someone as mighty as Piaf. She was the boss, and I didn't have any choice. It was like being a war correspondent!

The theatre-manager at Dreux tried to prevent Edith from going on stage – she remedied this by yelling down the tannoy, 'I love you! You're my life! Please, let me sing!' The people became so hysterical then that had she left the stage, there would almost certainly have been a riot. She sang 'C'est l'amour' and there was hardly a dry eye in the house. Then she clung to the edge of the piano and reached her seventh song before collapsing in a little black heap on the floor. The curtain closed slowly, and

Edith's admirers filed out in silence, and in tears. Some even made the sign of the Cross, believing that she had died – and no one asked for their money back. And by the time the theatre had emptied, Bruno Coquatrix and Louis Barrier were already *en route* with her for the hospital at Meudon.

Edith was literally days from her Olympia premiere, and still she refused to accept defeat. During the tour she had recorded more prolifically than at any other time in her career: twelve songs. With the exception of three, all were by Dumont. 'La vie l'amour' was a short, lively and extremely noisy piece by Robert Chauvigny. 'Jérusalem' was by Robert Chabrier and Jo Moutet, both one-off composers. It featured a most unusual un-Piaf-like but authentic Yiddish chant, the recurrent religious theme – in this case Jesus Himself – and though it is not one of her best-known songs, it should be. In France, 'Jérusalem' appeared on the flip-side of the original [ESRF 1303] pressing of 'Non je ne regrette rien', of which there were only several thousand copies. When this sold out, however, the song was replaced by 'Toujours aimer' and 'Mon vieux Lucien' . . . for the simple reason that Pathé-Marconi wanted to cash in on 'Piaf's resurrection' by having four songs by Charles Dumont on the same record. As for the English-language version, this was never released at all.

> In His eyes there is shining the sight of love,
> In His heart there is burning the light of love,
> In His hands is the power and might of love,
> And so He walks alone,
> On the way that He must go . . .
> In His eyes is forgiveness for all the world,
> From his heart pours salvation for all the world,
> From His hands comes creation for all the world,
> And for all time to come we pray His will be done!

When Pathé-Marconi's sister-company, Columbia, refused to issue 'In Jerusalem' as her next British single, Edith at once thought of Gracie Fields, whose recording of 'Ave Maria' had recently moved her to tears. Piaf and the woman revered as 'Our Gracie' had much in common – in spite of the diversity of their husbands and numerous lovers, both put the love of their public before that of any man in particular. Both had suffered hardship, only to profit by pouring their experiences into their work. Both were religious, praying on their knees each night, yet reluctant to attend church because they believed their faith too precious to be shared with the ever-present media. And for Edith, of course, Gracie Fields had always been the next best thing to Marie Dubas. 'I know you'll do justice to my song,' she told Gracie when she called her Capri home. 'That's why I'm entrusting it to you!' And Gracie did not disappoint: for its impeccable technique and sheer vocal brilliance, 'In Jerusalem' represents the British star at her most definitive, and is perhaps the best of all her later recordings.

Another song which suffered in the same way was 'Je m'imagine', the penultimate song to come from the pen of her great friend, Marguerite Monnot. Said to have been hurt by Edith's growing habit of substituting Dumont's songs for hers, Marguerite had been noticeably absent from the tour. She was in fact ill herself, though Edith had not been told. As for 'Je m'imagine', Edith had ideas of her own: she handed the song over to Yul Brynner, for the 'All-Star Festival' album which was being put together to raise money for the World Refugees Project. Maurice Chevalier, Bing Crosby, Nat 'King' Cole and Mahalia Jackson did likewise, and the album was a great success. The song told the story of a woman's admiration for a much younger man, and the fact that she was trying to imagine what it must have been like, watching him as he had been growing up. The subject of the song, however, was *not* Charles Dumont, as had been suggested – 'I've had it up to the chin with married men,' she told Roger Normand, 'And Dumont has kids, *quelle horreur!*' – but the still unreplaced Douglas Davies.

> Tu serais devenu mon maître,
> Moi ton esclave passionée . . .
> J'aurais aimé vivre dans l'ombre . . .
> Pour éclairer tes heures sombres,
> Faire partie de tes souvenirs.
>
> [You would have become my master,
> I, your passionate slave . . .
> I would have loved to live in the shadow . . .

To brighten your gloomy hours,
To be part of your memories.]

But if Edith was enraptured by Dumont, the composer, she was
not over-impressed by the man, as Roger Normand explained:

There was always a certain amount of distance between
them, even though at this point in their respective careers
they were hardly ever apart. With no man in her life –
indeed she was so preoccupied with what she called her
resurrection that she only had time for her work – Edith
was more ruthless than ever. She kept Dumont away from
his wife and daughters, then tried to convince everyone
that *he* was ashamed of being with them because he had
something to hide, which of course was not true! She
praised him every moment he was in the room yet he only
had to be out of it for five minutes and she'd begin yelling,
'Where's Dumont? Why has he walked out?' And one of
us would say, 'But Edith, he's only in the bathroom!' Then
she would bawl, 'The bathroom, be damned. The bastard's
on the phone to Delyle, or Patachou. Those two bitches
have spent their entire careers pinching other people's
songs!' Then Dumont would come back into the room, and
she'd start fussing over him again!

Dumont's rewards for what must have been his Job-like
patience were more than adequate. The seventeen new songs
expected to be included in the Olympia programme had been
well-aired in the provinces, and 'Non je ne regrette rien' had
proved the hit of the year in Europe. Edith was, however, still
very sick. She broadcast a personal message to her fans on
French radio, telling them that she was looking forward to
seeing them at the Olympia, thus ending any media speculation
that she might pull out at the last moment especially as, halfway
through rehearsals, her musical director Robert Chauvigny
himself became gravely ill and had to be replaced by the
younger, fitter Jacques Lesage.

Lesage and Edith had met in 1956, when he had been director
to Félix Marten. For Lesage, working with Piaf was a truly

monstrous ordeal, as Jean Noli points out in his moving biography of her last years: *Edith Piaf, trois ans pour mourir.*

> Jacques Lesage was a pitiful sight to see. At first he had
> appeared hale and hearty, solid as a bank. By the end of
> the month he had the transfixed expression of a Christian
> martyr. Like the rest of us he wore the stigmata common to
> the prisoners of the Boulevard Lannes – ashen complexion,
> rings around his eyes, a bitter taste in his mouth, joyless
> smile, vague, dimwitted . . .

Monique Lange, in her *Histoire de Piaf*, aside from Mômone's
book the only French biography to have any vestige of reality,
states, 'Piaf had decided to save the Olympia in the same way
that Joan of Arc had decided to save France.' There is no other
way of describing her ensuing triumph and that of the director,
Bruno Coquatrix. He too was ill with heart trouble, and he was
in debt to the tune of fifty million *anciens francs*. Aware of what
he might have been risking, Coquatrix had begged Edith to sing
at the Olympia, knowing that only she was capable of filling
the auditorium night after night, thus putting both their heads
above water again. It has to be said that for Edith, who was
incessantly in debt, financial reward did not figure highly on
her list of priorities. She sang because it was in her blood to do
so. She sang because she had to, otherwise life would have been
meaningless. When asked once what she would do if she had
to stop singing, she replied, 'I'd make films!' She was not being
serious, of course. The fact she might die at any moment did
not frighten her; the fact that she might not be able to sing on
any particular night filled her with terror.

Before the Olympia premiere there were two significant
events. Firstly, she appeared with Charles Dumont on the
popular television show *Cinq colonnes à la une*, hosted by Pierre
Desgraupes. He asked her, with absolute sincerity, what she
would have done if during her last visit to the hospital the
doctors had given her the ultimatum: to sing and die, or to stop
singing and live longer. Edith did not hesitate. 'If I had to
stop singing, then I would already be dead. And in any case,
the thought of growing old doesn't appeal to me. I would rather
die young!' For the time being, the French people were able to

see for themselves that she was in a fit state to sing. She and Dumont performed their latest collaboration, 'Les amants', and she sang 'Mon Dieu', leaning against his piano. Later, Dumont expressed his dislike of the former and branded the recording 'an amateur production' – Edith's voice only appears in the background, chanting and echoing fragments of the refrain. Even so the song, released on an EP with two other songs, under the title 'Edith Piaf et Charles Dumont chantent l'amour', sold 300,000 copies within a week of its release, and Dumont later had a big hit with the song on his own.

Secondly, whilst Edith was in the middle of her final rehearsal for the Olympia – at a Versailles cinema on Christmas Day, no less – she received a telegram from Marlene Dietrich:

> IMPOSSIBLE TO COME AND APPLAUD YOU
> GOOD LUCK AND GOOD HEALTH
> I KISS YOU ... YOUR MARLENE

Marlene was herself about to take on the most foreboding challenge of her later career: her first visit to the Germany she had turned her back on, on account of Hitler, in thirty years. This telegram dispelled any suggestion that Edith's friend had deserted her in her hour of need. Now, the show could go on!

Catherine Jan recalled the eve of the premiere:

> Boulevard Lannes was like a mad-house! Well-wishers filed in and out all day, most of whom were not sure whether they were helping Piaf prepare for a come-back, or encouraging her towards an early grave. Her new black dress and shoes arrived first thing, but at the last moment she changed her mind and wore an old pair of slip-ons and a dress she had been singing in for years. The stench of camphor was overpowering, but she declared that to wear anything else would have been unlucky. And I don't think I had ever seen her looking so radiant. She was literally dying on her feet, yet she'd managed to convince herself that she was invincible. We knew that it wouldn't last, but all that mattered was seeing her happy, *truly* happy for the first time in years!

Bruno Coquatrix had signed her up for four weeks – twice the length of a normal season in those days – but with as many two-week extensions as she wanted. Such was his confidence in her abilities, though the possibility of her suffering a relapse must have been at the back of his mind: the premiere had been set initially for mid-January, but because she was in such good form it was brought forward by several weeks. This presented her with some difficulties, for several songs, and 'Mon vieux Lucien' in particular, had not been rehearsed sufficiently. In fact, the evening of 29 December 1960 should have been little more than a rehearsal itself. It turned out to be the greatest and most significant performance she ever gave in her life. It was filmed and recorded for posterity: an entire book could be devoted to this one recital alone. Anyone who was anyone in Paris was there . . . including the sea of reporters and photographers who had come to witness the fulfilment of Edith's own prophecy that this time she really *would* die on the stage.

As the big red curtain swung back, the audience saw nothing but total darkness. Then Jacques Lesage's orchestra struck up 'Hymne à l'amour', and a miracle occurred as Edith emerged slowly from the back of the stage and approached the footlights. The crowd rose in one body and applauded her madly for almost half an hour. No other singer in the history of show-business could have achieved what Piaf did, that evening. Then, with a single movement of her tiny, deformed hands, she silenced them and announced her first song, 'Les mots d'amour', said to have been loosely based on the Cerdan theme.

> C'est fou c'qu'il me disait comme jolis mots d'amour,
> Et comme il les disait!
> Mais il ne s'est pas tué,
> Car malgré son amour, c'est lui qui m'a quitté!
>
> [It's mad, the way he said such lovely words of love,
> And how he said them!
> But he didn't kill himself,
> For in spite of his love, it was he who left me!]

It was a song which reminded the listener of a major philosophy in the Piaf dichotomy: dying for love. And it occurred in her next song, 'Les flons-flons du bal', which does not appear to have been Dumont's and Vaucaire's intention when they had written it, in 1959, for Lucienne Delyle. Edith, who took a great deal of persuading to perform a number created by the woman she often referred to as 'la vache de Monte-Carlo', had the whole central section changed . . . for amidst the boisterous sounds of the street-dancing there is an interlude wherein she confides,

> J'ai bien failli mourir
> Le jour où t'es parti . . .
>
> [I almost died the day you left . . .]

The third (album) song was the self-composed 'T'es l'homme qu'il me faut'. Though no longer lovers, Edith and Douglas Davies were still friends, and had kept in touch since his return to America. She therefore saw no reason why she should not sing about their happier moments on the Riviera, and the song was pleasantly if not unusually optimistic.

> Quand j'sors avec toi,
> J'm'accroche à ton bras,
> Les femmes, elles te voient,
> Toi, tu n'les vois pas!
> T'es l'homme qu'il me faut!
>
> [When I go out with you,
> I hang on to your arm,
> Women see you but you don't see them!
> You are the man for me!]

An interesting anecdote was attached to Dumont's and Vaucaire's 'Mon Dieu', which typified Edith's determination to get *exactly* what she wanted, regardless of the way this sometimes put her composers out. Dumont had brought her the song several weeks before the Olympia premiere: then it had been unimpressively entitled 'Toulon-Le Havre-Anvers'. Delighted with the music, she expressed such dissatisfaction with the lyrics, claiming that they reminded her too much of her tour, that she telephoned the hapless Michel Vaucaire at four in the morning, demanding a new lyric in time for her next rehearsal at five that very afternoon! Naturally, Vaucaire had obliged, and what began as a monumental headache became a resounding success. 'Mon Dieu', with its simple, heartfelt message and the backing of a choir and a single solo voice – as previously explained, often a weakening factor in Piaf songs – was one of her most highly acclaimed songs. She asks God to allow her lover back for a day, a week, two or three months, just enough time to invent a few memories, to start or finish, to burn or suffer, and ends:

> Mon Dieu . . .
> Même si j'ai tort,
> Laissez-le moi encore!
>
> [Please God,
> Even if I'm wrong,
> Let me have him again!]

Edith had truly despaired over her next song, 'Mon vieux Lucien'. Said to be based on an episode in the life of her chiropractor, Lucien Vaimber, it tells the story of a man about to kill himself . . . only to be saved from doing so by an old pal.

> Qu'est-c'que tu caches là?
> Là, dans ton tiroir?
> Donne-moi c'que t'as dans la main!
> C'est agréable d'être ton copain!
>
> [What are you hiding there?
> There, in your drawer?
> Give me what you have in your hand!
> It's nice being your friend!]

Dumont's music, slightly reminiscent of Edith's earlier 'La goualante du pauvre Jean', presented her with few problems. Michel Vaucaire's lyric, however, written entirely in tongue-twisting *argot*, was tricky. After the first verse she forgot the words, stopped the orchestra, and laughed over her mistake with the audience. Her jokes were as well-received as the song, and she began again, completing it to rapturous applause. Parisian audiences have always been notoriously hypercritical, and no other singer would have got away with it. Piaf, however, could do no wrong and would indeed have been capable of singing the contents of the telephone directory, as Juliette Gréco once suggested. She also later refused to omit the song from the recording of the recital because she claimed that she, like anyone else, was perfectly capable of making mistakes!

'La ville inconnue' must have reminded many people of Edith's 'suicide' tour. Each town seems like the last, with endless streets and deserted boulevards, where one wanders around like a lost dog, wanting only to sleep away each day with one's memories of love.

> Il y a des passants,
> Qui ont l'air de vous fuir,
> Et qui n'ont pas le temps
> De vous faire un sourire . . .

> [There are passers-by,
> Who seem to flee from you,
> And who haven't the time
> To give you a smile . . .]

The supreme triumph of Olympia 1961 was, of course, 'Non je ne regrette rien'. After surviving countless broken love affairs, four car crashes, several major operations, the suspicion of being an accessory to murder and receiving stolen goods, cures for drug and alcohol addiction, media assassination – and now with the threat of death hanging over her like a low, black cloud – she stood defiantly and proclaimed, 'I regret nothing. It's all behind me. I'm going back to zero!'

> Avec mes souvenirs,
> J'ai allumé le feu,
> Mes chagrins, mes plaisirs,
> Je n'ai plus besoin d'eux!

> [I've lit a fire with my memories,
> My griefs, my pleasures,
> I no longer need them!]

'La belle histoire d'amour', a formidable pastiche of love and hope, and a long song, was the last to be written by Edith in memory of Marcel Cerdan.

> Je cherche à t'oublier,
> Mais c'est plus fort que moi,
> Je me fais déchirer,
> Je n'appartiens qu'à toi . . .
>
> [I seek to forget you,
> But this thing's stronger than I,
> I tear myself apart,
> I belong to no one but you . . .]

The album of the Olympia performance contains just nine songs, and the applause between these had to be severely edited because it was longer than the songs themselves. Edith also sang ten of her old hits, including 'Comme moi', 'La foule' and 'Milord'. However, the phrase 'once more with feeling' could have been invented for one number alone. 'Les blouses blanches' was without any doubt the most disturbing song she ever sang – it had far-reaching effects on at least one member of a subsequent audience, who collapsed in the auditorium and had to be carried out on a stretcher. Like that other masterpiece of melodrama, 'Légende', it was recorded only on a stage and never in the studio. It was also Marguerite Monnot's last song for Piaf, with lyrics by Michel Rivgauche.

The 'white-coats' are the warders in the lunatic asylum . . .

> She's been locked up with the lunatics for eight years. It's because of the white-coats that she's there. They keep telling her she's not mad, she remembers a white dress she once had, a pretty dress with flowers. Then, a hand held hers, a beautiful hand with fingers which sang. But she isn't mad! She will go on loving – for ever!

Edith more than sang this song. She acted it, in as much as the great tragedienne Damia had acted 'La chanson du fou' whilst tearing at her hair, thirty years earlier. At the end of the song Edith almost became mad herself, screaming with manic laughter, 'I'm not insane! I'm not insane!' The song earned her twenty-two curtain calls, and at the end of her performance she was showered with flowers.

The recording of the Olympia premiere was the best-selling album in the *world* in 1961, since which time it has never been deleted – to date it has sold an estimated fifty *million* copies. One of Douglas Davies' lovely paintings appeared on the original cover, and on the sleeves of three of Edith's EPs there were the rough pencil sketches he had made of her in Cannes. 'Non je ne regrette rien' and 'Mon Dieu' were huge successes for Edith in English, but the German version of the former – complete with the 'cursing' interlude when she forgot her words! – was never released. Both of these were also recorded by Charles Dumont, and 'Souviens-toi', a revamped version of 'Les flons-flons du bal', with Edith's voice blending with his, was Dumont's personal tribute, released to coincide with the twentieth anniversary of her death. 'Les blouses blanches' was translated for a British revue and became 'The white-shirts', and I myself wrote an English adaptation of 'La ville inconnue'.

As for the Olympia, it had been saved! Edith's contract was extended, and if she was dying then at least she came alive each time she walked on to the stage to breathe in the undying love of her audiences. Indeed, at this stage in her career it seemed that she might go on for ever. Between January and April 1961 she recorded sixteen songs, again mostly by Dumont, Rivgauche, Vaucaire and Louis Poterat. An exception was 'Exodus', the Hebrew *chesed* from the film of the same name, with French words by Eddie Marnay which many claimed bespoke Edith's faith more than the original words by Pat Boone. Also, because she lived solely to perform on the stage, she began finding it difficult to cope in the recording studio. Although the end result was always her usual perfection, it had to be worked for. There were four takes for 'Qu'il était triste cet Anglais', six for 'Marie Trottoir', nine for 'C'est peut-être ça', and an incredible twenty-three for 'Exodus', all instead of the usual one. Two songs were taped, but not released until after her death: Jacques Larue's 'Les bleuets d'azur', and Jacques Prévert's poem, 'Quand tu dors'. The latter was actually recorded during Prévert's visit to Boulevard Lannes, and Edith seriously considered it for the title track of a forthcoming album.

The great poet, however, would not allow her to omit the final verse, which Edith found distasteful:

This can't go on between us/ One night I'll surely kill you/ Your dreams will end/ And since I will also kill myself/ My insomnia will be over/ Our two corpses reunited/ Together sleeping in a double-bed.

The soundtrack for the ballet *La Voix* was also test-recorded at about this time, with music by Claude Léveillé and lyrics by Edith and Michel Rivgauche. This time the orchestra leader was Christian Chevalier, the choreographer Pierre Lacotte, and the set-designer Pierre Clayette. In all, twelve songs were written for Edith to perform without actually being seen on the stage, and she took the idea very seriously, working on and off with the team for several weeks. As with 'Le vieux piano', she disapproved of one song, 'L'hiver', and ordered Léveillé to change the lyrics. It became 'Non, la vie n'est pas triste', and along with 'Kiosque à journaux' and 'Le métro de Paris' was taped during a rehearsal. Sadly, Edith never got around to singing the others and as a mark of respect when the piece was given its television premiere in 1965, the remaining songs were performed by a choir. In Canada, where Léveillé had dreamed up the idea for the ballet, 'Non la vie n'est pas triste' was given new, less-personal lyrics by the singer-songwriter Gilles Vigneault, and it was later a big hit for the Quebecoise singer Monique Leyrac.

On 13 April 1961 Edith closed at the Olympia and embarked on another tour. It was too much for her. On 25 May she collapsed and was admitted to the American Hospital at Neuilly, where an emergency operation was carried out for intestinal adhesions. There followed yet another convalescence with Louis Barrier at his house in Richebourg until, on 9 June, she suffered a relapse and was readmitted to the hospital with an internal blockage ... and if this was not enough, her great friend of twenty-five years, Marguerite Monnot, died suddenly of suspected peritonitis.

Edith was heartbroken. Marguerite Monnot was probably the only person in the world who really knew Piaf the woman. Yet they had been as different as chalk and cheese. Edith, though amongst the richest women in France, was no different class-wise at the height of her fame than she had been in the early thirties. She was still the little-girl-lost from Belleville, roughly spoken, hard as nails, and incredibly down to earth with absolutely no airs and graces. Adapting the old Fréhel maxim, she had said, 'I am as I am, and so is a stone – them that don't like me can leave me alone!' Marguerite, on the other hand, was well educated, sophisticated and refined. She was a very private person – almost reclusive, which must have been daunting for her if one considers the demands which Edith made on everyone, expecting composers and lyricists to be at her beck and call twenty-four hours a day, even if they were on holiday with their families.

Absent-minded often to the point of absurdity, Marguerite had usually travelled between her home and Edith's apartment on her *mobylette*, often losing it en route. In an exclusive interview for BBC radio's *Portrait of Piaf*, the film director Marcel Blistène recounted an interesting anecdote: one day Marguerite had been listening to a piece of music, and infatuated by its beauty and intensity she had demanded the name of the composer. Blistène had quietly told her – Marguerite Monnot.

Edith mourned her friend more privately than she had Cerdan or her father – a mixture of genuine grief, and guilt over the fact that only one Monnot song had appeared on the recording of the Olympia recital. She told her friends, 'Never speak to me of Marguerite again.' In a radio interview she said:

> I refuse to believe in her death. Marguerite isn't dead. She is still amongst us. She is beside me, listening to me. I will find her again, one day.

The radio tribute was followed by Edith's favourite song of the time, 'Toujours aimer', written some time before by Marguerite and Norman Newell as a tribute to Piaf, 'Little Sparrow of Paris', and Nita Raya had recently furnished it with a French lyric,

> J'aurai toujours assez de larmes pour pleurer,
> Je veux toujours aimer,
> Je veux toujours souffrir,

Si je n'dois plus aimer,
Moi je préfère mourir . . .

[I'll always have enough tears to cry,
I always want to love,
I always want to suffer,
If I mustn't love any more,
Then I prefer to die . . .]

Chapter Eleven

THÉO SARAPO:
LOVE CONQUERS ALL!

During her convalescence at Richebourg, Edith almost became a total recluse. Aside from the household staff from Boulevard Lannes, only a handful of people were allowed near her. One of these was a young reporter, Jean Noli, who was working at the time with Hughes Vassal of *France-Dimanche*. Initially, Noli had accompanied Vassal to her apartment in search of the usual sensationalism – never too far away where Piaf was concerned. 'Noli belongs to a rare breed of journalist,' she told Roger Normand, 'one with a heart and conscience.' In 1973 he would publish *'Edith Piaf, trois ans pour mourir'*, without any doubt the most honest account of her final years to date, complemented by Hughes Vassal's photographs. 'She always tried to hide her distress and loneliness behind the shell of the artiste,' he later said,' 'and I wanted everyone to have a better understanding of Piaf in her twilight years.'

But, there was more. Edith opened her heart to Jean Noli – something she had rarely done with any man – and these recollections, listed under tabloid-type headings ('My man, my men!', 'I drank to forget!', 'I'm unfaithful!', etc), her way of mocking the media for getting things wrong so many times in the past, were *not* published in *France-Dimanche*, but assembled by Noli to form her second autobiography, posthumously published as *'Ma vie'*. The book did not cause much of a stir in 1963, however. Much of the information had been collated between bouts of ill-health, and sceptics doubted its authenticity: not just how much of it was the result of Piaf's over-worked imagination, but how much had been fabricated by the editor. On careful inspection, now that more facts are known about Edith's life, the entire script would appear to be genuine – only some names had been changed, or omitted in the case of Gérardin and Moustaki. Edith knew that she had been living on borrowed time for three years, and she obviously wanted to go to her Maker with a clear conscience.

Another man almost eternally present during these last years was considered so important that she actually arranged a special radio message in his honour.

> Lucien Vaimber isn't a singer. In fact, he had nothing to do at all with the art of the *chanson*. Even so, I do owe him my life. He's my chiropractor, you see. So when you see me walking on to the stage, spare a thought for the man who made it all possible!

Initially, Vaimber had refused to treat her, well aware of her tendency to disregard medical advice. In fact, she obeyed him like a child, no matter how much the treatment hurt, and Vaimber did probably add a few more years on to her life, as his biographer Guillaume Hanoteau claimed in *Les doigts du miracle* published in 1972.

When Edith returned to Boulevard Lannes, the all-night parties were resumed, still as wild as ever, even though the woman everyone called 'La Patronne' soon tired. In spite of the noise and all the coming and going, she was probably better on her own territory because all her old friends were close at hand: Charles Aznavour, Suzanne Flon, Michel Emer, Henri Contet and Marlene all dropped by, as did Raymond Asso, said to have still been bearing a grudge after more than twenty years.

Edith was quietly launching Claude Figus' recording career and putting him through his paces on two new songs. 'Quand l'amour est fini' and 'La robe bleue' were not *bad* songs, otherwise they not have been given her seal of approval. They never amounted to much, quite frankly, because Figus did not have much of a voice and, according to many who knew him, even less of a personality. He was also criticized – even by Mômone, who should have been the last to pass judgement on anyone – for taking his male lovers back to Boulevard Lannes. Many of these were picked up in the seedy gay-bars he was known to frequent, and even from off the street, though within a few months few would have much to say against his latest 'flame', a young Greek hairdresser named Théophanis Lamboukas . . .

Meanwhile, Edith continued to further her own career. Charles Dumont was still her favourite composer. Thinking solely of her health – because of personal issues there could have been no romantic attachment even if Edith had wanted this, and she had already made it clear that she did not – in January 1962 he asked her to accompany him on a skiing holiday. She was sorely lacking a man in her life, having lived for more than two years in what may only be described as a somnambulant trance, drifting between theatres and hospitals, and far too often on the brink of death. Now, her tyranny reached an all-time high. Not only did she refuse to go on holiday with Dumont, she *forbade* him to leave Paris, vowing that if he 'deserted' her now, she would have nothing more to do with him.

Dumont left, and Edith was as good as her word, for a few months at least. She had already arranged to record six of his songs and she honoured her contract, not because she felt she owed Dumont any particular favours, but because the songs were so exceptional. One was amongst the noisiest she had ever sung: 'Toi tu l'entends pas' told of one lover's indifference to what was going on inside the other party's brain and heart – merry-go-rounds, circuses and grand-opéra, huge orchestras and even the Republican Guard! There was, however, a stern warning . . .

> Tous ces merveilleux poèmes,
> Dont chaque rime est 'Je t'aime!'
> Tu les entendras,
> Le jour où tu m'aimeras!
>
> [All those wonderful poems,
> Where each rhyme is 'I love you!'
> You will hear them,
> The day you come to love me!]

Dumont's absence gave Edith the opportunity to search further afield for fresh new talent, and she engaged young composers such as Michèle Vendôme and Florence Véran – the latter had worked with Aznavour on 'Je hais les dimanches'. She was also introduced to Noël Commaret and Francis Lai, who were doubly important because they were talented accompanists. And of course Michel Emer, that faithful old soldier, was never too far away.

At around this time, too, Pathé-Marconi released a new 'concept' album, 'Tête à tête avec Edith Piaf', within which eleven of her most celebrated songs were introduced by Edith, who recounted her personal philosophies on heart-to-hearts ('Heureuse'), friendship ('Mon vieux Lucien'), youth ('Avec ce soleil', 'L'homme à la moto', 'Le billard électrique'), and scandal ('Opinion publique'). Love, of course, took up a whole side of the album with 'C'est l'amour', 'Mon Dieu', 'La belle histoire d'amour', 'C'est peut-être ça' and 'Hymne à l'amour'. She concluded, obviously having decided that 'Chanson bleue' was no longer her favourite song,

> Destiny, sadness and death may separate us for a little while, but it's all in the cause of love. I have always sung about love because it's the one thing in life that interests us the most, whether it is the love of one's work, the love of humanity, or the love of a man. Love gives one courage, and suffering only adds to its value because true love can only be bought with tears . . .

At this time, Edith also drew Pathé-Marconi's attention towards her alter-ego, Marie Dubas, now retired and in the early stages of Parkinson's Disease. Calling several radio stations, she asked why they no longer played Marie's records. The response was that, unlike her contemporaries – Damia, Fréhel, Chevalier – none of Marie's songs had ever been transferred to vinyl!

In January 1961, Barbara, starting to make a name for herself having been awarded the Grand Prix du Disque for her interpretations of Georges Brassens, had visited Marie's apartment . . . with 4,000 letters from fans expressing their profound admiration for *La Fantaisiste des Années-Folles*. Always cagey where potential 'rivals' were concerned, Edith now got in touch with Barbara, and between them they composed a letter of complaint to Pathé-Marconi. And just to make sure he got the message, Edith told him over the telephone, 'Marie made a fortune for you during her hey-day. And what thanks does she get now that she's ill? Get off your backside and do something, otherwise *Piaf* will be leaving Pathé-Marconi!' Edith would never have gone this far even for Marie Dubas, but the ruse worked. The company released an album of Dubas songs which sold thousands of copies. As for Marie, she would live on until February 1972.

In February 1962, Edith was taken to the Ambroise Paré Clinic, at Neuilly, suffering from double bronchial pneumonia. She had probably forgotten Claude Figus's dishy Greek boyfriend, Théophanis Lamboukas, as Roger Normand explained,

> After their first meeting, she'd dismissed him as a 'brooding little shirt-lifter'. The first time I saw him, he was perched on the edge of the sofa, twiddling his thumbs and seemingly lost for words – hardly surprising, when one considers Piaf's powerful aura, and her insistence that all visitors to her court be spirited and cheerful, which she certainly *always* was, no matter how lousy she felt. Théo was a polite, well-spoken young man, and that got up her nose a bit. She went out of her way to be unpleasant and vulgar, going on about what men like him did in bed with each other. And Théo just sat there, smiling! Then, when Edith was ill, he accompanied Figus to the clinic, until one morning when he and Figus had a row, and he went alone. All her other friends took her huge bouquets of flowers, but Théo took her a bunch of daisies and a Greek doll. That did it, of course!

Two of Edith's former lovers had been Greek and during visiting hours, she and her young friend spoke lovingly of his homeland. Because she found his name too much of a mouthful, she shortened it to Théo. He told her that he lived with his parents and two sisters above their hairdressing salon at La-Frette-sur-Seine, just outside Paris, and that he would one day be expected to take over the family business. He also asked Edith if he might set her hair, without knowing how sensitive she was about the fact that she hardly had any hair left. Edith agreed, and she fell in love with him! She told a friend, 'Théo is the most beautiful man I have ever seen in my life.' For once she was not exaggerating, for Théo was by far the handsomest of her men, envied by many of her friends – male and female – who quite obviously would had liked to have had him for themselves. Théo and Figus continued sleeping together, too, long after he had become the new 'Monsieur Piaf'. 'Figus considered it his divine right because *he'd* brought them together in the first place,' Roger Normand said. 'And even Edith maintained that sharing Théo was better than not having him at all!'

Unlike any of his predecessors, Théo was shy, quiet and totally unassuming. He brought books to Edith, and read to her: she was still deeply into the classics, and adored Gide and others of his genre. On bad days, he cut up her food and spoon-fed her, and his infinite tenderness moved her. She told a reporter from *France-Soir* that Théo had given her the will to live at a time when she had thought herself way beyond redemption . . . and for the time being no one mentioned the fact that Théo had actually been born in 1935, two years *after* her long-dead daughter, Marcelle.

One day, Théo told Edith of his horrendous experiences when, as a soldier, he had spent his entire two-year military service at an outpost near Colomb-Bechar, in Algeria. Here, he had contracted dysentery and lost thirty pounds in weight, but his recovery had been aided by his portable record-player and collection of Piaf recordings. His favourite song: 'Hymne à l'amour'. And when Théo added that his own dream had always been to sing, Edith's recovery was little short of miraculous. Eleven of her lovers had become internationally renowned because of her, so why not this one? He certainly had the looks and more than his share of determination to succeed – but not, she declared, with a name like Théophanis Lamboukas, for the theatres would never fit it on to the billboards!

As usual, Edith came up with the ideal solution. During her brief fling with Takis Menelas in 1946 she had picked up quite a number of Greek phrases – most of them too filthy to repeat – but she had always remembered how to say 'I love you'. The Greek word for this was 'sarapo'. Thus her new protégé became known as Théo Sarapo – 'Théo I-love-you'. And if her critics scoffed at this, she quickly reminded them that her own name translated as 'spuggie'.

There is no doubt whatsoever – Théo Sarapo gave Edith Piaf a brand new lease of life. When they met, she already had one foot in the grave, yet thanks to this young man she lived another eighteen months – the happiest months of her life apart from her time with Cerdan, whom she would continue to mourn until the very end. Théo was Piaf's saving grace, her earthly saint. He did not simply teach her how to love again. He reformed her. He helped her to find her long-lost self-respect, and showed her how to have pride in her appearance again. And importantly, he 'softened' much of her tyranny. He did not do this by being a forceful man – far from it, he was passive and gentle as a lamb. Even Simone Berteaut, who galled many people by stating that even the most fervent of her lovers had only seen the words EDITH PIAF written in lights above the bed, was not scathing about this one and actually attacked those critics who suggested that Théo had only latched on to Edith for her money, which is certainly untrue. She was in debt when he met her, and always would be . . . and in the end, according to French law, Théo would inherit those debts. Very early in their relationship he was also told by her doctors that she did not have long to live, yet in this respect he was just as naive as Edith. Dreams were there to believe in: there would always be another miracle waiting around the next corner.

For Edith, however, there would be the penultimate shock.

In April 1962, Douglas Davies visited Paris, and naturally he was invited to stay *chez* Piaf – she hardly ever bore grudges, and was on speaking terms with all of her ex-lovers, even Moustaki. 'There was absolutely no rivalry between the two young men,' Roger Normand recalled. 'Far from it, for within days Douglas and Théo were sleeping in the same room, and I'm sure Edith knew.'

Without being badgered into doing so by Edith, Douglas painted Théo's portrait, and he was present when she recorded the sound-track for Mikis Théodorakis' film, *Les amants de Téruel*, which recounted the famous story of the star-crossed lovers whose only way out is suicide. Fortunately, she was unable to accompany the young man on his journey back to Orly airport during the morning of 3 June. Douglas' plane crashed just minutes after take-off, and there were no survivors.

For the second time, a plane had robbed Edith of a loved one. Théo and the household tried desperately to keep the news from her, worried that another relapse so soon after the last might prove fatal. Edith found out from the jealous Claude Figus and for two days locked herself in her bedroom, refusing to see anyone but Marlene Dietrich, and emerging only when Théo swore an oath on the Bible never to take a plane.

Thinking that it would do her good to get away from Paris for a while, Théo took Edith to Cannes, where they rented a suite at the Hôtel Majestic – not a good idea, considering she had stayed there with Douglas the previous summer, though Théo may not have known this, and it was of course a perfectly unselfish act on his part. Again she was seen in public wearing an antiquated bathing-costume, although this time she did not have to *forbid* her man to leave her side: Théo was besotted by her, and on 26 July he proposed to her. She was stunned! Nineteen years and a whole world of experience separated them, and initially she replied that she would 'have to think about it', suggesting that she should be given a month in which to make up her mind. She then offered him one excuse after another why they should *not* wed. *He* was young and strong, and handsome enough to have any woman he wanted, though she did know that sexually he was only interested in men. And *she*, in her own words, was 'An old wreck who's cheated on men all her life, an unscrupulous bitch who was renowned for her capriciousness and foul temper . . . who could not cook, or look after a house.'

Edith was being ridiculous, of course, yet those who knew her were well aware that in her whole life she had never once picked up a duster or washed a cup . . . and she herself told a reporter that whenever one of Théo's shirts needed washing, she simply threw it away and sent out for a new one!

The age-gap *did* worry her, but only because she thought a large section of her public might desert her if she ended up making a fool of herself. Théo, however, persisted and in the end she decided to meet him halfway: she would marry him, but only if Saint Thérèse gave her blessing! She told Jean Noli:

What woman of my age wouldn't be dazzled by loving such a man? And yet, when I analyze this love I don't find a mistress's love but something which until now has been refused me – a mother's love. Théo, with his laughter and youthful spirit, gives me the impression at times that I have been given a son. A mother sleeps within even the most voluptuous of mistresses! Only narrow-minded people are offended by what I have done – I know that my love of Théo is nothing to be ashamed of. Had this been the case, would I have taken him to Lisieux to crave Saint Thérèse's blessing? That would have been sacrilege, for when I was a child it was she who restored my sight. And I don't know if my wish will be granted. A year would suffice, or even a few months. I would thank Fate for that because I don't deserve such happiness. I don't think I ever did . . .

For decades, cynics have asked the same question: why? Edith was still the highest-paid female entertainer in the world, but she spent faster than she earned and would never change – and though she admitted that she had been 'a looker' when younger, she was fond of telling everyone that she was not so now. Maybe she had not heard of the saying, 'Beauty is in the eye of the beholder'. Illness had 'shrunk' her to 4 feet 7 inches, she weighed just eighty-four pounds, and she was so crippled with rheumatism that she could hardly walk. Eating was a horrendous ordeal, and much of the time she had to be fed like a baby. Her doctors reconfirmed that at best she would live another two years, and that she might have to stop singing at any moment – something that few people even *dared* to think of. So, why did Théo, a confessed homosexual to boot, insist on marrying her? Why not allow their affair to run its course like all the others, then move on, that much richer for the experience?

Quite simply, he loved her! They adored each other! 'We're what you might call a modern-day, noncomformist Romeo and Juliet,' she confided in Marlene Dietrich . . . whilst Roger Normand, who was never averse to crudity, was told, 'We both have the same taste in men – the stiffer the better!'

It was only after Saint Thérèse had 'given her blessing', however, that Edith gave Théo the go-ahead to ask his parents' permission to marry her – not necessary, of course, but ethical because of the way he had been raised. The meeting is said to have been fraught with worry. Théo spent some time in the garden, talking things over with his father, whilst the women – there were two younger daughters, Cathy and Christine – discussed what the bride would be wearing. There then followed a party, welcoming her into the family, and Madame Lamboukas asked Edith to call her Mamam ... oblivious to the fact that *she* was several months Edith's junior. The biggest surprise of all, however, was when one of Théo's sisters put on a record of Richard Anthony and persuaded Edith to dance le Twist!

Edith and Théo's engagement was officially celebrated at a rented villa in Cap Ferrat, with a group of hand-picked friends headed by Louis Barrier and her new nurse, Simone Margantin. The wedding-date was set for 9 October: and was it coincidence that it would be sixteen years to the day since she had recorded 'La vie en rose' and 'Mariage'? – though the latter number, in which the hapless bride goes to jail for murdering her husband, does not linger unduly on wedded bliss! Soon afterwards, inspired by her new-found joy and spurred on by Lucien Vaimber, Edith began working again. Louis Barrier had arranged a series of recitals on the Côte d'Azur, to be followed by what would be her final season at the Olympia.

One of the few friends who strongly disapproved of the forthcoming marriage was Marlene Dietrich. She told me:

> I had last seen Edith at Thionville, during her so-called suicide-tour. It was her forty-fifth birthday, and though she was still very sick, she seemed to be coping with her problems because there was no man around to complicate matters. I still loved her very much, but felt that she should have learned her lesson with Jacques Pills. He [Théo] was a nice young man, but I always thought he married her for her money. I later found out that he didn't. But he was *also* a homosexual, and I couldn't condone that.

As with Yves Montand and Les Compagnons de la Chanson, Edith insisted that Théo be given second-billing in all of their shows, *plus* the appropriate renumeration. This was asking too much, yet sick as she was, she had to be humoured if nothing else. For weeks she had been putting him through the mill, attempting to teach him the seemingly impossible: how to sing. Few people were allowed the privilege of sitting in on these 'workshops', but those who did agree unanimously that at the time he did not look as though he would make it. One onlooker, who specifically asked not to be named, said, 'Théo used to stand there, looking as though he had shit himself and singing down his nose all the time. He really was quite dreadful!' The latter fact was proved when he cut his first recordings: as a self-professed *chanteur-réalist* he was unbelievably bad. Louis Barrier, of course, was not just Edith's mentor and friend, he was also an astute businessman who believed, and rightly so, that no matter how lacking in talent Théo was, he would still pull in the crowds because of the sensationalist aspect of his relationship with Piaf. Thus the impresario persuaded most of the theatre-directors to engage Théo 'out of pity and in respect of Piaf's health'.

Edith ruled over the proceedings like a Tartar chieftain. Sometimes she became so aggressive with Théo that he would burst into tears and plead with her to stop. 'I'm surprised he didn't change his mind about marrying her,' recalled another friend, Claude Sounac, who later co-founded Les Amis d'Edith Piaf. 'She was so harsh with him. I'm sure he must have been thinking, "My God, what's it going to be like after October?" On one occasion she kept him on his feet for eight hours without a break. And yet, amazingly, by the time she'd finished with him, he *really* could sing!'

The recitals were attended mostly by tourists. Théo's entire repertoire had been written by Edith – who also stage-managed the shows – with music by Francis Lai, Noël Commaret and Charles Dumont, now welcomed back into the fold though not entirely forgiven. His best-received songs were 'Les enfants de la mode', 'Chez Sabine', and the clamorous 'La bande en noir' . . . the true story of a drug-runner friend of Claude Figus who had recently received his come-uppance from another thug he had wronged in the past.

> Pas une fille ne l'intéresse . . .
> Toute une jeunesse de foutue,
> Et ses vingt ans qu'il a perdu,

Étendu là sur le trottoir,
C'était pas joli à voir!

[Not one girl interested him . . .
An entire fucked-up youth,
And his twenty years which he lost,
There, stretched out on the pavement,
Not a pretty sight!

Théo's performances were by no means faultless, but they were sincere, unpretentious, and appreciated even by the hordes of media scandalmongers – and like any true *chanteur-réalist* he very quickly attracted a fairly large homosexual following. Many members of his audiences were shocked – and many more given a sharp thrill of excitement – when, during his fourth song, he stripped off his shirt and sang bare-chested. He was very tall, with a muscular, hirsute torso and Edith probably never realized the effect he was having on some people. Her husband-to-be did not have to sing a song like 'Les blouses blanches' to make his fans faint, for if anyone swooned during that magical fourth song, in spite of what Edith told everyone, it had nothing to do with the heat!

Edith's own recitals were short – sometimes as few as ten songs – and she was so ill that instead of silencing the audience with the customary wave of her hand after each song, she allowed the applause to run on so as to enable her to recover her strength. Her new songs included 'Fallait-il', 'On cherche un Auguste' and 'Polichinelle', all delivered in the upper register, and with comparative ease once she had recovered her breath. One song alone, however, proclaimed the couple's private ecstasy to the cynical world – Michel Emer's 'A quoi ça sert l'amour?', which was first performed on the television programme, *Cinq colonnes à la une*. It was Edith's first true duet with another artiste since those with Constantine and Pills, and remains her most famous. Its couplets, alternated by the two singers, form a series of pertinent questions and philosophical replies. Théo would ask:

A quoi ça sert l'amour?
On raconte toujours

Les histoires insincères.
A quoi ça sert d'aimer?

[What's the use of love
One always tells insincere stories.
What's the use of loving?]

Edith's response would then come with her cocking her head to one side and gazing up into her lover's eyes. 'You're the last! You're the first!' And, she concluded:

Avant toi y avait rien,
Avec toi je suis bien!
C'est toi qu'il me fallait!
Toi que j'aimerai toujours!
Ça sert à ça, l'amour!

[Before you I had nothing,
With you I'm fine!
You are the one I needed
The one I'll always love
That's the point of, love.

Performing on a television show, Edith declared, was considerably less satisfactory than airing the song before a live audience. She therefore decided that 'A quoi ça sert l'amour?' should be given its 'proper' premiere under the most arduous circumstances imaginable, at least for herself – at Chez Patachou, the chanteuse's posh nightclub off the Plâce du Tertre! 'I've decided to forgive her for all the terrible things she's said about me,' she told Roger Normand, when in fact *she* had done all the insulting, over the years! Exactly what Patachou had to say about the matter is not known – she was not in Paris at the time, though once Théo stepped on to the stage, she had more than enough to cope with when the audience began booing and he rushed off the stage in tears. Wearing an old cardigan over her dress, Edith led him back on, and held his hand whilst they sang their song. Only *then* did Théo appear to be appreciated and afterwards, at Boulevard Lannes, he confided in Edith that he would *never* make it as a singer. She told him, truthfully,

'*That's* exactly what Montand and Aznavour said to me, and look where *they* are today!'

The incident at Chez Patachou was followed by a thoroughly heartless and debasing article in *Noir et Blanc* on 3 August 1962 which caused Edith such distress that Théo at once demanded to meet its author, Jean Louville, and give him a good hiding – something the young man was more than capable of doing, according to those who knew him. Fortunately, Louville failed to turn up at the meeting.

EDITH PIAF: 'MY MARRIAGE WITH THÉO IS MY CHALLENGE TO DEATH!'

A scrap of cardboard headed HÔTEL MAJESTIC, CANNES. Clumsily written words: EDITH PIAF AND THÉO SARAPO HAVE JOY IN ANNOUNCING THEIR MARRIAGE AT THE END OF OCTOBER '62. Signed by the fiancés, this distinctly exceptional, unexpected invitation! The public found it unbelievable when Edith began her 'adventure' with Théo Sarapo, but this marriage exceeds the bounds of understanding. One tries to discern why the *grande chanteuse*, not content with this conspicuous liaison, has to leap the ultimate hurdle and MARRY him. She could easily be his mother, and it is this enormous age difference which shocks us. He is handsome, ambitious. Like others who have become stars, he COULD take her advice and live with Edith for a while, adding a little more to the gossip columns.

One can only repeat . . . UNBELIEVABLE!

For some years, Edith's friends had been urging her to take legal action against the more scurrilous journalists. She never did, always claiming that even the most scurrilous tittle-tattler had his living to earn, the same as anyone else. She did, however, lash out on the radio when a reporter dismissed one of her recitals as 'mediocre'.

A journalist goes to see an artiste once, then he goes around saying that he's an experienced critic. This is something for which I reproach him. How dare he judge me after a single recital! He must come and see me – oh, three or four times before making up his mind. And before he starts pulling me to pieces for not being on form, does he ever stop to think if he's always on cue? Somehow, I don't think so . . .

It was true, of course, that Edith was old enough to be Théo's mother – the cynical tabloids of today would have branded him a 'toy boy'. She retaliated to the article in *Noir et Blanc* not with hostility, but by asking her friend Jean Noli to place an advertisement in his newspaper, asking for her public's approval and blessing. She and Théo received considerably more than this: in the space of a week she received several thousand letters, cards and gifts from well-wishers. From her suite at the Hôtel Majestic Edith also granted an interview – in English – to Victor Newson of the *Daily Express*, stating that in her 'experienced and unbiased opinion' the British were still not ready to hear her sing because of their 'attitude towards love'. It is thought that she feared being mocked if she sang there now, on account of her relationship with Théo, though they would later spend a clandestine weekend in London. Newson himself delighted her by telling her that he approved of the marriage, and wrote, 'The love between Piaf and Sarapo is a love-affair which all France loves.' Even so, she did not change her mind about the British.

The premiere of Olympia '62 was fixed for 27 September, but Edith's health was so uncertain that Louis Barrier and Bruno Coquatrix agreed on just a two-week stint this time. For Edith this was a period of worry and indecision. Morally, audiences at the Olympia were much more reserved than their counterparts on the Riviera, and though her Paris public had seen her on the television with Théo, this had been before the announcement of their engagement. Edith was therefore worried that this time she might have gone too far – somewhat surprising, when one considers how her public had stood by her during her affairs with Cerdan and Toto Gérardin.

Edith therefore decided to put her public to the test, and two days before the Olympia she sang in her last gala performance . . . a concert from the top of the Eiffel Tower for the premiere of the film *The longest day*. Quite literally, her voice soared over the rooftops of the city, via loudspeakers attached to the actual structure, and as she finished 'Non je ne regrette rien' the sky exploded in a terrific display of fireworks. The show was preceded by a sumptuous banquet in the Palais de Chaillot gardens, and the audience of three thousand was the most distinguished she had ever faced: Lord Mountbatten, the Shah of Iran, Montgomery and Churchill, Queen Sophia of Greece, Prince Rainier of Monaco, Richard Burton, Elizabeth Taylor, Maria Callas, Audrey Hepburn and Sophia Loren were but a few. From Edith's point of view, however, the occasion was doubly important because it reunited her with her old friend President Eisenhower, and it was probably he who suggested that she sing on a raised platform similar to the one she had used at the Versailles. Of her fourteen songs, 'Le diable de la Bastille' and 'Le rendez-vous' had been written for her to sing at the Olympia. She also sang her most portentous song, 'Le droit d'aimer', by Robert Nyel and Francis Lai. It would become her personal credo, and it was her last European hit during her lifetime.

> À la face des hommes,
> Au mépris de leurs lois . . .
> Quoi qu'on dise ou qu'on fasse,
> Tant que mon coeur battra,
> Jamais rien ni personne
> M'empêchera d'aimer!
> J'en ai le droit d'aimer!
>
> [Facing men, scorning their laws . . .
> No matter what anyone says or does,
> So long as my heart's beating,
> Nothing, no one
> Will stop me from loving!
> I have the *right* to love!]

If anyone had the right to love – through fear of losing everything and even at the risk of destroying herself, as is indicated in the song – that person was Edith Piaf.

On the opening night of Olympia '62 Edith faced dozens of press reporters and photographers, good, bad and indifferent.

Tonight, there would be no prophecy of death: the only cloud which hung above her head was a silver-tinged cloud of love. The audience was a tough one, even by French standards, for the sheer sensationalism connected with her forthcoming marriage had attracted a curious cross-section of the public. The genuine fans were there, of course, but they were vastly outnumbered by cynics who wanted to see if she could stay up on her feet. Here was her *honorable sociéte* again, but if many of them – 'having heard certain rumours' – were expecting the spectacle of Sarapo, *torse nu*, they were to be disappointed. Edith had given her fiancé strict instructions to keep his shirt *on*!

Vocally, Edith was in impeccable form, and she excelled herself with a wider range than usual: Francis Lai's 'Musique à tout va', had it been written then, might have defied her during the mid-fifties when she had been at the peak of her physical fitness. Now it and her other numbers were delivered with relative ease. Her opening song, the self-composed 'Roulez tambours', was one of the rare protest songs she sang after her visits to the United States.

> Pour ceux qui meurent chaque jour,
> Pour ceux qui pleurent dans les faubourgs,
> Pour Hiroshima, Pearl Harbour!
> Pour l'heure et pour la fin des guerres,
> Allez, roulez tambours!
>
> [For those who are dying each day,
> For the ones crying in the suburbs,
> For Hiroshima, Pearl Harbour!
> For the present, for an end to war,
> Come on, roll the drums!]

When Edith bawled out for Théo to join her on the stage, there was an outburst of mocking laughter, perhaps on account of the seventeen-inch difference in their heights. However, once the audience had listened to 'A quoi ça sert l'amour?', the applause spoke for itself and she was more than convinced that her marriage had been given the invaluable Parisian seal of approval.

After the premiere, she was interviewed by Pierre Desgraupes:

DESGRAUPES: There's something invincible about you. People say you're finished, you'll never sing again. Then, a miracle! You always return. How do you explain this?

PIAF: My fight! As long as there's a breath of life left in my body, I'll fight!

DESGRAUPES: You've been singing for twenty-seven years with constant success. How do you explain this?

PIAF: I've been sincere, I think, in giving all to my art. My heart ... my life. And I regret absolutely nothing! I only thank God for the joys and the pains that He's given me ...

DESGRAUPES: You always sing about love. It isn't just another word to you. You've had a lot of love in your life. Don't you regret the men who deceived you?

PIAF: One can't live without love. And no one deceived me ... ever!

DESGRAUPES: But one of your lovers stood out from all the others, didn't he?

PIAF: There was one. He was genuine. But I'm not going to tell you who he was.

DESGRAUPES: And ... are you singing as well now as you were fifteen years ago?

PIAF: Oh, only the public can tell you that!

Edith and Théo's wedding on 9 October 1962 was a feast for public and Press alike. Around 10,000 well-wishers gathered outside the Mairie of the 16th arrondissement: the police had to be brought in to restore order before Edith arrived, wearing a black alpaca dress ... and her old mink coat. She resembled a fragile doll, but was smiling radiantly. According to her nurse Simone Margantin, her closest woman friend now that Marguerite Monnot was gone, she had developed cold feet a few hours before the ceremony, and had had to be coaxed into Théo's brand new white Mercedes – after her injection.

The civil ceremony was followed by a religious one at the Greek Orthodox Church on Rue Daru, which was filmed. Edith and Théo exchanged rings and crowns, which were placed on their heads by Louis Barrier – Marlene Dietrich, unable to stand in as witness this time, had sent a telegram. The couple were blessed by the same priest who had married Edith's friend Sacha Guitry to Lana Marconi, some years before. Outside the church, the fanatical crowd chanted 'Vive la Mariée!'. This delighted Edith, who until that moment had not considered herself the typical bride. One or two onlookers were interviewed by the media, and a variety of reasons were given for being there. Most were genuine admirers, fighting to embrace or even touch the hem of her dress during her brief walkabout. Others were there out of curiosity, to scoff and jeer at the bridegroom, who took their insults 'on the chin' like the mild-mannered young man he was. An interesting clip of newsreel shows one elderly female admirer's attitude towards a snooty woman who told a reporter that she was only there 'to get a glimpse of the gigolo' – she belted her with her handbag, then broke through the barrier to kiss the bride before being moved on by a burly gendarme!

The couple returned to Boulevard Lanne for the first time in several weeks. Upon leaving the Hôtel Majestic in Cannes, Théo had rented a suite at the George V in Paris, having taken it upon himself to have the apartment refurbished and made to look like a home even if, according to Jean Noli, his tastes, were decidedly eccentric. He had done his best, and as far as Edith was concerned, it was the thought which counted. The new furniture was Danish, the divans and armchairs had been suitably re-upholstered in black velvet, and the wall coverings were of red silk. She did, however, strongly disapprove of the carpets because these were an unlucky green.

Edith and Théo's wedding presents to each other were equally strange. For her, a collection of rare first editions of Balzac and Baudelaire, and an enormous teddybear. The latter is now in the Piaf museum, at the headquarters of Les Amis d'Edith Piaf in Paris – to see it, and Edith's other effects, one has to make an appointment, then hurry around in an austere atmosphere governed by the curator's watchful gaze and rattling tin. As for Edith, she bought her husband an exercise cycle and an enormous electric train set: one of Hughes Vassal's photographs shows him playing with it, whilst Edith is sitting in a corner . . . sewing absent-mindedly!

For several days, Boulevard Lannes was busier than it had been on the eve of Olympia '61 – a seemingly incessant stream of interviews with the media. This time, Edith had little patience. It had taken her thirteen years to replace Cerdan – if indeed she had – and for the first time she branded some reporters 'vultures' to their faces. She took others for a ride. One in particular amused her, and needless to say the name of the interviewer has never been revealed.

TO THEO: What effect will it have on you, marrying a woman twenty years your senior?
RESPONSE: Edith has the character of a child . . .
TO EDITH: What effect does it have on you, marrying a man twenty years younger than yourself?
RESPONSE: The effect that I was lucky to find a man who's so gentle . . . and handsome!
TO THEO: Will you have any children?
RESPONSE: If my wife wishes . . .
TO EDITH: Do you want to have children?
RESPONSE: Sure! Why not!

Soon after her wedding, Edith entered a detoxification clinic: through no fault of her own, this time, she had become dependent on the needle. Fortunately the visit was brief. When she returned to Boulevard Lannes, accompanied by Simone Margantin – from now on she would always be at Edith's side – she seemed strong enough to take on her next venture, a tour of Holland and Belgium. She had been engaged to appear at L'Ancienne Belgique, in Brussels. This was a large, expensive cabaret noted for the noise its clientele made with their knives and forks whilst the artistes were on stage. Edith, of course, laid down several conditions of her own. Charles Dumont, who for some reason was back in her bad books, was ingloriously informed that she was going to remove 'Non je ne regrette rien' from her programme, as its subject matter meant that it could no longer be included on the same bill as 'Le droit d'aimer'. Then, several days before she left France, she summoned

Dumont to her court. She told him that she had only sung his 'Le diable de la Bastille' at the Olympia as 'a favour', and that now it was time for him to pay his debt. She had written a poem, 'Le chant d'amour', which she wanted set to music. Dumont obliged, and Edith in turn agreed to retain 'Non je ne regrette rien' in her repertoire!

'Le chant d'amour' was the very last song which Edith wrote for herself, though she wrote others for her husband. It was a great success, though she never got as far as recording it in the studio. During the afternoon of 3 December 1962 she paid a visit to Pathé-Marconi and, in a single take, cut 'Le rendez-vous' by René Rouzaud and Francis Lai. There would be no more.

Barbara, who since her last meeting with Edith had enjoyed considerable success with an album of songs by Jacques Brel, watched this final session through a security window. She told me:

> I had just taken to performing my own songs, and was at the studio to rehearse 'Chapeau-bas' in the very next room, the one and only time that our names appeared on the same bill – in this instance, in chalk on the blackboard just inside foyer! I was excited because I was hoping to arrange another visit to see Marie Dubas, and was sure Piaf would come with me. Like a fragile little black bird, but with a voice capable of silencing a thunderstorm, she sang her song. Then she collapsed into a heap. My heart skipped a beat. I was sure she was dead. Then her husband scooped her up like a bundle of rags and carried her to the car. I held the door as they passed through, and that's the nearest I ever got to meeting her again.

Edith's tour proved too much for her, but she stuck it out, even though she was twice rushed back to Paris to be given vital blood transfusions. At L'Ancienne Belgique she premiered 'Le chant d'amour' – she later claimed that whilst writing it she had seen beyond her own death, for the lovers in the song both die and are reunited in heaven to share the same griefs. Ironically, less than eight years on, her prophecy would come true.

On 12 December, she gave a splendid recital at Nijmegen, in

Holland. This was filmed, and until recently believed to have been lost. Then, in 1989, it was edited and released in Europe on a video – the only complete record of a Piaf performance and one which keeps the observer on the edge of his seat for almost an hour. What is incredible is that she did not look ill – just a little nervous and shy, and seemingly embarrassed by all the standing ovations, particularly after 'Emporte-moi', at the end of which she had broken down. One song, which was not included in the edited version of the film was 'J'en ai tant vu', another optimistic work from the pen of Michel Emer which she could sing, now, with utter confidence.

> Je croyais que j'avais tout vu,
> Tout fait, tout dit, tout entendu,
> Et je m'disais, 'On n'm'aura plus!'
> C'est alors qu'il est venue!
> C'est vrai je marche plus . . . je *cours*!

> [I thought I'd seen everything,
> Done, said, heard everything,
> I told myself, 'Nobody will want me any more!'
> That's when he came along!
> I don't walk any more, it's true . . . I *run*!]

Time was swiftly running out, yet Edith still insisted that her precognitive dream would see her through the very worst of her traumas. Alas, there would be few more miracles. She had been booked for a series of recitals at the Bobino, and Louis Barrier was inundated with offers from around the world. She was invited to tour Japan, at a time when Damia was *still* one of the biggest record-sellers there ten years after retiring, but she declined. Japan, she said, was too far away should the need arise for her to be rushed back to Paris, and in any case she would never forgive the Japanese for their atrocities during the war. She *did* agree to visit Canada, and meticulously planned a proposed recital at the White House, before President Kennedy. Little did the world know that they would both be dead before the year was out.

For thirty years now, Edith's life had represented a dichotomy of male-inspired dramas – the irony of the eagerly awaited train which never seems to arrive, the coat thrown over the shoulders during the early hours of the morning, or the optimistically blue sky which is somehow always tinged with grey. And yet, at the end of her life she did manage to find that elusive crock of gold which had always been beyond her particular rainbow – an answer to the cry for help which she had first made during the early thirties, in the streets as Edith Gassion.

> J'aurais préférer malgré tout,
> Un homme qui peut m'aimer d'amour,
> Pour avec lui finir mes jours,
> Dans un nid chaud comme deux moineaus . . .

> [In spite of everything I would have preferred
> A man who can love me for love's sake,
> To end my days with him in a warm nest,
> Like two sparrows . . .]

Edith and Théo opened at the Bobino on 18 February 1963. Their recitals could be compared, almost, with the wave of Beatlemania which swept across the world later that year – even Théo received a twelve-minute standing ovation before being allowed to sing. Eight of his twelve songs were written by Edith, including the somewhat over-strident 'Défense de . . .', an attack of her still-critical *honorable société*. And as an introduction to yet another proposed tour of Britain which would not take place – she said she had already commissioned an English lyric, which has yet to come to light – there was 'Un dimanche à Londres'. The inspiration for the song had come from a clandestine weekend visit to the British capital, shortly before her marriage. The public and most of the critics observed that Théo's act was more polished than it had been at the Olympia, and if his voice was still a little nasal, his performances were dramatic and well-received. Some years later another of his songs, 'Les mains', would be adapted into English and incorporated in Libby Morris' London revue.

Edith's opening performance was more hysterically received that any other she ever gave – at one stage the fans became so rowdy that the theatre staff braced themselves for a riot and thought about calling in the police. The public, as if aware that they were hearing the Great Piaf for the last time, went crazy. Six of the songs were new to her Paris audience. 'Traqué' traces the familiar pattern of the man being hounded for the crime he has not committed. 'Monsieur Incognito', also by Florence Véran and Robert Gall, tells the story of a *male* prostitute who works the beat outside the narrator's Métro station: with his fine clothes, well-shined shoes and gentle disposition, he could be taken for just another passer-by, but *she* knows what he is up to and instinctively hates him because when she was alone and feeling wretched, there were never such men on the street to comfort *her*! Therefore all she can do is scream, 'Go away!' 'Tiens v'la un marin', by Julien Bouquet, proved that the years had not depreciated Edith's fondness for sailors, and the catchy 'Margot Coeur-Gros' was by Michèle Vendôme: in English it became 'Poor little lost Louise'. And of course, there was 'Le chant d'amour'.

One song drove the audience into a frenzy. This was 'C'était pas moi' by Robert Gall and Francis Lai, which some critics declared was even more disturbing than 'Les blouses blanches' had been, and which Edith acted out so dramatically that most of the audience were convinced she was having a fit. Even now it is impossible to listen to the song without feeling that 'something' has walked over one's grave. It tells the story of a man who has been thrown into prison for a murder he did not commit, and really has to be heard to be believed. 'It wasn't me! It wasn't me!' Edith screams, at the top of her voice as the curtain falls. And finally she sang 'Les gens', a subtle slap in the face for those who still criticized her marriage.

> Comme ils baissaient les yeux les gens,
> Comme ils nous regardaient les gens,
> Quand tous deux on s'est enlacé,
> Quand on s'est embrassé . . .
>
> [How the people lowered their eyes,
> How the people looked at us,
> When we hugged one another,
> When we kissed each other . . .]

After the Bobino, Edith and Théo toured again, though by now she was so ill that it was an effort to sing more than ten songs, and as with her previous tour she had to keep returning to Paris for medical treatment. The public were ready to believe that she would go on for ever: she had already announced that she would never retire. And she was of course only forty-seven, the age when most *chanteuses-réalistes* are reaching their peak.

Then, on 18 March 1963 Edith Piaf sang in public for the last time, at the Opera House in Lille.

She returned to Boulevard Lannes and, shelving the idea of visiting America for the time being, she began rehearsing for what would have been her first visit to Germany since entertaining the prisoners of Stalag III during the war. A demonstration tape 'Non je ne regrette rien', sung phonetically in German (although Simone Margantin claimed that she could speak the language just as fluently as she could English) had already been made, and there were to be others. Edith had never forgiven the Germans for their atrocities during the Occupation, and Charles Dumont and Michel Vaucaire had written 'Le Mur', a somewhat harrowing song about the Berlin Wall. It is a fine, dramatic work which Edith did get around to taping, though the recording has since conveniently become 'lost' and will no doubt turn up some day in a compilation album to increase its commerciality, as 'Dans ma rue' and 'Sans y penser' did for the twenty-fifth anniversary of her death. In 1966, after a great deal of deliberation by the composers, an English adaptation of the song, 'I've been here' – which lyrically has absolutely nothing to do with the Berlin Wall – was given to Barbra Streisand. When Streisand heard the French version, however, she recorded the song in *both* languages and the result was a performance of which Piaf would have been proud.

Another 'German' song was 'L'homme de Berlin', by Francis Lai and Michèle Vendôme, and unlike the previous number was much in keeping with the well-rehearsed Piaf subject of prostitution. The woman has just arrived in Berlin, searching to find a way of forgetting. She sees the man through the drizzle, standing under the grimy, anxiously weeping sky, and imagines that life with him would work out fine, if only she were not in Berlin. One wonders, however, what the Germans might have thought of the song and Edith's interpretation, had she sung it there.

Ne me parlez pas de Berlin,
Puisque Berlin n'a rien pour moi!
Y'a pas qu'un homme dans c'foutu pays,
Il n'y a pas que lui . . .

[Don't speak to me about Berlin,
For Berlin has nothing for me!
There's only one man in this fucking country,
There's only him . . .]

Edith recorded 'L'homme de Berlin' on 7 April 1963, on a bedside tape recorder at Boulevard Lannes, accompanied by Noël Commaret on the piano, and with Francis Lai on the accordion. The German tour never took place, and Théo Sarapo kept the tape in a locked chest until 1968, when the media – and a lack of funds – persuaded him to hand it over to Pathé-Marconi, who issued it on an EP with 'Le diable de la Bastille' and two of the songs from Edith's last Bobino recital, with the applause edited out. The cover photograph, from her concert in Lille, was the last of her to be taken on the stage. Critics said at the time that her voice sounded cracked and worn-out, and that she could be heard gasping for breath between stanzas. This is untrue: though she was dying and her voice had dropped a whole tone, her powers had diminished only slightly and her performance was well above average, marred only by the accoustics and the primitive recording technique. Neither was it her last recording, as will be revealed.

During the spring of 1963 Edith befriended a young *chanteuse* by the name of Jacqueline Danno – a former student with Mireille's Petit Conservatoire de la Chanson, my godmother, and today one of the most acclaimed and respected actresses in France. Never overtly fond of other female singers, Edith had been impressed with Jacqueline's 'Chez Lolita' and 'Mère doul-oureuse' – the latter, by Gilbert Bécaud, tells of a mother's anguish after finding her twenty-year-old son dead at the bottom of a ravine. 'Formidable,' she told the composer, 'Danno's found a new way to die. Get her to come and see me!' The meeting, however, could just as easily have ended in disaster, as Jacqueline explained:

I had also been the first to record Dumont's 'Les amants', and I was terrified in case this was brought up. It was, and she stunned me by telling me that my version was better than hers – such a *compliment*! Then we discovered that we had something else in common other than our record producer, Michel Poisson – she called him, in English, 'Mister Fish' – and that was our birth-signs. She was very much into birth-signs and lucky omens, and Sagittarius was, she said, the luckiest one in the zodiac, closely followed by Capricorn, Marlene's and Jesus's sign. After that I visited the apartment every week, until later that summer when Théo took her to the South. The last words she said to me were, 'Don't forget our dinner-date when I get back from my holidays!' I'm sure she was convinced that she'd beaten her illness.

On 10 April Edith was rushed into the Ambroise Paré Clinic at Neuilly, where doctors diagnosed an oedema of the lung. She lapsed into a coma, and for two weeks lay on the brink of death. Her recovery was nothing short of miraculous, and at the end of the month Théo took her to Cap Ferrat. Here he rented a villa, La Serena, initially for two months. For a little while she at least seemed to rally, and spent much of her time 'cheating at Scrabble' and living pretty much how she had lived at Boulevard Lannes – planning tours, rehearsing new songs and poring over manuscripts. Her strength returned sufficiently for her to have a violent quarrel with Claude Figus. The troublesome little secretary had revealed 'certain secrets' about Théo's private life to the press – one can only surmise what these must have been, and one wonders how much more he might have revealed had not Edith sent him packing. 'Théo put it about rather a lot,' one friend said, 'boys and girls, they were all the same to him, though nothing would have prevented him from worshipping the ground Piaf walked upon. He absolutely adored her!' Simone Margantin, the faithful but shrewd nurse, agreed, but added, 'There was never anything *physical* between Edith and Théo. She would never allow him to see her naked, and always locked the bathroom door in case he wandered in. No man had seen her naked since Cerdan, not even Jacques Pills.' Edith's argument with Figus took place after a journalist turned up at Boulevard Lannes, claiming that he had been invited there by 'Madame Piaf's secretary', who had said over the telephone that he had a story to sell concerning Théo's private life. Figus claimed that in his youth, Théo had worked as a rent-boy, which considering some of the company he kept before meeting Edith – Figus especially – may well have been true. Figus had also told the journalist, from the scurrilous *Noir et Blanc* which had already incurred her wrath, of Théo's involvement with Douglas Davies, which was *certainly* not an invention of his jealousy. As with Jean Louville, in Cannes, Théo threatened to sort out both Figus and the offensive reporter with his fists. Edith used a better tactic: she paid him to keep his mouth shut.

At La Serena, Edith entertained all her old friends, and there was even talk of an Olympia '63, with Théo as *vedette-américaine* and a place on the bill for his sister, Christine Lamboukas, whom she was 'coaching' – the first time she had ever played Svengali to another woman, and a venture which proved a dismal failure. Charles Aznavour and Denise Gassion were regular visitors. Jean Noli was there most of the time, adding the final touches to 'Ma vie', and there was a new song – 'Je m'en remets à toi', with music by Charles Dumont and astonishingly lovely lyrics by Jacques Brel. Edith did get around to taping the song: like 'Le Mur' and Georges Moustaki's 'Un jour' and 'Les filles d'Israël', it has never been released commercially for the world to appreciate and enjoy. Out of respect for Edith, Brel never sang the song himself.

In June 1963, Edith despatched a telegram to Raymond Asso, now sixty-two and himself ailing. If one is to believe the long-deposed poet, Edith was in a pretty despairing state and this was a plea from the heart, not unlike that other one after Leplée's murder. Even so, Asso did not go to her straight away, though when he did reach La Serena in the July, he was clearly shocked:

> I will not dwell on the lamentable picture that I saw. Sump-tuously clean, surrounded by an evil, pitiful band of clowns, like in a Pirandello drama, I discovered an absol-utely unrecognizable Piaf. She took me to one side, she weighed her words carefully. Raymond, it's very bad – I

think I'm done for, this time. Perhaps I still have a chance, with you. Since you're free, when I return to Paris you must come and live with me and rid me of all this trouble – all these people around me.'

'*All* of them?' I asked.

'Yes,' she said. 'All except for Loulou.'

It would have delighted Asso to have had her all to himself again after so many years, and no doubt he would have possessed a great deal more willpower than Théo, whose devotion towards Edith was so all-consuming that he tended to ignore much of what was going on around him. Asso promised Edith that they would set up house together in that October, and added that even if she *was* on the verge of death, then at least with him she would be able to die in an atmosphere of serenity. It never happened, of course, and when Théo discovered what had transpired, his reaction was to threaten Asso with legal action. It may also be that Edith's husband had begun to fear for his future, whether she recovered or not: even if a miracle did occur and she did get better, Théo was only too well aware of Edith's track-record for dumping her men once they had outlived their usefulness, or as in the case of Moustaki and Marten, become too big for their boots. He may have feared that, with her, even a husband would not be regarded as indispensable – as indeed had been proved by Jacques Pills. Had Edith been in better health, and effectively more active in music-hall circles and thus capable of taking on new challenges, then there would always have been the danger of her meeting someone new who might have posed as a threat to Théo, whose sexuality was perpetually in danger of exposure by the press. She was not, and as such he had nothing to worry about so long as she kept forking out hush-money.

Meanwhile, Edith continued working, although Simone Margantin banned her from staying awake all night. Friends have said that if Théo was the new Monsieur Piaf, he was never regarded by any of the household staff as *le patron*. This honour went to the stalwart nurse, who ruled over the proceedings like a benevolent dictator. Early in June, Edith and Théo made a tape recording on 'Un dimanche à Londres', an arrangement not unlike that for Dumont's 'Les amants', with Théo singing

Edith's lyrics whilst she chanted in the background. The quality was above average, though this did not prevent the 'owners' from hogging the recording for almost thirty years before handing it over for public consumption. It was released by Pathé-Marconi as a single, with Edith's September 1962 recording of 'Légende' . . . a 'send-up' of the song she had sung so dramatically at the Olympia in 1955.

Eventually, because the sea air was proving too much for her, Edith's doctors advised Théo to take her to Gatounière, a peaceful mountain retreat near Mougins. On 20 August she lapsed into a hepatic coma and was taken to the Meridien Clinic, at Cannes. Miraculously, she still clung to life and a few days later she was discharged and transferred yet again to Plascassier, a village near Grasse. The house, l'Enclos de la Bourre, has been described by one of the friends who visited her there as 'the most depressing prison on God's earth'.

Edith, confined to a wheelchair most of the time, was too ill to be aware of her surroundings, just as she was too frail to be told of the latest events in Paris. Jean Cocteau had already suffered one heart-attack. He sent her a message, which she may or may not have been shown. It read, 'My Edith. You and I have a knack of cheating death. You are one of the seven or eight people of whom I think lovingly each day of my life.' Now the great man was reputed to be close to death again.

Théo, too, was not much of a comfort simply because he was not always there. The film director Georges Franju had offered him a quite substantial role in *Judex*, which necessitated his making regular trips to Paris – Edith would not hear of him sacrificing his career for her, and it must be said that as an actor he showed great promise.

There were further complications when, on 5 September, the exiled Claude Figus was found dead in a Saint-Tropez hotel room. The official verdict was that he had taken an overdose of drugs, some said in a fit of remorse after being ousted by Piaf. An article, printed some years later in *Paris-Match* as part of Théo Sarapo's obituary, suggested that Figus may even have been murdered. This would have surprised few of those who knew him, considering the crowd he mixed with outside the Piaf household.

Simone Margantin gave strict instructions to the household

staff: Edith was not to be informed of Figus' death, for fear of the shock proving fatal. For more years than anyone cared to remember this peculiar little man had been Piaf's slave – her court jester, the butt of her cruellest jokes, who had also frequently taken the brunt of her unpleasant temper. Once, he had been imprisoned for several days for frying eggs for her breakfast – over the Flame at the Arc de Triomphe!

Between bouts of unconsciousness, Edith made the best of her time at Plascassier, though she pestered Théo to take her back to Paris as soon as he could. And during the afternoon of 20 September she gave her last press-interview, for *France-Soir*, concluding:

> Evidently there are always going to be these minor setbacks, though at the moment I'm very well and I expect to be back in Paris in about a month's time. There are going to be lots of new songs – I'm preparing for a new series of recitals. I've seen my doctor, and he changed my medication. It cost me a lot of money, but right now I'm fine. I expect to be recording in a couple of months, all being well . . .

After the interview, Edith and Théo were photographed in the garden at L'Enclos de la Bourre, taking a stroll with their black poodle – the first time, apparently, that she had taken much interest in anything with four legs since 'baptizing' her camel in North Africa. She also put on an impromptu 'fashion-show' for the reporter, proudly showing off the new coat which her husband had bought her in advance of their first wedding anniversary.

Théo Sarapo's surprisingly vicious temper has been mentioned, and although it took a great deal to actually *get* him angry, few people provoked him more, it would appear, than the irascible demon-spirit, Mômone. 'He loathed her and once said that he'd love nothing more than to strangle her with his bare hands,' Roger Normand said. 'Théo always believed that she and Denise Gassion were fakes who were only after Edith's money, but that she was scared of sending them packing in case they spun some yarn to the newspapers.'

Even so, when Mômone and her daughter turned up at the

beginning of October – 'on the cadge', as Edith put it – Simone Margantin's otherwise indomitable authority was overruled when Théo allowed Mômone to see Edith, but only as a last resort, to get rid of her. According to the nurse, the meeting lasted but a couple of minutes. Mômone, however, tells an entirely different story in her biography:

> Like a faithful dog, Théo stretched out at the foot of her bed, and that is how I shall always think of him – as a faithful dog with living eyes which would not face up to the reality that I had sensed straight away. The curtain was about to come down. At breakneck speed, she and I relived our forgotten hours. Edith saw her life so clearly, it frightened me. Then she looked up at Théo, and in her eyes I saw reflected all the joy that he gave her. Like a little sparrow's claw, her fingers closed over mine. The current between us flowed strongly, and warmly. I would have done anything to keep that current alive: I did not know then that there was nothing left to keep. Then she said, 'Watch out for yourself, Mômone. In this life you only pay for the stupid things you do. I can die now – I've lived twice already!' I kissed her, and said goodbye . . .

Many of Edith's friends believed that Edith had never forgiven her 'demon spirit' for stealing Marcel Cerdan's letters, and that it was probably Mômone who told Edith of Figus' death – adding as she did in her book, 'Little Claude had taken his own life to open the gates of heaven for my sister.' A great many people, myself included, firmly believe that this final, spiteful act only hastened Edith's end.

On 9 October 1963 – her first wedding anniversary – Edith sent Théo a card upon which she had scrawled, almost illegibly, 'I don't deserve a man like you, yet you're here all the same!' It was whilst he was reading this that she lapsed into the hepatic coma from which she never emerged.

Simone Margantin was sitting at her bedside when, at around midnight, her condition became critical and she suffered an internal haemorrhage. There was a storm brewing and the doctor, who in any case would not have been able to save her, could not reach the house until five the next morning. When he arrived he confirmed the worst: the world's greatest ever *chanteuse-réaliste* was dying. At noon, Danielle Bonel, Edith's secretary and the wife of Marc, her accordionist, was asked to summon a priest. Tragically, because of the storm she was unable to get through on the telephone.

The faithful, loving nurse spoke of Edith's last moments with infinite tenderness, 'At ten minutes past one her eyes opened . . . they seemed to be shining. Then they closed again, and her head drooped forwards.'

Edith had once said, 'I'm determined to come back to earth after my death . . .'

Epilogue

LES CLOCHES
SONNENT

Saint Thérèse did not allow Edith her dearest wish: to die in Paris, with a priest at her bedside. Although she actually died on 10 October, the newsflashes did not go out until seven the next morning. Edith Piaf, who had loved Paris like a lover, could not die in some provincial village, severed from her second heart – the people there would never have forgiven her, and even today there is a plaque over the entrance to Boulevard Lannes stating that she died there. Therefore, knowing that they were breaking the law, Théo and Simone Margantin travelled overnight with her body in the back of an ambulance; in her hands was a spray of mimosa which was preserved and kept by Théo for several years.

Edith was laid in state in her vast salon, her coffin surrounded by her *fétiches*: the statuette of Saint Thérèse, an epaulette from a légionnaire's uniform, letters from Marlene, Cerdan and Cocteau, a sailor's beret given to her in 1936 when she had visited Brest, and her rabbit's foot. All of these items would be buried with her.

Throughout the day, French radio stations played solemn music. The world wept, and Paris went mad with grief. No one, not even a president or any member of a defunct royal family, had been revered quite so much as the courageous little singer in the black dress who, for the best part of thirty years, had been its very soul. Even in Moscow, where she had never sung, a two-minute silence was observed. For a decade the people had truly believed this energy-charged soldier to be utterly invincible, immortal even. They had shared her joys and sorrows; they had helped her fight her final battle. Now, this army of admirers steadfastly refused to believe in her death. Within hours of the first newsflash, every Piaf record in France had been snapped up by bereaved fans. Boulevard Lannes was blocked by a 20,000-strong crowd of weeping admirers, chanting her name and saying prayers outside the railings of 67-bis.

For weeks, Edith would occupy the front pages of newspapers all over the world, and the obituaries and eulogies would be legion. Only one, however, by Jean Monteaux of *Arts*, ventured to declare what the others had been thinking:

> She picked *exactly* the right time to die. It's atrocious of me to say so, but only too true. And now she passes into the realm of legends. I could never imagine Edith Piaf dying at the age of eighty in an old people's home, with her finest years behind her. In leaving us at forty-seven, she remains immortal – indeed, her legend will only grow in future years.

Within the apartment, Edith had been embalmed. There was a constant stream of visitors: ashen-faced friends, colleagues, and ex-lovers. Her entourage were alarmed, fearing a riot as there had been at Valentino's funeral thirty-seven years before. Théo was advised to call in police reinforcements. In fact, he did exactly what Edith would have wanted him to do. He opened the doors of the apartment to the crowd – *la foule*, that contingent of unseen lovers to whom she had cried, 'I love you! You are my life!'

For two whole days a constant stream of people filed past her coffin, draped with the French flag as a tribute to all she had done for her country during the war. Incredibly, journalists and press photographers were allowed into the room. In order to camouflage the mortician's chin-rest, Simone Margantin had wound a length of green silk around Edith's face, securing it with a large bow. One reporter wrote that her head looked like an undersized Easter egg. Even more appalling was the sketch executed by Charles Kiffer on 12 October: this appeared in newspapers and even on an album cover with the words, Edith n'est plus!

On the morning of 11 October the television producer Louis

Mollion telephoned Jean Cocteau to arrange a radio broadcast: the poet, though very ill, had wanted to read a personal eulogy to his great friend. By the time Mollion and his crew arrived at Milly-sur-Forêt, they were too late. Cocteau had succumbed to a heart-attack. He had once said, 'If Piaf dies, part of me will die too.'

Edith was buried in the Père Lachaise cemetery on Monday 14 October, amidst one of the most emotional scenes Paris has ever seen. Her funeral remains the largest there has ever been for a popular personality: Valentino's had been almost as large, with the 'record' in Europe going to the Anglo-Belgian singer Harry Fragson, in 1914, and more recently to Fréhel in 1951. It is estimated that two *million* people lined the streets of Paris along the funerary route – almost the city's entire population – and as the cars passed by, eleven of them piled fifteen feet high with flowers, the people fell to their knees, making the sign of the Cross. Their devotion was quite extraordinary.

Within the cemetery, 40,000 people jostled and clambered over the gravestones, causing no little damage. Beside the grave, a detachment from the Foreign Legion stood to attention and gave a salute of honour – a year before they, like the OAS after the Algerian war, had adopted 'Non je ne regrette rien' as their theme song. Their enormous wreath of purple wild flowers was inscribed: A leur Môme Piaf – La Légion. Maurice Chevalier's wreath read: Sleep in peace, courageous little Piaf. Marlene Dietrich had arrived at the cemetery alone, dressed in black and wearing no make-up, and carrying a single rose. She turned to the crowd as she walked slowly towards the graveside and said, 'God, how they must have loved her!'

Edith's devotion towards God and Saint Thérèse had never been short of profound, even though she had not regularly attended Mass. 'The people would only stare,' she had said. Yet she had never been seen on stage or in public without her medallion or crucifix, and religion had played an important role in so many of her songs. 'She prayed like a little child,' Simone Margantin said. 'She never said Lord or Saviour. It was always Little Lord Jesus.' Now, she was given the supreme insult. The Pope, in his infinite wisdom, denied her a requiem mass and Christian burial, proclaiming that she had lived a life of public sin. 'She was but a prefabricated icon, and as such *deserves* no religious honours,' declared the *Osservatore Romano*. This caused a massive swell of public outrage, so much so that the Roman Catholic Archbishop of Paris, Cardinal Feltin, was forced to issue a formal statement to the effect that the Pope had turned his back on Edith because she had been a divorcée.

> The honours that the Church reserves for its dead cannot be rendered towards Edith Piaf because of this very irregular situation. Those who have appreciated the talents of Madame Piaf are deeply moved by her sudden death. Christians aware of her faith and charity will not fail to beseech Divine Mercy for her soul at the sacrifice of the Mass.

A priest, Père Thouvenin, and Bishop Martin kindly offered to say prayers over Edith's grave, to an unearthly silence. Théo could barely stand, and had to be supported by Louis Barrier – and Mômone, still craving attention, pushed her way to the front line of mourners which comprised Marlene, Aznavour, Jacques Pills, Herbert and Denise Gassion, Théo's parents and sisters, Suzanne Flon, Charles Dumont, Marcel Cerdan Jr, and almost every one of the Piaf Boys – not in Edith's favourite blue, this time, but in black.

Then, as *le fanion de la Légion* fluttered in the warm, autumnal sunshine, Edith's coffin was lowered end-first into the vault. In a moment's panic, the crowd surged forward and the barriers around the 97th Division gave way. Louis Barrier and Marlene managed to shove Théo into the back of his car, and climbed in after him – Marlene lost a shoe, which figured amongst the two hundred or so collected by the cemetery guardian the next day. The unfortunate Bruno Coquatrix was pushed into the grave, but was unhurt. Elsewhere an elderly admirer collapsed and died of a heart-attack and was taken away in the back of the hearse.

It was over.

During the next few days, over five million people filed past her expensive black marble tomb. After the funeral, Marlene had called in at Boulevard Lannes to bid farewell to Théo, before leaving for Cocteau's funeral at Milly-la-Forêt. Edith's death had affected her deeply, as she recalled:

> As you know, I myself was very busy travelling around the world with my stage-show, so there wasn't much time for us to meet during that last year. Thank God for the telephone. And thank God for that young man, who *had* been good for her, after all. He and I spoke many times on the telephone, and in the end I grew to like him. But, two funerals in as many days was more than anyone could bear, and after embracing the second widow [Jean Marais, Cocteau's long-time partner] I came to the conclusion that the next funeral I would be going to would be my own.

Marlene would stick to her word: after 1963 she would attend no more funerals, not even that of her own husband in 1976.

For a whole week, Théo shut himself away at Boulevard Lannes – even the household staff were not allowed near him, such was his wish to be left alone, and the telephone was left off the hook. Then, on 22 October, flinging open the shutters and opening the curtains, he set about fulfilling all the dinner engagements that Edith had arranged before leaving Paris. Jacqueline Danno was one of the first visitors to the apartment:

> It was both strange, and moving. No kinder, more generous a person than Théo has ever walked this earth, and the poor boy was *lost*. Everything in the apartment was exactly as Edith had left it, save for the living room, where every wall was covered in her photographs and posters. And at the head of the dining table, her place had been set as usual – only on her chair he had placed the mimosas which she had clasped in her dead hands during that last journey back to Paris. I felt so *numb*, watching him, that I could hardly eat. And even now I'm unable to remember who else was sitting at that table. It was soon after that dinner that all the staff were forced to leave. Poor Théo couldn't afford to keep them on, and they were just as distressed to be leaving him as he was, having to let them go.

On Christmas Eve 1963 – deliberately ill-timed – the bailiffs turned up at Boulevard Lannes and drew up a list of items to be sold in order to pay off some of Edith's debts. Amongst the items seized was an abstract painting by the Russian-born artist, André Lanskoy. This was bought back by André Schoeller, the director of an art gallery in Rue de Miromesnil who was now revealed as having had a brief, secretive affair with her during her 'adventure' with Moustaki. Schoeller had wanted to give her the painting as a gift: Edith had insisted on paying for it, and there had even been talk of Schoeller moving in with her and her adopting his child. For the last few years of her life the painting had hung over the television set in her room.

Théo Sarapo was left with an immense legacy of debts. For several years he worked hard in theatres – and was not always very well received, with the shouts of 'gigolo' still ringing loudly in his ears – until most of them had been paid off. *Judex*, his film with Georges Franju, was not the commercial success everyone had anticipated. In 1964 he honoured a contract which had been signed some time earlier with the Bobino, and aware that he was not yet ready for top-billing he pleaded with the management to be 'demoted' to someone else's *vedette-américaine*. Appallingly there was not one artiste in France who would agree to appear with him, and he battled through his short season of recitals alone. One song endeared him to his limited public. Written by Noël Commaret and Francis Lai, 'La maison qui ne chante plus' may now be regarded as Théo Sarapo's epitaph.

> Je partirais de la maison,
> La maison qui ne chante plus.
> Je n'aurais pour l'horizon
> Pour toujours que le monde inconnu.
> Je fermerais la porte
> Sur elle, et notre amour . . .
>
> [I will leave the house,
> The house which sings no more.
> My horizon evermore will be
> Only the unknown world.
> I will close the door
> On her, and our love . . .]

Bad luck dogged Théo for another six years. *Un conte*, his second film within which he starred opposite Michel Bouquet, was an above-average success in France and because of this he was offered a leading role in Jacques Fabbri's comedy-musical, *Les deux orphélines*. He should have made the grade as a singer – Bruno Coquatrix of the Olympia declared that had Edith lived a little longer, he would have done, for in France the age of the *yé-yé* had brought about a great change. Middle-of-the-road *chanteurs* of his calibre were much in demand, to cater for that section of the public who flocked to see the likes of Serge Lama and Claude Nougaro, then at the start of their careers.

Some of the songs which Théo recorded in the mid-sixties are astonishingly lovely and extremely well-performed: Edith's all-powerful influence, even from beyond the grave, afforded him only the best writers and composers. 'Sainte Sarah' came from the pen of Charles Aznavour, Moustaki wrote him 'Nous n'étions pas pareils', and from Maurice Vidalin there was perhaps the best song of his brief career, 'La ronde'.

Théo's last minor hit record in France was ironically entitled 'Oui je veux vivre' – Yes, I want to live. A few weeks after recording it, on 28 August 1970, he was killed in a car-crash outside Limoges, and it has subsequently proved difficult for anyone to prove that this was not suicide – close friends have stated persistently that Edith's death had robbed him of the will to go on living. He was just thirty-five, and perhaps his greatest consolation is that he now lies next to his wife, her father, and little Marcelle Dupont in the Père Lachaise cemetery where, until it was stolen, the plaque bore their photographs and the inscription which has become synonymous with the Piaf legend: 'Toujours avec nous'.

At the time of his death, Théo Sarapo was Honorary President of the Paris-based 'Les Amis d'Edith Piaf', founded in 1967 by a group of young admirers and still going strong, though today many of its big-name founder members are dead. The society holds regular meetings, there is an annual rally, and the 'Grand Prix Edith Piaf' is a prestigious award in its own right for amateur and professional singers alike.

Many of the old friends and retainers, alas, are also gone. Robert Chauvigny, her former musical director and arranger, died three months after Edith. Her first husband, Jacques Pills, died of a heart-attack a few weeks after Theo, just days after giving his last interview for the BBC. Edith would have been amused to observe that for once the newspapers revealed his *real* age – he was sixty-four.

Since then, others have passed on: Simone Margantin, Jean-Louis Jaubert, Francis Blanche, Paul Meurisse, René Rouzaud, Lucien Baroux, Julien Bouquet, Louiguy, Pierre Hiègel, Louis Dupont, Michel Simon, Marcel Achard, Manouche, Marcel Blistène, Damia, Marie Dubas, Michel Vaucaire, Bruno Coquatrix, Chevalier and Yves Montand. Marlene, the close friend we shared, died in May 1992.

Simone Berteaut, the incorrigible and frequently obnoxious demon spirit Mômone, succumbed to a heart-attack in May 1975. She had just completed her autobiography, *Mômone*, before retiring to Chartres with a homosexual companion, but he had recently walked out on her. Incredibly, although her famous biography had made her a millionairess virtually overnight, she died in debt, just as Edith had done, but much less loved and weighed down by remorse and regrets. At the time of writing her daughter runs a chain of clothes shops in one of Paris' notorious red-light districts.

A year or so before her death, Simone Berteaut sold the film rights to her book. The ensuing film, *Piaf*, was not a resounding success though it remains the best film-tribute thus far. Many of her songs in the film were sung by Betty Mars – the originals from the thirties could not be used because of the worn quality of the recordings, and Betty sang several songs which Piaf had sung in the streets. Her version of Jean Lenoir's 'Comme un moineau' is so breathtakingly superb that it brings tears to the eyes. Betty herself was a lovely lady, whose own life was hounded by sadness and tragedy. She sang for my wife and I in October 1982, on the occasion of our tenth wedding anniversary. Then, in February 1989 finding the pressures of life just that much too hard to bear, she took her own life.

There was another posthumous accolade in Paris in September 1981 when the Mayor, Jacques Chirac, inaugurated the Place Edith Piaf – this is at the crossing of Rue Belgrano and Rue Capitaine Ferber, not far from where Edith was born. It has the most delightful little bar where her records are played non-stop, and where the walls are filled with moving portraits and the instruction, PHOTOGRAPHIE INTERDIT. There is also a plaque on the wall in Rue Pierre-Charron, marking the spot where Gerny's once stood.

Since 1963 there have been innumerable contenders for the Piaf crown. Performers such as Patachou, Juliette Gréco, Colette Renard and Catherine Sauvage were unique whilst Edith was alive, and for many years continued a tradition which is now, sadly, dying out in an age when the intimacy of the theatre has given way to the greed-inspired world of the stadium. In the mid-sixties the stages of the Bobino and the Olympia were graced by the presence of three Piaf 'sound-alikes'. Betty Mars was by far the most convincing because, like Edith, she was a true 'enfant du faubourg'. Georgette Lemaire and Mireille Mathieu are still popular today, but decidedly middle-of-the-road. In 1985 the latter recorded an album of Piaf classics which, compared to her own big hits such as 'La dernière valse' and 'Mon credo', was poor.

The *réaliste* tradition in France was continued single-handedly in France by a woman of phenomenal talent: Barbara, recognized as the greatest European female entertainer since Piaf, and the only one who has been capable of surpassing her. Moreover, her lengthy career was never marred by scandal. Barbara emulated no one, and like her alter-idol always refused to sing in Britain, even though she asked me to adapt several of her songs into English. A tireless campaigner against injustice, the death penalty, sexual and racial prejudice, and for AIDS awareness, Barbara died in November 1997, whilst this book was in preparation. At the time of her death she had raised a staggering two hundred *million* francs for charity, and this book is dedicated to her.

DISCOGRAPHY

1935–45 Polydor; 1946–63 Pathé-Marconi; 1947–48 Decca; 1956 CBS (USA).

A complete guide to the recorded output of Edith Piaf which includes lyricists, composers, tape recordings (TR), acetates (AC) and live (LR) recordings of songs not recorded in the studio. The dates refer to the actual recording sessions and are not release dates. In her formative years Piaf frequently worked with musicians and orchestras provided by the studio. Between 1946 and 1962, however, her musical director was Robert Chauvigny, and unless otherwise stated it is he who was responsible for her arrangements and accompaniment during these years.

1935

15 October — *La java en mineur* [1] (Léo Poll, Raymond Asso, Marcel Delmas) TR made in Marie Dubas' dressing-room, ABC Music-Hall. Piano: Raymond Asso.

18 December — *Les mômes de la cloche* [1 & 2] (Decaye, Vincent Scotto); *La java de Cézigue* (Eblinger, Groffe); *Mon apéro* (Robert Juél, Robert Malleron). With Les Accordéons Médinger.
L'étranger [1] (Robert Juél, Robert Malleron, Marguerite Monnot).
L'étranger [2]. With slightly different lyrics. Both with piano accompaniment by Marguerite Monnot.

1936

10 January — *Les hiboux* [1] (E Joullot, P Dalbret). Accompanied by Les Accordéons Médinger.

15 January	*La fille et le chien* [1] (Jacques-Charles, Charles Borel-Clerc, Charles Pothier). Piano: Raymond Asso.
	Je suis mordue (Jean Lenoir, L Carol, R Delamare). Accompanied by Les Accordéons Médinger.
	Reste [1] (Will Léardy, Pierre Bayle, Jacques Simonot). Piano: Raymond Asso.
7 March	*Mon amant de la coloniale* (Raymond Asso, Robert Juél). Orchestra: Emile Stern.
24 March	*Fais-moi valser* (Charles Borel-Clerc, Telly); *Va danser* (Maurice Legay, Gaston Couté); *La Julie Jolie* (Léo Daniderff, Gaston Couté). Orchestra: Emile Stern.
	Quand-même (Louis Poterat, J Mario, Jean Wiener). From the film, *La Garçonne*. Piano: Jean Wiener.
31 March	*La fille et le chien* [2] Piano: Jacques-Charles. Guitar: Django Reinhardt.
7 May	*Les deux ménétriers* (Jean Richepin, Louis Durand). Orchestra: Emile Stern.
	Il n'est pas distingué (Paul Maye, Marc Hélly). Orchestra: Georges Aubanel.
8 May	*Y avait du soleil ce jour-la* (Jean Lenoir). Orchestra: Georges Aubanel.
23 October	*'Chand d'habits* (Jacques Bourgeat, R Alfred). Orchestra: Georges Aubanel. Directed by Emile Stern.
28 October	*La petite boutique* (Roméo Carlès, O Hodeige). Orchestra: Georges Aubanel.

1937

28 January	*Le contrabandier* (Gilles, Raymond Asso). Orchestra: Georges Aubanel.
	Ne m'écris pas (René Cloërec, Louis Lagard, Jean Rodor); *Mon légionnaire* [1] (Raymond Asso, Marguerite Monnot); *Le fanion de la Légion* [1]. In the latter the verse has a different melody to the 'regular' version. Orchestra: Emile Stern.
12 April	*Corrèque et reguyer* (Paul Maye, Marc Hélly).

Orchestra: Wal-berg, directed by Emile Stern. *

Dans un bouge du vieux port (André Liaunet, André Deltour). Orchestra: Wal-berg. *

Entre Saint-Ouen et Clignancourt (Adelmar Sablon, André Mauprey). Orchestra: Wal-berg. Accordion: Maurice Alexander. *

Mon coeur est au coin d'une rue (Henri Coste, Albert Lasry). Orchestra: Wal-berg. *

* On these recordings and on the corresponding sheet music Piaf is billed, 'Edith Piaff'.

24 June	*C'est toi le plus fort* [1] (Raymond Asso, René Cloërec). Piano: René Cloërec. *Browning* (Gilles, Raymond Asso); *Paris-Méditerranée* (Raymond Asso, René Cloërec); *Un jeune homme chantait* [1] (Raymond Asso, Léo Poll). Orchestra: Jacques Métehen.
12 November	*Ding din don* (Raymond Asso, Pierre Dreyfus); *Tout fout le camp* (Raymond Asso, Robert Juél); *Le fanion de la Légion* [2]. The latter is the 'regular' version. Orchestra: Jacques Métehen.
16 November	*Le chacal* (Raymond Asso, Charles Seider, Robert Juél); *J'entends la sirène* (Raymond Asso, Marguerite Monnot); *Le mauvais matelot* [1] (Raymond Asso, Pierre Dreyfus); *Partance* (Raymond Asso, Léo Poll). The last two songs are sung with Raymond Asso. Orchestra: Jacques Métehen.

1938

15 March	*Le fanion de la Légion* [3] Orchestra: Wal-berg. *Madeleine qu'avait du coeur* [1] (Raymond Asso, Max d'Yresne); *Les marins ca fait des voyages* (Raymond Asso, Mitty Goldin). Billed 'Edith Piaff' on labels and sheet-music. Orchestra: Jacques Métehen.
? September	*Le fanion de la Légion* [4]; *Madeleine qu'avait du coeur* [2]. Both AC. Orchestra: Wal-berg.
3 October	*C'est lui que mon coeur a choisi* (Raymond Asso, Max d'Yresne); *Le grand voyage du pauvre nègre* (Raymond Asso, René Cloërec); *Madeleine*

qu'avait du coeur [3]; *Le mauvais matelot* [2] solo version. Orchestra: Jacques Métehen.

12 November   *Mon légionnaire* [2] Orchestra: Jacques Métehen. Solo violin thought to be Stephane Grapelli.

? November   *La java en mineur* [2] Full-length version. Piano: Raymond Asso.

1939

31 May   *Les deux copains* (Raymond Asso, Charles Borel-Clerc); *Je n'en connais pas la fin, Le petit monsieur triste* (Raymond Asso, Marguerite Monnot): *Elle fréquentait la rue Pigalle.* The latter with dialogue by Raymond Asso. Orchestra: Jacques Métehen.

1940

18 March   *C'est la moindre des choses* [1], Sur une colline (Paul Misraki). Orchestra: Jacques Métehen.

20 March   *C'est la moindre des choses* [2] AC; *On danse sur ma chanson* (Raymond Asso, Léo Poll); *Y'en a un de trop* (Edith Piaf, Marguerite Monnot). Orchestra: Jacques Métehen. The latter song, written for Damia with a lyric entitled 'Un coin tout bleu', was not recorded at once by her: Piaf therefore wrote an 'alternative' lyric for herself.

5 April   *L'accordéoniste* [1] (Michel Emer); *Elle fréquentait la rue Pigalle* [2] AC, *Embrasse-moi* [1] (Wal-berg, Jacques Prévert); *Jimmy c'est lui* [1] (Kamkë, Wal-berg). The latter sung with Adrian Lamy. Orchestra: Wal-berg.

27 May   *L'accordéoniste* [2] Orchestra: Walberg. Accordion: Gus Viseur. This is the version usually issued on Philips-Polydor compilations.
Embrasse-moi [2]; *Escale* [2]; *Jimmy c'est lui* [2]; *C'était la première fois* (Edith Piaf, Marguerite Monnot). All AC. Orchestra: Jacques Métehen.

1941

27 May   *C'était un jour de fête* [1 & 2], *Où sont-ils mes petits copains?* [1 & 2], *J'ai dansé avec l'amour* [1] * (Edith Piaf, Marguerite Monnot); *C'est un*

monsieur très distingué (Edith Piaf, Louiguy). Orchestra: Jacques Métehen.
* from the film *Montmartre-sur-Seine*.

? November   *L'homme des bars* (Edith Piaf, Marguerite Monnot). Taken from the soundtrack of *Montmartre-sur-Seine* and released 1982. Orchestra: Johnny Uvergolts.

1942

9 February   *Le vagabond* [1] (Edith Piaf, Louiguy). Orchestra: Claude Normand. Sung with Yvon Jean-Claude and the Claude Normand Ensemble.

13 November   *Les hiboux* [2]; *Le vagabond* [3] AC. Orchestra: Claude Normand.

25 November   *Simple comme bonjour* (Roméo Carlès, Louiguy) written for *Montmartre-sur-Seine* but subsequently dropped; *Un coin tout bleu* (Edith Piaf, Marguerite Monnot), see also 20 March 1940; *Tu es partout* (Edith Piaf, Marguerite Monnot), also written for Damia, from film *Montmartre-sur-Seine*. Orchestra: Johnny Uvergolts.

1 December   *Le vagabond* [3 & 4] Orchestra: Paul Durand. Solo versions.

15 December   *C'était une histoire d'amour* (Henri Contet, Jean Jal). Orchestra: Claude Normand. From the film, *Étoile sans lumière*. Sung with Yvon Jean-Claude.

31 December   *Le disque usé* [1] (Michel Emer), *J'ai qu'a l'regarder* (Edith Piaf, Alex Siniavine). Orchestra: Paul Durand.

1943

2 January   *Je ne veux plus laver la vaiselle* (Henri Contet, Marguerite Monnot). Piano and orchestra: Paul Durand.

8 January   *Le brun et le blond, C'était si bon* (Henri Contet, Marguerite Monnot); *La valse de Paris* (Edith Piaf, Marguerite Monnot); *La demoiselle du cinquième* (Henri Contet, Louiguy). Orchestra: Paul Durand.

12 January   *Y'avait ses mains* (Edith Piaf, Raymond Asso).

Orchestra: Paul Durand.

18 January	*Le disque usé* [2], as Version 1; *Tu es partout* [2], as Version 1. Both AC.
10 February	*Monsieur Saint-Pierre* [1] (Henri Contet, Johnny Hess). Orchestra and children's choir: Guy Luypaerts.
14	*Chanson d'amour* (Henri Contet, Marguerite Monnot), *Monsieur Saint-Pierre* [2]. Orchestra and choir: Guy Luypaerts.
24 April	*Histoires de coeur* (Henri Contet, Marguerite Monnot, based on a concept by Edith Piaf). Orchestra: Claude Normand.
7 April	*C'est l'histoire de Jésus, Mon amour vient de finir* (Edith Piaf, Marguerite Monnot). Orchestra: Claude Normand. The latter song was written for *Montmartre-sur-Seine* but dropped when Piaf gave it to Damia.

1944

20 January	*Un monsieur me suit dans la rue* (Jean-Paul Lechanois, Jacques Besse). Orchestra: Guy Luypaerts. Piano solo: Georges Bartholé.
21 January	*Coup de grisou* (Henri Contet, Louiguy). Orchestra: Guy Luypaerts. Two versions exist of the same take, which runs at 4'20. The one frequently released runs at 3'18 and is minus the lengthy introduction.
27 January	*Le chasseur de l'hôtel* (Henri Bourtayre, Henri Contet); *C'est toujours la même histoire* (Daniel White, Henri Contet). Orchestra: Guy Luypaerts.
4 July	*Y a pas de printemps* [1] (Henri Contet, Marguerite Monnot) 'regular' version, 2'37, see also 9–3–46; *Les deux rengaines* (Henri Bourtayre, Henri Contet). Orchestra: Guy Luypaerts.
13 May	*Les gars qui marchaient* (Henri Contet, Marguerite Monnot). Orchestra and choir: Guy Luypaerts.
14 May	*Celui qui ne savait pas pleurait* (Henri Contet, Claude Normand); *Il riait* (Georges Bartholé, Henri Contet); *Regarde-moi toujours comme ça*

(Henri Contet, Marguerite Monnot). Orchestra: Guy Luypaerts.

26 June   *De l'autre côté de la rue* (Michel Emer); *Escale* [3]. Orchestra: Guy Luypaerts.

1946

Y a pas de printemps [2] Longer (4'35) version, with extra verse and chorus. Accordion: Marc Bonel. Piano: Robert Chauvigny. LR. Radio Suisse-Romande.

23 April   *Adieu mon coeur, C'est merveilleux, Le chant du pirate* (Henri Contet, Marguerite Monnot). Orchestra: Guy Luypaerts. From the film, *Étoile sans lumière*.

? May   *Johnny Fedora et Alice Bonnet-Bleu* (Allie Weubel, Ray Gilbert, Edith Piaf). Orchestra unknown. 'Mixed' to include a backing from the Andrews Sisters, for the film, *La boîte à musique* (US: *Make mine music*).

4 June   *Miss Otis regrette* (Cole Porter, Henneve, Palex); *Monsieur est parti en voyage* (Stephen Beresford, Jacques Larue). Both LR. Radio Suisse-Romande. Piano: Robert Chauvigny.

25 June   *Céline, Dans les prisons de Nantes, La complainte du roi Renaud, Le roi a fait battre tambour.* Traditional songs arranged by Marc Herrand and Louis Liebard. Sung with Les Compagnons de la Chanson. No musical accompaniment.
Les trois cloches (Gilles). Sung with Les Compagnons de la Chanson. No musical accompaniment. From the film, *Neuf garçons et un coeur*.

9 October   *Je m'en fous pas mal* (Michel Emer); *Le petite homme, Mariage* (Henri Contet, Marguerite Monnot) the latter from the film, *Étoile sans lumière*; *La grande cité (Comme c'est drôle)* (Edith Piaf, Marguerite Monnot) AC; *Un refrain courait dans la rue* (Edith Piaf, Robert Chauvigny), *La vie en rose* (Edith Piaf, signed for publication by Louiguy and created by Marianne Michel in

1945) The last two songs from the film, *Neuf garçons et un coeur*. Orchestra, all: Guy Luypaerts.

6 December — *Une chanson à trois temps* [1] (Anna Marly). Orchestra: Guy Luypaerts.

7 December — *C'est toi le plus fort* [2] *, *Sans y penser* (Norbert Glanzberg) *, *Dans ma rue* (Jacques Datin) **, *La fille en bleue* (Traditional, arranged by Marc Herrand) *** Four songs performed live on Radio Suisse-Romande.
* Piano: Norberg Glanzberg. ** Piano: Jacques Datin. *** With Les Compagnons de la Chanson, no accompaniment.

1947

6 January — *Le rideau tombe avant la fin* (Jean-Marc Thibault, Jacques Besse), *Elle avait son sourire* (Daniel White, J P Laspeyres). LR. Radio Suisse-Romande.

6 February — *Les cloches sonnent* (Edith Piaf, Marguerite Monnot), *Le geste, Monsieur Ernest a réussi, Si tu partais* [1] (Michel Emer). Orchestra: Raymond Legrand.

7 February — *Une chanson à trois temps* [2], *Sophie* (Edith Piaf, Norbert Glanzberg). The latter from the film, *Neuf garçons et un coeur*. Orchestra: Raymond Legrand.

6 October — *Douce nuit* (F Gruber, Jean Brousolle). AC. Sung with Les Compagnons de la Chanson. No accompaniment. *Qu'as tu fait John?* (Michel Emer).

7 October — *C'est pour ca* [1] (Henri Contet, Marguerite Monnot) sung with Les Compagnons de la Chanson, from the film, *Neuf garçons et un coeur*; *Un homme comme les autres* (Edith Piaf, Pierre Roche).

? October — *Un air d'accordéon, Black boy* (Michel Emer), *Clair de lune*. All AC. No other details.

1948

11 June	*Monsieur Lenoble* (Michel Emer), *Boléro* (Henri Contet, Paul Durand). Orchestra: Guy Luypaerts. *Les amants de Paris* (Léo Ferré, Eddie Marnay), *Il pleut* (Charles Aznavour, Pierre Roche).
12 July	*Monsieur X* (Michel Emer, Roger Gaze), *Les vieux bateaux* (Jacques Bourgeat, Jacqueline Batell). Orchestra: Raymond Legrand.
21 July	*Il a chanté* (Cécile Didier, Marguerite Monnot) Sung with Marcel Jiteau.
6 August	*Amour du mois de mai* (Jacques Larue, Norbert Glanzberg), *Cousu de fil blanc* (Michel Emer). Orchestra: Raymond Legrand.

During 1946–8, whilst deciding whether to extend her contract with Decca, or record exclusively for Pathé-Marconi, Edith Piaf made acetates and tape-recordings of a number of songs which subsequently were released by neither. It is not always known which company was responsible for each song, and other details are sketchy. The songs are: *Vol de nuit, Blues de février, Pas une minute de plus, Monsieur Lévy* (Edith Piaf, Marguerite Monnot, possibly for Decca, 12/7/48); *Le gilet, J'ai dansé avec l'amour* (with amended lyrics), *Moi je sais qu'on se reverra* (Edith Piaf, Marguerite Monnot, 1948); *Le pauvre homme, Blues d'octobre* (Michel Emer, 1948); *Poker* (Charles Aznavour, Pierre Roche, 1948); *Pourquoi m'as-tu trahi?, Le routier, Sans faire de phrase, Les yeux de ma mère, Y'avait une voix qui se lamentait* (Edith Piaf, Marguerite Monnot, May 1948).

1949

3 February	*Dany* (Edith Piaf, Marguerite Monnot); *Le prisonnier de la tour* (Francis Blanche, Gérard Calvi); *Paris* (André Bernheim). The latter from the film, *L'homme aux mains d'argile*.
9 February	*Pour moi toute seule* (Michel Philippe-Gérard, Flavien Monod, Guy Lafarge), *Tu n'as pas besoin d'mes rêves* (Edith Piaf, Marguerite Monnot).
1 March	*Bal dans ma rue* (Michel Emer).

| 21 July | *Pleure pas* (Henri Contet, Aimé Barelli), *L'orgue des amoureux* (Francis Carco, André Varel, Charlie Bailly). |
| ? December | *You're too dangerous chéri* (Edith Piaf). First English version of 'La vie en rose', written by Piaf in 1948 for Gracie Fields. Orchestra: Daniel White. LR. Copacabana Club, Paris. |

1950

2 May	*Hymne à l'amour* (Edith Piaf, Marguerite Monnot). From the film, *Paris chante toujours!*
11 May	*La petite Marie* (Edith Piaf, Marguerite Monnot).
19 June	*Tous les amoureux chantent* (Jean Jeepy, Marguerite Monnot), *Le ciel est fermé* (Henri Contet, Marguerite Monnot).
20 June	*La fête continue* (Michel Emer), *Il fait bon t'aimer* (Jacques Plante, Norbert Glanzberg), *Le chevalier de Paris* (Angèle Vannier, Michel Philippe-Gérard). The latter obtained le Grand Prix du Disque, 1952.
7 July	*C'est un gars* (Charles Aznavour, Pierre Roche), *C'est de la faut à tes yeux* (Edith Piaf, Robert Chauvigny).
8 July	*Hymn to love* [1] (Edith Piaf, Marguerite Monnot, Eddie Constantine), original title, 'Hymne à l'amour'; *Just across the way* (Michel Emer, Christopher Hassall), original title, 'De l'autre côté de la rue'; *The three bells* (Gilles, Bert Reisfeld), solo version, original title, 'Les trois cloches'; *La vie en rose* [1] (Edith Piaf, Louiguy, Mac David), sung in English, 'drums' version. *If you go* (Michel Emer, Geoffrey Parsons), sung in English, original title 'Si tu partais'; *All my love* (Paul Durand, Mitchel Parish) original title, 'Boléro'.
10 July	*Il y avait* (Charles Aznavour, Pierre Roche), *Simply a waltz* (Norman Wallace). An original song, never sung in French, written especially for Piaf to sing before General Eisenhower.
11 July	*Don't cry* [1] (Edith Piaf, Eddie Constantine), original title, 'C'est de la faute à tes yeux', *'Cause*

I love you [1] (Edith Piaf, Eddie Constantine), original title, 'Du matin jusqu'au soir'.

? July   *Je n'attends plus rien* [1] (Melleville, Guillermin, Cazaux), *Le dénicheur* [1] (Gibert, Agel, Daniderff) both TR extracts; *Les feuilles mortes* (Joseph Kosma, Jacques Prévert). AC, for release in USA.

1951

6 April   *Demain il fera jour* (Marcel Achard, Marguerite Monnot) *

11 April   *Du matin jusqu'au soir* (Edith Piaf) *, *L'homme que j'aimerais* (Marcel Achard, Marguerite Monnot) *

13 April   *Avant l'heure, Si si si* (Marcel Achard, Marguerite Monnot) * the latter sung with Eddie Constantine; *Rien de rien* (Charles Aznavour, Pierre Roche) *

15 April   *Chanson bleue* [1] (Edith Piaf, Marguerite Monnot), *Du matin jusqu'au soir* [2]. Piano: Marguerite Monnot. LR broadcast from Orly airport, Paris; *Dans tes yeux, La valse de l'amour, C'est toi* [1 and 2] (Edith Piaf, Marguerite Monnot) * the latter sung French/English with Eddie Constantine, *Chanson bleue* [2].
     * From the operetta, *La p'tite Lili*.

4 July   *Chante-moi* (Edith Piaf) sung with Marcel Jiteau, *Une enfant* (Charles Aznavour, Robert Chauvigny).

15 October   *Plus bleux que tes yeux* (Charles Aznavour), *Je hais les dimanches* (Charles Aznavour, Florence Véran), *Padam padam* (Henri Contet, Norbert Glanzberg).

8 November   *Jézèbel* (Wayne Shanklin, Charles Aznavour) an adaptation of the American song created by Frankie Laine; *La chanson de Catherine* (Pierre Damine, Joumiaux, Youri) awarded Prix Concours de Deauville, 1951; *La rue aux chansons* (Michel Emer).

23 November   *A l'enseigne de la fille sans coeur* (Gilles), *Noël de la rue* (Henri Contet, Marc Heyral).

25 November   *Télégramme* [1] (Michel Emer).

1952
28 June   *Mon ami m'a donné* (Raymond Asso, Claude Valéry), *Au bal de la chance* (Jacques Plante, Norbert Glanzberg); *Je t'ai dans la peaux* [1] (Jacques Pills, Gilbert Bécaud) from the film, *Boum sur Paris!*

3 September   *Les amants de Venise* [1 and 2] (Jacques Plante, Marguerite Monnot) the latter with extra couplet at end; *Bravo pour le clown* (Henri Contet, Louiguy), *Les croix* (Gilbert Bécaud, Louis Amade), *Jean et Martine* (Michel Emer), *Pour qu'elle soit jolie ma chanson* (Edith Piaf, Louiguy) the latter sung with Jacques Pills, from the film, *Boum sur Paris!*

11 December   *Et moi, Soeur Anne, N'y va pas Manuel* (Michel Emer); *Le diable est près de moi* (Edith Piaf, Marguerite Monnot).

14 December   *L'effet qu'tu me fais* (Edith Piaf, Marc Heyral), *Cri d'amour* (André Varel, Charlie Bailly).

24 December   *Heureuse* [1] René Rouzaud, Marguerite Monnot); *Johnny tu n'es pas un ange* (A traditional Romanian folk-song arranged by Les Paul, Paddy Roberts and Marcel Stellman as 'Johnny is the boy for me'. French lyrics by Francis Lemarque).

1954
16 February   *La goualante du pauvre Jean* (René Rouzaud, Marguerite Monnot).

10 April   *Le 'ça ira'* [1] (Ladré, Bécourt) sung with male voice choir; *Le 'ça ira'* [2] sung without choir. From the film, *Si Versaille m'était conté*.

20 October   *Avec ce soleil* [1] (Jacques Larue, Michel Philippe-Gérard), *Sous le ciel de Paris* [1] (Jean Dréjac, Hubert Giraud) sung with choir; *Avec ce soleil* [2], *Sous le ciel de Paris* [2] sung without choir.

27 October   *Mea culpa* (Michel Rivgauche, Hubert Giraud), *Enfin le printemps* (René Rouzaud, Marguerite Monnot).

23 November   *L'homme au piano* (Henning and Terningsohn, Jean-Claude Darnal), original title, 'Mein Klavier'.

13 December   *Sérénade du pavé* (Jean Varney). Created by Eugénie Buffet in 1895, from the film, *French Can-Can*.

19 December   Medley: *Le dénicheur/Je n'attends plus rien/Dans les bars c'est la nuit*. TR. Sung in a Paris street, with accordion accompaniment by Maurice Alexander; *Tous mes rêves passés* (Edith Piaf, Marguerite Monnot) AC.

1955

27 January   *L'accordéoniste* [3] LR, Paris Olympia. This version, with the applause edited out, remains the best-known; *Légende* (Edith Piaf, Gilbert Bécaud) TR, Paris Olympia.

28 February   *C'est à Hambourg* (Michèle Senlis, Claude Delécluse, Marguerite Monnot), *Le chemin des forains* (Jean Dréjac, Henri Sauget), *Un grande amour qui s'achève* (Edith Piaf, Marguerite Monnot), *Miséricorde* (Jacques Larue, Michel Philippe-Gérard).

1956

4 January   *Allentown Jail* (Irving Gordon) TR: Carnegie Hall.

8 February   *Les amants d'un jour* (Michèle Senlis, Claude Delécluse, Marguerite Monnot), *Soudain une vallée* (Charles Meyer, Biff Jones, Jean Dréjac), original title: 'Suddenly there's a valley'.

28 February   *L'homme à la moto* (Jerry Lieber, Mike Stoller, Jean Dréjac), original title: 'Black denim trousers and motorcycle boots'.

8 March   *Avant nous* (René Rouzaud, Marguerite Monnot).

20 June   *Toi qui sais, Une dame* (Michel Emer).

4 July   *Et pourtant* (Michel Emer, Pierre Brasseur); *Marie la Francaise* [1 and 2] (Jacques Larue, Michel Philippe-Gérard) the latter with different

	musical arrangement; *Dis-moi* (Charles Aznavour, G Wagenheim) AC.
11 July	*Heaven have mercy* ['Miséricorde'], *One little man* ['Le petit homme'], *I shouldn't care* ['Je m'en fous pas mal'] English lyrics by Rick French; *My lost melody* ['Je n'en connais pas la fin'] English lyrics by Harold Rome; *La vie en rose* [2] English version, without drums; *Hymn to love* [2], *'Cause I love you* [2], *Don't cry* [2] new arrangements by Edith Piaf; *Autumn leaves* [2] English lyrics by Johnny Mercer; *Suddenly there's a valley*; *Chante-moi darling sing to me* ['Chante-moi'] English lyrics by Mac David.
16 November	*Une jeune apatride, Pleine de la nostalgie* (Edith Piaf, Marguerite Monnot). LR, A la Porte St-Jean, Quebec.

1957

13 January	*C'est pour ça* [2], *Je t'ai dans la peau* [2], *Les grognards* [2], *Heureuse* [2], sung in English/French, English lyrics by Edith Piaf; *Lovers for a day* ['Les amants d'un jour'], *The highway* ['Un jeune homme chantait'] English lyrics by Rick French; *Autumn leaves* ['Les feuilles mortes'] rearranged version; *La vie en rose* [3] sung in English/French; *If you love me, really love me* ['Hymn à l'amour'] English lyrics by Geoffrey Parsons. All LR, Carnegie Hall, New York.
25 November	*La foule* (Angel Cabral, Michel Rivgauche), original title: 'Amor di mis amores', created by Carmella. *Les grognards* (Pierre Delanoë, Hubert Giraud) studio version, sung in French; *Opinion publique* (Henri Contet, Marguerite Monnot); *Salle d'attente* (Michel Rivgauche, Marguerite Monnot); *Les prisons du roi* (Irving Gordon, Michel Rivgauche), original title: 'Allentown Jail'.
7 December	*Comme moi* (Michèle Senlis, Claude Delécluse, Marguerite Monnot).

1958

21 March | *Mon manége à moi* (Jean Constantin, Norbert Glanzberg).

27 March | *Les amants de demain* (Henri Contet, Marguerite Monnot), *Fais comme si* (Michel Rivgauche, Marguerite Monnot). From the film, *Les amants de demain*.

3 July | *Un étranger* [1] (Georges Moustaki, Norbert Glanzberg), *Le ballet des coeurs* (Michel Rivgauche, Norbert Glanzberg).

2 September | *Les neiges de Finlande, Tant qu'il y aura des jours* (Henri Contet, Marguerite Monnot). From the film, *Les amants de demain*.

3 September | *C'est un homme terrible* (Jean-Pierre Moulin); *Le gitan et la fille, Les orgues de barbarie, Eden blues* (Georges Moustaki); *Un étranger* [2] (Georges Moustaki, Evan, Robert Chauvigny) different melody, the version regularly issued on compilations.

4 September | *Je me souviens d'une chanson* (Jean-Pierre Moulin, Félix Marten); *Tatave* (Albert Simonon, Henri Crolla); *Je sais comment* (Julien Bouquet, Robert Chauvigny); *Mon amour je t'aime* (Michel Rivgauche, Marguerite Monnot) TR.

? October | *When the world was young* ['Le chevalier de Paris'] with English lyrics by Johnny Mercer. TR, New York.

1959

? January | *Faut pas qu'il se figure* [1] (Michel Rivgauche, Georges Moustaki) TR, New York.

24 February | *Milord* (Georges Moustaki, Marguerite Monnot, Rick French), *The gypsy* ['Le gitan et la fille'] English lyrics, Rick French; *Madame la Vièrge Marie* (Georges Moustaki). All TR, New York.

5 August | *T'es beau tu sais* (Henri Contet, Georges Moustaki), *Milord*, sung in French.

1960

? January   *C'est l'amour* [1] (Edith Piaf, Marguerite Monnot). Piano: Marguerite Monnot. TR.

? April   *Embrasse-moi* [2] Piano: Robert Chauvigny. TR.

13 May   *Ouragan* (Claude Léveillé, Michel Rivgauche), *C'est l'amour* [2] Studio version.

20 May   *Les amants merveilleux* (Robert Gall, Florence Véran), *Cri du coeur* (Jacques Prévert, Henri Crolla), *Je suis à toi* (Julien Bouquet), *Le vieux piano* (Henri Contet, Claude Léveillé).

27 May   *Le long des quais, Rue de Siam* (Henri Contet, Claude Léveillé); *Boulevard du Crime* (Michel Rivgauche, Claude Léveillé).

? October   *C'est fous que j'peux t'aimer* [1] (Michel Rivgauche, Charles Dumont). Later known as 'Les mots d'amour'. TR.

10 November   *Non je ne regrette rien* (Michel Vaucaire, Charles Dumont), *La vie l'amour* (Michel Rivgauche, Robert Chauvigny).

24 November   *Les mots d'amour* [2], *Jérusalem* (Jo Moutet, Robert Chabrier).

12 December   *Mon Dieu* (Michel Vaucaire, Charles Dumont) sung in French, *Des histoires* (Michel Vaucaire, Charles Dumont).

15 December   *La ville inconnue* (Michel Vaucaire, Charles Dumont), *Je m'imagine* (Nita Raya, Marguerite Monnot).

22 December   *T'es l'homme qu'il me faut, La belle histoire d'amour* (Edith Piaf, Charles Dumont); *Les flons-flons du bal* (Michel Vaucaire, Charles Dumont).

29 December   *Les blouses blanches* (Michel Rivgauche, Marguerite Monnot) LR, Paris Olympia.

? December   *Kiosque à journaux, Le métro de Paris* (Pierre Lacotte, Michel Rivgauche, Claude Léveillé); *Non la vie n'est pas triste* (Edith Piaf, Claude Léveillé). These songs, extracts from the ballet, *La voix*, were recorded on tape and released posthumously. The latter was given a new arrangement by Gilles Vigneault and became 'L'hiver'.

1961

25 January   *Toujours aimer* (Nita Raya, Charles Dumont), *Dans leur baiser* (Michel Vaucaire, Charles Dumont), *Mon vieux Lucien* (Michel Rivgauche, Charles Dumont).

3 February   *Marie Trottoir* (Michel Vaucaire, Charles Dumont), *Exodus* [1 and 2] (Eddie Marnay, Ernest Gold). Version 2 has a different arrangement.

2 March   *Le billard électrique* (Louis Poterat, Charles Dumont), *Faut pas qu'il se figure* [2] (Michel Rivgauche, Charles Dumont). This was the version released by Pathé-Marconi, though on stage Piaf always sang the Moustaki melody.

13 March   *Mon Dieu*, English lyrics by Dallas; *No regrets* ['Non je ne regrette rien']. English lyrics by Hal David; *In Jerusalem* [Jérusalem]. English lyrics by Dallas.

23 March   *Le bruit des villes* (Louis Poterat, Charles Dumont), *C'est peut-être ça* [1] (Michel Vaucaire, Charles Dumont).

4 April   *Carmen's Story* (Michel Rivgauche, Charles Dumont). Sung in French; *Qu'il était triste cet anglais* [1 and 2]. Sung partly in English.

? April   *C'est peut-être ça* [2]. Piano: Charles Dumont. TR.

17 May   *Les amants* (Edith Piaf, Charles Dumont). Sung with Charles Dumont.

? May   *Non je ne regrette rien* (lyricists unknown). Sung in German; *Les bluets d'azur* (Jacques Larue, Guy Magenta); *Quand tu dors* (Jacques Prévert, C Verger). Piano: Charles Dumont. All TR.

1962

26 January   *Fallait-il* (Michel Vaucaire, Charles Dumont), *Toi tu l'entends pas* (Pierre Delanoë, Charles Dumont).

15 February   *Polichinelle, Une valse* (Jacques Plante, Charles Dumont).

22 February   *Ca fait drôle* (Jacques Plante, Charles Dumont),

	On cherche un auguste (Robert Gall, Charles Dumont).
19 April	*Inconnu excepté de Dieu* (Louis Amade, Charles Dumont). Sung with Charles Dumont.
20 April	*Les amants de Téruel, Quatorze juillet* (Jacques Plante, Mikis Théodorakis). From the film, *Les amants de Téruel*.
4 May	*Le petit brouillard* (Jacques Plante, Francis Lai).
3 September	*Musique à tout va* (René Rouzaud, Francis Lai), *Emporte-moi* (Jacques Plante, Francis Lai), *A quoi ça sert l'amour?* (Michel Emer). The latter sung with Théo Sarapo.
20 September	*Légende* [2]. Satirical arrangement of the Michel Emer song by Edith Piaf. Piano: Noël Commaret, TR; *Le diable de la Bastille* (Pierre Delanoë, Charles Dumont); *Le droit d'aimer* [1] (Robert Nyel, Francis Lai). Orchestra: Jean Léccia.
21 September	*Roulez tambours* (Edith Piaf, Francis Lai).
13 November	*Le droit d'aimer* [2]. Orchestra: Robert Chauvigny.
3 December	*Le rendez-vous* [1]. (René Rouzaud, Francis Lai).
12 December	*Le rendez-vous* [2]. Reworked LR, Nimegue, Holland.
? December	*Les amants du dimanche* (Edith Piaf, Francis Lai).

1963

? January	*Les filles d'Israël* (Georges Moustaki, C Rolland, G Bonnin) TR.
18 February	*Les gens* (Michèle Vendôme, Francis Lai), *C'était pas moi* (Robert Gall, Francis Lai); *Monsieur Incognito, Traqué* (Florence Véran, Robert Gall); *J'en ai tant vu* (Michel Emer); *Tiens v'là un marin* (B Labadie, Julien Bouquet); *Le chant d'amour* (Edith Piaf, Charles Dumont); *Margot Coeur-Gros* (Michèle Vendôme, Florence Véran. Orchestra: Noël Commaret. LR Bobino Music-Hall.
7 April	*L'homme de Berlin* (Michèle Vendôme, Francis Lai) TR. Accordion: Francis Lai. Piano: Noël Commaret. Recording first released 1968.
? June	*Un dimanche à Londres* (Edith Piaf, Florence

	Véran) TR. Orchestra: Noël Commaret. Sung with Théo Sarapo.
? August	*Un jour* (Georges Moustaki, C Rolland); *Je m'en remets de toi* (Jacques Brel); *Le mur* (Michel Vaucaire, Charles Dumont). Piano: Noël Commaret. All TR made in Cannes.

RECORDINGS:
Around ninety-five per cent of the Piaf output has been released in France between 1936 and the present day. Most of her songs have been released in Britain, but her actual recordings are far too numerous to mention. Worldwide, her (and Théo Sarapo's) most sought-after recordings have been the extended-play and ten-inch LPs released in France between 1952 and 1970. All are now deleted, and are as follows:

EXTENDED PLAY
SCRF 103:	Je t'ai dans la peau; Monsieur et madame.
SCRF 121:	Bravo pour le clown; Les amants de Venise.
SCRF 126:	Les croix; Jean et Martine.
SCRF 134:	La goualante du pauvre Jean; Soeur Anne.
ESRF 1022:	La goualante du pauvre Jean; Heureuse; Johnny tu n'es pas un ange; Soeur Anne.
ESRF 1023:	Padam padam; Jézébel; Mariage; Les amants de Venise.
ESRF 1036:	C'est à Hambourg; Le chemin des forains; L'homme au piano; Retour.
ESRF 1051:	La vie en rose; Les trois cloches; Hymne à l'amour; L'accordéoniste.
ESRF 1070:	Soudain une vallée; L'homme à la moto; Avant nous; Les amants d'un jour.
ESRF 1135:	Les grognards; Les prisons du roi.
ESRF 1136:	La foule; Comme moi; Salle d'attente.
ESRF 1174:	Mon manège à moi; Fais comme si; Le ballet des coeurs; Étranger.
ESRF 1197:	*Edith Piaf chante Jo Moustaki*: Eden blues; Les orgues de barbarie; Le gitan et la fille. Sleeve notes: Georges Brassens.
ESRF 1198:	*Edith Piaf chante les airs du film 'Les amants de demain'*: Les amants de demain; Les neiges de

Finlande; Fais comme si; Tant qu'il y aura des jours. Sleeve notes: Marcel Blistène.

ESRF 1215: C'est un homme terrible; Je me souviens d'un chanson; Tatave.

ESRF 1245: Milord; Je sais comment.

ESRF 1262: Boulevard du Crime; La ville inconnue; La vie l'amour.

ESRF 1289: Les amants merveilleux; Cri du coeur; C'est l'amour. Cover: Douglas Davies.

ESRF 1292: Ouragan; Opinion publique; Le vieux piano. Cover: Douglas Davies.

ESRF 1303: Non je ne regrette rien; Les mots d'amour; Jérusalem. First pressing. Cover: Leloir.

ESRF 1305: *Edith Piaf chante Charles Dumont*: Mon Dieu; Les flons-flons du bal; La belle histoire d'amour. Sleeve notes: Edith Piaf.

ESRF 1306: Exodus; Marie Trottoir; Dans leur baiser.

ESRF 1312: Non je ne regrette rien; Les mots d'amour; Toujours aimer; Mon vieux Lucien. Second pressing. Cover: Levin.

ESRF 1319: *Edith Piaf et Charles Dumont chantent l'amour*: Les amants; C'est peut-être ça; La fille qui pleurait dans la rue.

ESRF 1357: *Chansons à la Une*: Toi tu l'entends pas; Ça fait drôle; Fallait-il, Polichinelle.

ESRF 1361: Emporte-moi; Le petit brouillard; Musique à tout va; A quoi ça sert l'amour?

ESRF 1371: Le droit d'aimer; Le rendez-vous; Roulez tambours.

ESRF 1466: *Edith Piaf avec Les Compagnons de la Chanson*: Les trois cloches; Dans le prisons de Nantes; Le roi a fait battre tambour; Céline.

ESRF 1921: L'homme de Berlin; Traqué; Le diable de la Bastille; Les gens. Sleeve notes: Francis Lai.

EDITH PIAF LONG PLAY

FS 1008: La vie en rose; C'est de la faut à tes yeux; La fête continue; Hymne à l'amour; Je hais les dimanches; Padam padam; Plus bleu que tes yeux; Jézébel.

FS 1037: Soeur Anne; Heureuse; N'y va pas Manuel; Et moi; Les amants de Venise; La goualante du pauvre Jean; Johnny tu nees pas un ange; Le 'ça ira'; Bravo pour le clown; L'éffet que tu me fais.

FS 1049: *Edith Piaf à l'Olympia*: Heureuse; Avec ce soleil; C'est à Hambourg; Légende; Enfin le printemps; Miséricorde; Je t'ai dans la peau; La goualante du pauvre Jean; Bravo pour le clown; Padam padam.

FS 1075: *Edith Piaf à l'Olympia*: Comme moi; Salle d'attente; Les prisons du roi; La foule; Les grognards; Mon manége à moi; Bravo pour le clown; Hymne à l'amour.

FS 1083: *Huit chansons nouvelles*: C'est l'amour; Ouragan; T'es beau to sais; Cri du coeur; Le vieux piano; Les amants merveilleux; Je suis à toi; Opinion publique.

FS 1103: Le billard électrique; Faut-pas qu'il se figure; Carmen's Story; Qu'il était triste cet anglais.

FS 1104: Les amants de Teruèl; Quatorze juillet; Toi tu l'entends pas; Polichinelle; Ça fair drôle; On cherche un Auguste; Une valse; Fallait-il.

THÉO SARAPO EXTENDED PLAY

ESRF 1366: Pour qui tu prends (song by Piaf-Lai); Départ (Piaf-Lai); Chez Sabine (Piaf-Véran).

ESRF 1374: Les enfants de la mode (Piaf-Lai); Pense à moi (Piaf-Lai); Les mains (Piaf-Lai); Garce de vie (Piaf-Lai).

ESRF 1383: Un dimanche à Londres, La bande en noir (Piaf-Véran); A l'aube (Piaf-Lai); Les rebelles (Vendôme-Véran).

ESRF 1393: Chanson d'amour d'aujourd'hui, Bluff! (Piaf-Lai); Ce jour viendra (Delanoë-Denoncin); Pourquoi je l'aime (Raya-Maine).

ESRF 1450: La maison qui ne chante plus (Gall-Commaret); Les filles c'est comme ça (Berney-Fontenoy-Kesslair); J'ai laissé (Nencioli, Revaux); La vie continue (Delanoë-Stanrey).

ESRF 1771: Le jour où tu sauras (Fontane); La solitude

(Commaret-Richit-Carriere); Le coeur au soleil (Commaret-Carriere); New York (Commaret-Carriere).

ESRF 1851:   L'age ingrat (Commaret-Sarapo); Dis-moi Alice (Commaret-Sarapo); J'préfère aller au cinéma (Commaret-Sarapo); Les amours sans issus (Commaret-Sarapo).

SCRF 627:   Les rebelles; La bande en noir.

ESRF 1906:   Tous mes chemins (Sarapo-Commaret); Sainte Sarah (Aznavour-Dimay); Quand (Sarapo-Commaret); Si moi je t'aime (Baschung-Dousset).

C016–10056   Les aventuriers (Roubaix-Lang); Dans la nuit (Senlis et Delécluse-Lai); Oui je veux vivre (Dona-Demarny); A tort ou à raison (Dona-Nyel).

THÉO SARAPO LONG PLAY/COMPACT DISC

FSX 144:   *Recital 1963 à Bobino.* Piaf sings: Monsieur Incognito; Tiens v'la un marin; Le chant d'amour; J'en ai tant vu; C'était pas moi; Margot Coeur-Gros. Sarapo sings: Défense de . . .; Les mains; La bande en noir; Un dimanche à Londres; Chez Sabine. They duet on A quoi ça sert l'amour. Orchestra: Noël Commaret; arrangements by Francis Lai.

2527542   *Collection La Chance aux Chansons* (CD): A quoi ça sert l'amour; Un dimanche à Londres; La vie continue; Sainte Sarah; La maison qui ne chante plus; Chez Sabine; On se croit libre (Lai-Barouh); Nous nétions pas pareils (Moustaki); Revenir de Grèce (Botton); La ronde (Vidalin-Magne); J'avais le ciel (Rivat-Fumière); Le jour ou tu sauras; La solitude; Moi qui passe (Hadjidakis-Barouh); Départ; New York; Les Espagnols (Nyel); Si moi je l'aime.

SONGS WRITTEN BY EDITH PIAF FOR YVES MONTAND

La grande cité (Comme c'est drôle); Elle a . . .; Mais qu'est-de que j'ai?; Il fait des . . .

FILMOGRAPHY

LA GARÇONNE   1936
Director: Jean de Limur, Script: Albert Dieudonné, Music: Jean
Wiener, Photography: Roger Hubert/Charlie Bauer. Based on
novel by Victor Marguerite. 90 minutes B/W.
Monique: MARIE BELL, Niquette: ARLETTY, Anika: SUZY
SOLIDOR, Tante Sylvestre: MARCELLE GENIAT, Boisselot:
HENRI ROLLAN. With Marcelle Praince, Jean Worms, Maurice
Escande. Piaf played 'une jeune chanteuse des rues'.
Song: 'Quand-même'.

MONTMARTRE-SUR-SEINE   1941
Director: Georges Lacombe, Script: Georges Lacombe/ André
Cayette, Photography: Nicolas Hayer, Music: Marguerite
Monnot. 110 minutes B/W.
Lily: EDITH PIAF, Moussette: DENISE GREY, Maurice: HENRI
VIDAL, Michel: JEAN-LOUIS BARRAULT, Paul: PAUL MEUR-
ISSE, Mme Courtin: LOUISE SYLVIE. With Huguette Faget,
Roger Duchesne, Gaston Modot.
Songs: 'L'homme des bars'; 'Tu es partout', 'Un coin tout bleu',
'J'ai dansé avec l'amour'.

LE CHANT DE L'EXILÉ   1942
Director: André Hugon, Script: André Hugon/ Yves Mirande,
Music: Edith Piaf/ Maurice Vandaire, Photography: Raymond
Agnel. 90 mins B/W. This film which starred Tino Rossi, Gaby
Andreu, Luis Mariano and Ginette Leclerc, was to have featured
Piaf in second female lead, but she turned the role down.

ÉTOILE SANS LUMIÈRE   1946
Director and Script: Marcel Blistène, Photography: Paul Cotteret,
Music: Guy Luypaerts/Marguerite Monnot, Band: Jacques
Hélian. 85 minutes B/W.
Madeleine: EDITH PIAF, Pierre: YVES MONTAND, Gaston

Lansac: SERGE REGGIANI, Stella Dora: MILA PARELY, Billy Daniel: JULES BERRY. With Mady Berry, Colette Brosset, Jean Raymond, Paul Frankeur.
Songs: 'C'était une histoire d'amour', 'Adieu mon coeur'; 'C'est merveilleux'; 'Mariage'; 'Le chant du pirate'.

LA BOÎTE À MUSIQUE [THE MUSIC-BOX/ MAKE MINE MUSIC] 1946
Script: Walt Disney. Voices included: Edith Piaf, André Dassary, The Andrews Sisters, Nelson Eddy.
Song: 'Johnny Fedora et Alice Bonnet-Bleu'.

NEUF GARÇONS ET UN COEUR
Director: Georges Freedland, Script: Georges Freedland/ Norbert Carbonnaux, Photography: Charlie Bauer, Music: Robert Chauvigny, Marguerite Monnot, Kurt Lewineck, Anne Bariset, Raymond Legrand, Norbert Glanzberg, Charles Trenet, Gilles, Louiguy, Mireille. 85 minutes B/W.
Christine: EDITH PIAF, Christine's friends: LES COMPAGNONS DE LA CHANSON, Lisa: ELISABETH WELLS, Victor: LUCIEN BAROUX. With Marcel Vallée, Lucien Nat.
Songs: 'La vie en rose'; 'Les trois cloches'; 'Un refrain courait dans la rue'; 'Sophie'; 'C'est pour ça'.

PARIS CHANTE TOUJOURS! 1951
Director: Pierre Montazel, Script: Jacques Chabannes/Roger Féral, Photography: Armand Thirard, Music: Raymond Legrand. 85 minutes B/W. With Lucien Baroux, Clément Duhour, Madeleine Lebeau, Line Renaud, Les Compagnons de la Chanson, Luis Mariano, Georges Guétary, Yves Montand, Tino Rossi, Jean Sabion, André Dassary, Van Doude, Edith Piaf, Les Petits Chanteurs à la Croix de Bois, Les Petits Poulbots de Montmartre.
Song: 'Hymne à l'amour'.

BOUM SUR PARIS! 1953
Director: Maurice de Canonge, Script: Maurice de Canonge/ Roger Féral/ Jacques Chabannes, Photography: Jean Bachelet, Music: Louiguy. 95 minutes B/W.
Young man: JACQUES PILLS, His girlfriend: DANIÈLE

GODET, Detectives: ARMAND BERNARD, LUCE FEYRER. With Edith Piaf, Charles Trenet, Mick Micheyl, Mouloudji, Juliette Grèco, Aimé Barelli, Jean Nohain, Les Quatre Barbus, Jacqueline Francois, Lucienne Delyle, Annie Cordy, Martine Carol, Giselle Pascal, Gary Cooper, Gregory Peck.

SI VERSAILLES M'ÉTAIT CONTÉ   1953
Director and Script: Sacha Guitry, Photography: Pierre Montazel, Music: Jean Francaix. 160 minutes Colour.
Louis XIV: SACHA GUITRY, Fénelon: JEAN-LOUIS BARRAULT, Une fille du peuple: EDITH PIAF, Molière: FERNAND GRAVEY, D'Artagnan: GÉRARD PHILIPE, Un gondolier: TINO ROSSI. With Claudette Colbert, Georges Marchal, Gaby Morlay, Jean Marais, Mary Marquet, Pauline Carton, Jean-Pierre Aumont, Giselle Pascal, Jeanne Fusier-Gir, Micheline Presle, Bourvil, Annie Cordy, Gino Cervi, Daniel Gélin, Danièle Delorme, Nicole Courcel, Orson Welles, Jean Richard, Charles Vanel, Raymond Souplex, Robert Hirsch, Jean-Claude Pascal, Jean Desailly, Brigitte Bardot, Aimé Clariond, Howard Vernon, Louis Seigneur.

FRENCH CAN-CAN   1954
Director: Jean Renoir, Script: Jean Renoir/André-Paul Antoine, Photography: Michel Kelber, Sets: Max Douy, Music: Georges Van Parys. 85 minutes Colour.
With FRANCOISE ARNOUL, JEAN GABIN, MARIA FÉLIX, PHILIPPE CLAY, VALENTINE TESSIER, DORA DOLL, JEAN PARÉDÈS, JEAN-ROGER CAUSSIMON, JEAN-MARC TENNBERG, GIANNI ESPOSITO, MICHEL PICCOLI, MAX DALBAN, GASTON MODOT. Guest artistes: Edith Piaf, Patachou, Cora Vaucaire, Albert Rémy, Annick Morice, France Roche, André Claveau, Claude Berri, Jean Raymond, Léo Campion.
Song: 'Le sérénade du pavé'.

LES HÉROS SONT FATIGUÉS   1955
Director: Yves Ciampi, Script: Yves Campi/Jacques-Laurent Bost/ Jean-Charles Tacchella, Photography: Henri Alekan. 85 minutes B/W. With YVES MONTAND, MARIA FÉLIX, CURT

JURGENS, Jean Servais, Gérard Oury, Elisabeth Manet, Gert Froebe and the *voices* of Edith Piaf and André Dassary.
Song: 'Le vagabond'.

LES AMANTS DE DEMAIN   1958
Director: Marcel Blistène, Script: Marcel Blistène/Jacques Sigurd/Pierre Brasseur, Photography: Marc Fossard, Music: Marguerite Monnot. 75 minutes B/W.
Simone: EDITH PIAF, Pierre Montfort: MICHEL AUCLAIR, Louis: ARMAND MESTRAL, Charles: RAYMOND SOUPLEX, Yvonne: JOËLLE BERNARD. With Olivier Hussenot, Georges Aminel, Mona Goya, Robert Dalban, Gina Manes, Robert Castel. Songs: 'Les amants de demain', 'Les neiges de Finlande', 'Fais comme si', 'Tant qu'il y aura des jours'.

UN COEUR GROS COMME ÇA   1961
Director: Francois Reichenbach. With Michèle Morgan, Abdou Faye. The soundtrack included Piaf singing 'Les mots d'amour'.

THEATRE PRODUCTIONS

LE BEL INDIFFÉRENT   1940
Théâtre des Bouffes Parisiens
followed by tour.

Script: Jean Cocteau.
Cast: Edith Piaf, Paul Meurisse (replaced by Jean Marconi).
Song: 'C'est lui que mon coeur a choisi'.

LA P'TITE LILI   1951
ABC Music-Hall

Script: Marcel Achard, Producer: Raymond Rouleau, Sets: Lila de Nobili, Music: Marguerite Monnot.
Lili: Edith Piaf, Spenser: Eddie Constantine, Mario: Robert Lamoureux, Eric: Howard Vernon, Martine: Nora Coste, Iréne: Katharine Kath, Henriette: Edith Fontaine. With Praline, Huguette Faget, Marcelle Praince, Jeanne Silvestre, Joëlle Robin, Robert Dalban, Buguette, Henri Polage, Edith Jablan, Ketty Albertini, Micheline Cevennes, Marie-Geneviève Parmentier, Annie Duck, Maurice Nasil, Dangelys, Robert Rollis, Germond, Gérard Kérise.
Songs: 'Demain il fera jour', 'L'homme que j'aimerais', 'Rien de rien', 'Avant l'heure', 'Si, si, si', 'Petite si jolie', 'Dans tes yeux', 'Du matin jusqu'au soir', 'C'est toi'.

LE BEL INDIFFÉRENT   1953
Théâtre Marigny

Script: Jean Cocteau.
Cast: Edith Piaf, Jacques Pills.
Song: 'Je t'ai dans la peau'.

SELECTED FILM TRIBUTES

Edith Piaf 1968
Trianon Films produced this short but excellent biography in black and white, which was narrated by Alan Badel. Piaf was seen singing 'La foule' at the Olympia in 1962, and other songs complementing the newsreel footage were 'Entre St-Ouen et Clignancourt', 'Mon légionnaire' and 'Milord'. The film is important in that it also depicts Belleville during the early thirties.

I Regret Nothing 1970
BBC Television. Producer: Michael Houldey. Narrator: David de Keyser. With Charles Aznavour, Bruno Coquatrix, Jacques Pills, Simone Margantin, Eddie Constantine, Michel Emer, Yves Montand, Les Compagnons de la Chanson, Marcel Blistène, Théo Sarapo.
Songs: 'Non je ne regrette rien', 'Je sais comment', 'Si, si, si', 'Les mômes de la cloches', 'Entre St-Ouen et Clignancourt', 'Mon légionnaire', 'C'est merveilleux', 'Les trois cloches', 'Bravo pour le clown', 'N'y vas pas Manuel', 'L'accordéoniste', 'Télégramme', 'Enfin le printemps', 'Une enfant', 'La vie en rose', 'Les gens', 'La goualante du pauvre Jean', 'Je t'ai dans la peau', 'Heureuse', 'La foule', 'L'homme à la moto', 'Le droit d'aimer', 'Milord', 'A quoi ça sert l'amour?', 'Hymne à l'amour', 'C'est à Hambourg', 'No regrets', 'Mon manège à moi'.
To date, *the* unsurpassed British documentary about Piaf.

All You Need is Love 1973
London Independent Television. The section devoted to Piaf included rare footage of her singing 'Milord', 'A quoi ça sert l'amour?', 'La vie en rose', 'Hymne à l'amour' and 'Non je ne regrette rien'.

Piaf [Great Britain: **Piaf the Early Years**] 1974
Director: Guy Casaril, Script: Guy Casaril/Francoise Ferley. Photography: Edmond Sechan, Music: Ralph Burns. French and English language versions. Based on the biography by Simone Berteaut. Edith Piaf: BRIGITTE ARIEL; Louis Leplée: GUY TREJEAN; Mômone: PASCALE CHRISTOPHE. With Jacques Dubay, Pierre Vernier, Francois Dyrek, Sylvie Joly, Anouk Ferjac, Yvan Varco, Michel Beditti. Songs interpreted by Piaf: 'La vie en rose', 'Les flons-flons du bal', 'Paris', 'Padam padam', 'L'accordéoniste', 'Non je ne regrette rien'. By Betty Mars: 'La trompette en bois' (Boyer-Scotto), 'Les petits qui n'ont pas de nid' (E Dumont-Bénoch), 'Sur le bord de la Riviera' (Bertal-Daniderff), 'Comme un moineau' (Hély-Lenoir), 'Titania' (Roydel), 'Où sont mes amants?' (Vandair-Cachant), 'Les mômes de la cloche', 'Elle fréquentait la rue Pigalle'.

The *supreme* Piaf biopic, much-criticized in France because its star was chosen by computer after several actresses – including, believe it or not, Liza Minelli! – turned the part down. In fact, Brigitte Ariel possesses the exact *titine du faubourg* qualities required to play Piaf in her formative years – the film ends with her singing 'L'accordéoniste' in 1940 – qualities which would not have easily been found in a more professional actress, and as the sound quality of Piaf's early recordings is relatively poor, no finer substitute than Betty Mars could possibly have been found.

Piaf 1979
Arena, BBC Television. Featuring the actress Jane Lapotaire, promoting her role in Pam Gems' play, *Piaf*. The short programme included rare footage of Piaf, and recorded scenes from the play. Songs: 'La vie en rose', 'Les mots d'amour', 'L'accordéoniste', 'A quoi ça sert l'amour?', 'Le droit d'aimer', 'Les mômes de la cloche'.

Edith et Marcel 1983
Director and Script: Claude Lelouche, Photography: Jean Boffety, Music: Francis Lai. Additional lyrics: Charles Aznavour. 160 mins. Edith Piaf: EVELYNE BOUIX, Marcel Cerdan: MARCEL CERDAN JR, Louis Barrier: JEAN-CLAUDE BRIALY, Lucien Roupp: JEAN BOUISE, Ginout: CHARLOTTE DE

TURCKHEIM. With Jacques Villeret, Francis Huster, Charles Aznavour, Maurice Garrel, Jean-Pierre Bacri, Jani Gastaldi, Charles Gérard, Micky Sebastian, Ginette Garcin, Philippe Khorsand. Songs interpreted by Piaf: 'Et moi', 'Le diable de la Bastille', 'Hymne à l'amour', 'Les mots d'amour', 'Je t'ai dans la peau', 'Le chant d'amour', 'C'est de la faute à tes yeux', 'C'est peut-être ça', 'Mon Dieu', 'Comme moi', 'Bal dans ma rue', 'La vie en rose', 'C'est merveilleux', 'L'homme que j'aimerais', 'Un homme comme les autres', 'Margot Coeur-Gros', 'La foule', 'C'est un gars'. Songs interpreted by Charles Aznavour and/or Mama Béa: 'C'est un gars', 'Le fanion de la Légion', 'Je n'attendais que toi', 'La prière', 'Avant toi', 'Viens pleurer au creux de mon épaule', 'Avec toi', 'L'éffet que tu me fais'.

An over-hyped, basically poor bio-pic. Evelyne Bouix is unconvincing in the lead: she does not resemble Piaf, her gestures and miming are contrived, clearly indicating that she has not taken the time to study film footage of her subject. Marcel Cerdan Jr, replacing Patrick Dewaere – who committed suicide halfway through filming – is equally wooden, though he does excel in the fight scenes. Worse still, sadly, is the spectacle of a fifty-nine-year-old Charles Aznavour playing himself at twenty-five, and the dreadful 'cover' singing by Mama Béa.

The Man Who Lived at the Ritz 1988
Director: Desmond Davis. This multinational TV movie was based on the novel by A E Hotchner, and co-produced by Piaf's friend Henri Spade, the man responsible for the 'Joie de vivre' series. The part of Madame Ritz was played by Patachou, and in a brief sketch Piaf (Nathalie Cerda) sings 'L'accordéoniste', whilst the heroine pronounces Cocteau's words, 'Piaf speaks for everyone who has been used or abandoned.'

Edith Raconte Piaf 1988
French Television. Directed by Gilles Delannoy and narrated by Piaf herself, this film ingeniously tells her story up to her marriage to Théo Sarapo. It includes dozens of her songs, and clips of on-stage performances of 'Non je ne regrette rien', 'Le fanion de la Légion', 'L'accordéoniste', 'Tu es partout', 'Monsieur Saint-Pierre', 'C'est merveilleux', 'Les trois cloches', 'La vie en rose', 'Hymne à l'amour', 'La goualante du pauvre Jean', 'Pour qu'elle

Selected Film Tributes

soit jolie ma chanson', 'Je t'ai dans la peau', 'Gypsy', 'L'homme
à la moto', 'Bravo pour le clown', 'La foule', 'Milord', 'Mon
vieux Lucien', 'Mon Dieu', 'Le petit brouillard', 'A quoi ça sert
l'amour?', 'Le billard électrique', 'Emporte-moi'.

Eve Raconte Piaf   1990
French Television. Director: Patrick Bureau. Presented by
Evelyne Ruggieri. A series of ten fifteen-minute programmes
packed with a wealth of anecdotes and rare footage: Piaf at the
Versailles and on the *Ed Sullivan Show,* Marie Dubas and Simone
Berteaut. An otherwise excellent series which is marred by sud-
denly cutting the rare closing-shots of Piaf on stage at the
Olympia.

Edith Piaf à Nimegue [Nijmegen]   1991
Proserpine Video. Recorded 14 December during Piaf's last tour
of Holland. The picture quality is sometimes poor, but this is
wholly immaterial as, to date, this is the only complete recital
of her to have emerged on film.
Songs: 'Le chant d'amour', 'Roulez tambours', 'Le petit brouil-
lard', 'Le rendez-vous', 'Musique à tout va', 'Emporte-moi',
'Margot Coeur-Gros', 'Le droit d'aimer', 'Le billard électrique',
'A quoi ça sert l'amour?', 'Non je ne regrette rien', 'La foule',
'Milord'.

Edith Piaf: Ma Vie en Rose   1993
TF1 Video, France. Directors: Philippe Fortin/ Jacques Rouhaud.
By far the best 'behind-the-scenes' Piaf collage ever assembled,
the film contains almost one hour of home-movies shot by Piaf's
accordionist, Marc Bonel, and his wife Danielle. Its importance
cannot be over-emphasized. Piaf is seen singing at the ABC
Music-Hall in 1937, touring Switzerland with Les Compagnons
de la Chanson, in *La p'tite Lili,* in Casablanca with Cerdan, on
tour with Pills, at the Coney Island funfair, with Jean Dréjac,
frolicking around Ginger Rogers' pool, singing 'La vie en rose'
to Chevalier, with Moustaki and Douglas Davies, singing 'La
foule' at the Waldorf Astoria, convalescing at Richebourg,
rehearsing 'Non je ne regrette rien' at Boulevard Lannes with
Dumont, and in the South of France a few days before her

death. Amongst those interviewed are Charles Dumont, Moustaki, Fred Mella, and the Bonels themselves.

Edith Piaf: Ses Plus Belles Chansons 1993
René Château Video, France. A compilation of clips, mostly of complete songs, from Piaf's films. The publicity for this claimed it to be an 'intègrale', though there are several omissions, and the editing is shaky in parts.
Montmartre-sur-Seine: 'Un coin tout bleu', 'Tu es partout', 'J'ai dansé avec l'amour'; *Etoile sans lumière*: 'C'est merveilleux', 'Le chant du pirate', 'Mariage'; *Neuf garçons et un coeur*: 'C'est pour ça', 'Sophie', 'La vie en rose'; *Les amants de demain*: 'Tant qu'il y aura des jours', 'Les amants de demain', 'Les neiges de Finlande'; *La Garçonne*: 'Quand même'; *Paris chante toujours*: 'Hymne à l'amour'; *French Can-Can*: 'Sérénade du pavé'; *Si Versailles m'était conté*: 'Le "ça ira" '.

Edith Piaf: La Cassette D'or 1995
Welcome Video, France. A unique compilation of songs, performed in their entirety, taken from numerous stage-performances and television shows in France and the United States. The quality and content are remarkable. Only one clip, 'La foule', has had to be reconstructed. Songs: 'La foule', 'La vie en rose', 'Mon Dieu', 'Hymne à l'amour', 'Hymn to love', 'L'accordéoniste', 'Le petit brouillard', 'Le fanion de la Légion', 'Les trois cloches, 'Faut pas qu'il se figure', 'Le gitan et la fille', 'A quoi ça sert l'amour?', 'La goualante du pauvre Jean', 'L'homme à la moto', 'Emporte-moi', 'Bravo pour le clown', 'Non je ne regrette rien', 'Milord', 'Padam padam'.

SELECTED THEATRE PRODUCTIONS

Edith Piaf, Je Vous Aime   1977
London stage. Devised and produced by Libby Morris. Music:
Chuck Mallett and Frank Stafford. Additional English lyrics:
Fran Landesman, Ronnie Bridges, Peter Reeves. Performers:
Libby Morris, Peter Reeves, Maureen Scott, Clifton Todd. The
brainchild of Canadian star Morris, this revue was thoughtfully
assembled and performed, and should be more widely known.
Songs: 'Under the skies of Paris' (Sous le ciel de Paris); 'Little
Sparrow of Paris' (Toujours aimer); 'My friend John' (La goual-
ante du pauvre Jean); 'Milord'; 'The accordionist'
(L'accordéoniste); 'In Amsterdam' (C'est à Hambourg); 'Lovers
in Paris' (Les amants de Paris); 'It's lovely loving you' (Il fait
bon t'aimer); 'If you love me really love me'; 'Padam padam';
'I don't care' (Je m'en fous pas mal); 'Gypsy boy' (Le gitan et
la fille); 'Song of Catherine' (La chanson de Catherine); 'Poor
little lost Louise' (Margot Coeur-Gros); 'Les flons-flons du bal';
'Bravo for the clown'; 'My lost melody'; 'Love is like champagne' (Mon manège à moi); 'I hope' (Faut pas qu'il se figure);
'An exceptional spring' (Il y avait); 'Strange town' (La ville
inconnue); 'Beside my legionnaire' (Mon légionnaire); 'The
crowd' (La foule); 'The devil who danced' (Le diable de la
Bastille); 'La vie en rose'; 'In a world of our own' (Les gens);
'The right to love' (Le droit d'aimer); 'La vie l'amour'; 'Two
people kiss' (Dans leur baiser); 'The lovers' (Les amants); 'Please
God' (Mon Dieu); 'In the waiting room' (Salle d'attente); 'Hands'
(Les mains); 'The white-shirts' (Les blouses-blanches); 'Cri du
coeur'; 'The way love goes' (A quoi ça sert l'amour?); 'Non je
ne regrette rien'.

Piaf   1978

Dramatic play with songs, by Pam Gems. The finest tribute to Piaf *ever*, this masterpiece, albeit based on Simone Berteaut's controversial biography – presenting Piaf exactly as she was, warts and all – works tremendously well because it convinces us of her deep love and understanding of the human condition. It started out in a small provincial theatre and was an immediate hit, progressing via London's West End to Broadway, since which time it has been put on in theatres around the world ina dozen languages. The original production contained a character-ization of Marlene Dietrich: this was replaced by one of Piaf's contemporary, Joséphine Baker, when Marlene objected to anyone portraying her whilst she was alive. The original pro-duction, which opened at The Other Place, Stratford-upon-Avon, was directed by Howard Davies and designed by Douglas Heap, with the following cast:

Jane Lapotaire (Piaf); Zoë Wanamaker (Toine); Carmen du Sautoy (Madeleine); Darlene Johnson (Marlene); Susannah Bishop (Nurse); Conrad Asquith (Inspector/Georges/Barman); Bill Buffery (Louis/Butcher/Lucien/Dope-pusher); Ian Charleson (Pierre/Man at rehearsal); Geoffrey Freshwater (Manager); James Griffiths (Leplée/Jean); Allan Hendrick (Emil/Jacko/Eddie); Anthony Higgins (Angelo/German soldier); Ian Reddington (Paul/American sailor/Physiotherapist); Malcolm Storry (Légionnaire/Jacques/German soldier/American sailor/Marcel/Théo).

Edith Piaf, Parmi Nous   1983

Bobino Music-Hall, Paris. An intimate audio-visual revue, inter-spersed with Piaf's recorded speaking voice and featuring her most celebrated songs performed by Betty Mars and Jack Mels, both sadly deceased. Accompanied by the Jean Sala Trio, with Serge Tomasi on the accordion. Arguably the best-ever stage tribute in France. Songs performed by Betty Mars: 'Tu es née à Belleville', 'Comme un moineau', 'Les mots d'amour', 'Non je ne regrette rien', 'Mon manège à moi', 'L'homme à la moto', 'Milord'. Songs performed by Jack Mels: 'Je m'imagine', 'Je n'en connais pas la fin', 'Marie la Francaise', 'Avec ce soleil', 'Retour', 'Mon Dieu', 'Bravo pour le clown', 'Eden Blues'. Songs per-formed as a duo: 'A quoi ça sert l'amour?', 'Moi je sais qu'on se reverra', 'Roulez tambours', 'Les trois cloches', 'Hymne à l'amour', 'C'est peut-être ça', 'Légende', 'Petit bout de femme'.

Piaf   1993

A revival of the Pam Gems play, even more stunning than the original production, opened at the Thorndike Theatre, Leatherhead, on 22 September 1993, and after a lengthy tour transferred to London's Piccadilly Theatre. The new cast was as follows: Elaine Paige (Piaf); Wendy Morgan (Toine); Greg Hicks (Legionnaire/Jacques/German soldier/Marcel/ American sailor/Théo); Dawn Hope (Joséphine); John Arthur (Manager); Lorren Bent (Nurse); Polly Kemp (Madeleine); Ron Emslie (Inspector/Georges/Barman/Doctor); Joe Jones (Pierre); Stephen Noonan (Emil/Jacko/French sailor/Eddie); Rocky Marshall (Butcher/Lucien/Dope-pusher/Louis); Steven Serlin (Angelo/German soldier); Michael Roberts (Leplée, Jean); Andrew Vezey (Paul/American sailor/Physiotherapist).

TRIBUTE ALBUMS

There have only been two tribute albums worthy of note: one in England and the other in France.

ELAINE PAIGE: *Piaf* 1994
'If you love me really love me'; 'Harbour girl' (C'est à Hambourg); 'La vie en rose'; 'The ballad of poor old John' (La goualante du pauvre Jean); 'The three bells'; 'Mon Dieu'; 'Lovers for a day'; 'La belle histoire d'amour'; 'All this I know' (Je sais comment); 'Non je ne regrette rien'; 'The accordionist' (L'accordéoniste).
Produced by Mike Moran. WEA 4509–94641–2

JACQUELINE DANNO: *Il était une fois Edith Piaf* 1996
'Le chemin des forains'; 'Mon légionnaire'; 'Dans leur baiser'; 'C'est à Hambourg'; 'Je m'en fous pas mal'; 'La fête continue'; 'Bal dans ma rue'; 'Les flons-flons du bal'; 'Mon Dieu'; 'Et pourtant'; 'Les croix'; 'Le prisonnier de la tour'; 'Les neiges de Finlande'; 'Les blouses-blanches'; 'Hymne à l'amour'.
Produced by Yvon Chateigneur. SACEM 080164

SELECTED BRITISH
RADIO BIOGRAPHIES

There have been numerous 'biographies' broadcast in Britain (*The Legend Lives On, Troubadours of French Song, Nights at the Paris Olympia*, etc), but these have represented sketchy and inaccurate accounts of the singer's life. Only two are therefore worthy of mention.

Piaf the Entertainer   1973
BBC Radio. Producer: Stanley Williamson. Narrator: Geoffrey Wheeler. Miriam Karlin narrated passages from *Ma vie*, and the programme included extracts of interviews from the BBC's *I regret nothing*. Songs: 'Non je ne regrette rien', 'Milord', 'Mon légionnaire', 'Hymn to love', 'L'accordéoniste', 'No regrets', 'La vie en rose', 'Je t'ai dans la peau', 'Bravo pour le clown', 'Mon Dieu', 'A quoi ça sert l'amour?'

Portrait of Piaf   1974
BBC Radio. Producer: Lawrence Bedford. Script: Thomas Thompson. Presenter: Elizabeth Welch. This astonishing three-part programme, unlikely to be bettered on account of its tight, accurate script and Elizabeth Welch's warm, vibrant narration. It featured more than 100 famous Piaf songs, and several rare ones – including the Radio Cité broadcast, in 1936, of 'Le fanion de la Légion'. There were extracts of interviews from *I regret nothing*, with supplementary tributes from Juliette Gréco, Nana Mouskouri, Moustaki, Jacques Canetti and Charles Dumont. Passages from her biographies were read by Nicolette Bernard. The theme for the programmes was 'My lost melody', Piaf's signature tune in America during the late fifties.

273

BIBLIOGRAPHY
PRIMARY AND SECONDARY
SOURCES

Berteaut, Simone: *Piaf* (Laffont, 1969).

Blistène, Marcel: *Au revoir Edith* (Gerfaut, 1963).

Bret, David: *The Piaf legend* (Robson, 1988).

Bret, David: *Marlene my friend* (Robson, 1993).

Crosland, Margaret: *Piaf* (Hodder & Stoughton, 1985).

Dureau, Christian: *Edith Piaf, 20 ans après* (Sipe, 1982).

Gassion, Denise: *Piaf ma soeur* (Authier, 1977).

Gassion, Denise: *Edith Piaf secrète et publique* (Ergo, 1988).

Lange, Monique: *Histoire de Piaf* (Ramsay, 1979).

Noli, Jean: *Edith Piaf; Trois ans pour mourir* (Stock, 1973).

Piaf, Edith: *Au bal de la chance* (Jeheber, 1958).

Piaf, Edith: *Ma vie* (with Jean Noli, Union Général des Editions, 1963).

Routier, Marcelle: *Piaf l'inoubliable* (Renaudot & Cie, 1990).

Saka, Pierre: *Hymne à l'amour* (texts to 200+ songs, L-poche, 1994).

Various: *Piaf, sacrée Môme* (Télérama, 1993).

Publications quoted in this book:

Accordéon; *France-Soir*; *New York Herald Tribune*; *France-Dimanche*; *Paris-Presse*, *Paris-Théâtre*; *Le Soleil* (Quèbec); *Paris-Match*.

PERMISSIONS

I would like to thank the following for giving me permission to quote extracts from the songs of Edith Piaf:

SEMI, France:
'Je m'imagine' (1960); 'L'étranger' (1936); 'Fais-moi valser' (1936); 'Toi tu l'entends pas' (1962); 'Mon vieux Lucien' (1961); 'Comme un moineau' (1933); 'Si tu partais' (1947); 'Les croix' (1952) 'Les grognards' (1957); 'Miséricorde' (1955); 'Avec ce soleil' (1954); 'Comme moi' (1957).

Southern Music Publishing Company, London:
'Paris-Méditeranée' (1937); 'Le fanion de la Légion' (1936); 'Les mots d'amour' (1960); 'L'accordéoniste' (1940); 'Les flons-flons du bal' (1959); 'La belle histoire d'amour' (1960); 'A quoi ça sert l'amour?' (1962); 'La ville inconnue' (1959); 'Toujours aimer' (1961); 'Les gens' (1963); 'Les trois cloches' (1944); 'Chanson bleue' (1950); 'Bravo pour le clown' (1953); 'Légende' (1955); 'La foule' (1957); 'Mon manège à moi' (1958).

EMI, France.
'Jérusalem' (1960).

Editions Salabert, Paris:
'Le vieux piano' (1960); 'Padam padam' (1951)', 'Opinion publique' (1960); 'Au bal de la chance' (1952); 'Boulevard du Crime' (1959); 'Je sais comment' (1958); 'Milord' (1958).

Chappell Music, London:
'Mon légionnaire' (1936); 'Mon Dieu' (1960); 'De l'autre côté de la rue' (1943); 'Hymne à l'amour' (1950).

Editions Intersong, Paris:
'Le droit d'aimer' (1962); 'Roulez tambours' (1962).

Edition Fortin, Paris:
'Les mômes de la cloche' (1933).

Editions Les Auteurs, Paris:
''Chand d'habits' (1936); 'La goualante du pauvre Jean' (1954).

Editions Paul Beuscher, Paris:
'Elle fréquentait la rue Pigalle' (1939); 'Browning' (1937); 'Où sont-ils mes copains?' (1940); 'C'est un monsieur très distingué' (1942); 'Tous mes rêves passés' (1953); 'Un grand amour' (1955); 'Les amants d'un jour' (1956); 'La grand cité' (1945); 'La vie en rose' (1945); 'Demain il fera jour' (1951).

Editions Raoul Breton, Paris:
'Le prisonnier de la tour' (1949); 'Paris' (1949); 'Je t'ai dans la peau' (1953).

Britico/SDRM:
'Les neiges de Finlande' (1958); 'Je hais les dimanches' (1951); 'Une enfant' (1952).

Editions Métropolitaines, Paris:
'C'est un homme terrible' (1958); 'Le gitan et la fille' (1958).

Shapiro-Bernstein, London:
'Non je ne regrette rien' (1960).

Editions Patricia, Paris:
'L'homme de Berlin' (1963); 'J'en ai tant vu' (1963).

Warner-Chappell, Paris:
'La bande en noir' (1963); 'C'est l'amour' (1960); 'L'homme à la moto' (1956).

INDEX